PATTERN CUTTING

LAURENCE KING

Published in 2011 by

LAURENCE KING PUBLISHING LTD

361–373 City Road, London,
EC1V 1LR, United Kingdom
T +44 20 7841 6900
F +44 20 7841 6910
enquiries@laurenceking.com
www.laurenceking.com

Reprinted 2012, 2013, 2014, 2015

A catalogue record for this book is available
from the British Library.

ISBN: 978 1 85669 750 7

TEXT BY Dennic Chunman Lo

CAD/CAM CONSULTANT
Megan McGuire

TECHNICAL DRAWINGS BY
Alina Moat

DESIGN BY Melanie Mues,
Mues Design, London

SENIOR EDITOR Gaynor Sermon

PICTURE RESEARCHER Evi Peroulaki

The author dedicates this book to 'B'
and the Lo Family.

Printed in China

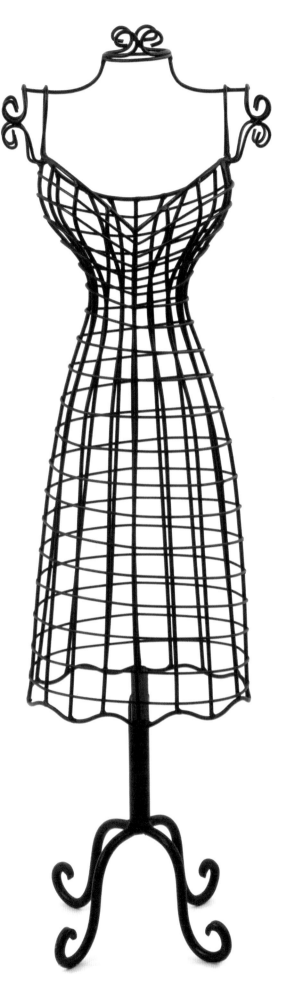

PATTERN CUTTING

DENNIC CHUNMAN LO

LAURENCE KING PUBLISHING

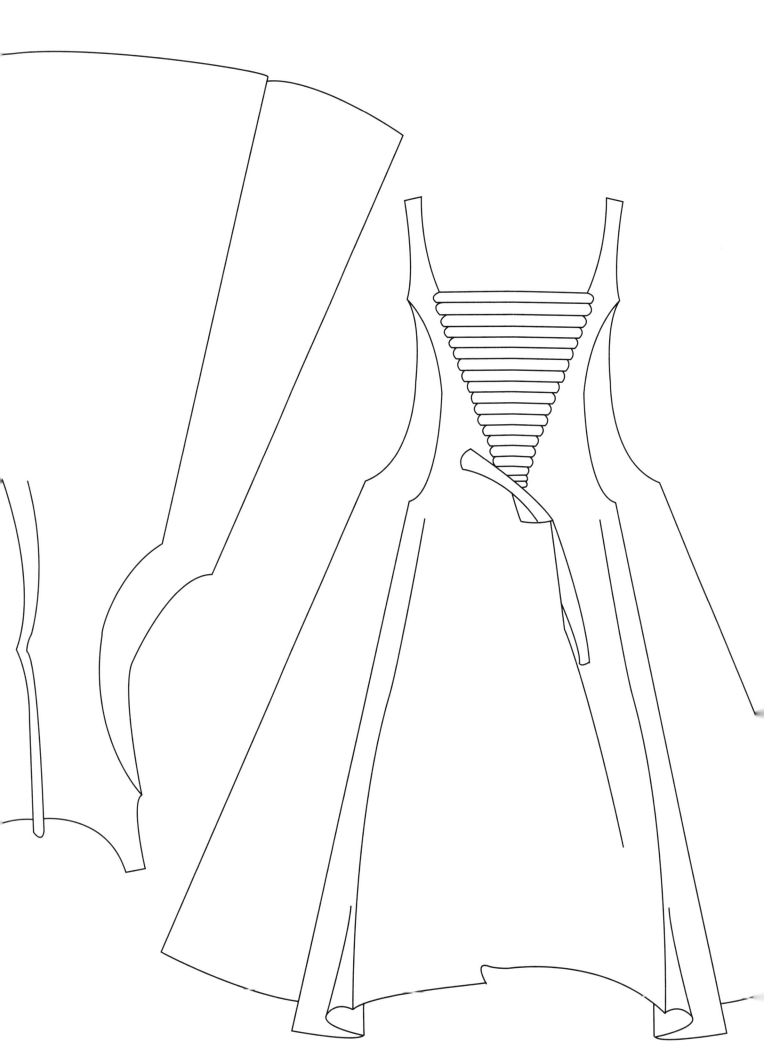

CONTENTS

Related study material is available on the Laurence King website at www.laurenceking.com

ABOUT THIS BOOK

Pattern cutting is the art of producing a paper pattern from which a beautifully cut garment that fits well can be made. This book explores the process of flat pattern cutting, providing a thorough grounding in the skills that are essential for both designers and pattern cutters, combining basic knowledge about fabrics, styles and sizing systems with step-by-step instructions on how to create blocks and patterns.

In industry, pattern cutting is usually undertaken by a pattern cutter who is either employed directly by a fashion house or who works freelance. The fashion industry, like most industries, is changing rapidly; new technologies are introduced and impact on construction methods, trends are constantly updated, customers' needs change as lifestyles evolve, and at the same time the fine line changes between what is acceptable and what is not.

In the 1980s when the Japanese designers (such as Rei Kawakubo of Comme des Garçons) started to showcase their collections in Paris, the influence of deconstruction began to evolve. The question was raised as to whether it was acceptable to wear garments with raw edges. Now this invisible boundary has been breached and many would no longer see the presence of a raw edge as an issue. In the same way there is no longer a right or a wrong answer to the correct fit of a garment. What is beautifully cut? What is beautifully made? What fits well? What doesn't fit? Everyone has a different answer to each of these questions, and this book will not only assist you in developing your pattern cutting skills, but also open your eyes to the potential for experimentation in this exciting industry.

WHAT IS PATTERN CUTTING?

Flat pattern cutting means drafting the paper pattern 'flat' on a piece of paper, relying on the measurements of the human body as a guide. To achieve high accuracy you must be experienced in drafting the paper pattern first then making it into a toile/test garment quickly and precisely. Another method of creating a design is called draping on the stand, or 'moulage': this is literally draping a piece of fabric directly onto the mannequin, using dress pins or adhesive tape to secure the material, in order to achieve the design of the garment without needing to gauge the shape on paper first. The final paper pattern would be created by taking the draped piece of fabric off the mannequin, laying it flat, then tracing its shape onto a piece of paper.

This book focuses on flat pattern cutting, though both are useful and interchangeable skills, each supporting the other. For example, patterns made by flat pattern cutting need to be made into toiles to test accurate fitting on the body or mannequin, and knowledge of how fabric hangs on the body is essential; those who primarily create patterns through draping must still understand the principles of flat pattern cutting in order to produce a set of professional paper patterns for storage, archive or mass production. Some pattern cutters find that it saves time to combine both flat pattern cutting and draping methods, and this is evidenced in constructing the convertible collar in Chapter 5.

THE ROLE OF THE PATTERN CUTTER

The role of a pattern cutter in the industry is primarily as a link between the designer/design team and the manufacturer/manufacturing process. For this reason, fashion students may see a pattern cutter's job as removed from the creative process because the design team would have completed the designs of the garments and the pattern cutter's job is to merely translate them into a three-dimensional form. This is entirely untrue.

A truly talented pattern cutter needs to produce accurate and speedy patterns for the garments designed, and this very process is not possible without the pattern cutter's ability and talent to interpret a garment in terms of proportion, technical possibility, details, comfort, fit and – most importantly – an accurate eye for the 'flair' and the soul of the garment. Take the examples of John Galliano, Alexander McQueen and Yohji Yamamoto: their creations carry a unique signature in terms of cut, silhouette and shape because they were trained as pattern cutters as well as designers.

Recently, at the high-end of the market, a new trend has surfaced; many designers and design houses are beginning to recruit for designers/pattern cutters. This means that candidates must together be capable of designing garments from generated ideas, create sketches, identify fabrics, produce working drawings, and understand pattern cutting (flat or draping) in order to create test garments which they can then follow through the sampling and production processes. As a result, fashion colleges all over the world are also starting to offer courses and training for creative individuals to join forces, namely designers/pattern cutters, or, indeed, courses for creative pattern cutters.

THE DESIGN PARTNERSHIP

The best balance in this partnership is achieved when the pattern cutter is flexible and open-minded while the designer understands the art of pattern cutting, exploring its possibilities and accepting its limitations. The key for the pattern cutter is always to know how to do things in various ways to be able to accommodate different companys' systems, designers' signatures or individuals' aesthetic sense. After all, a good pattern cutter is a translator of ideas into fabric, but isn't this also what a designer should be?

Pattern cutting is a collaborative process between the designer, pattern cutter and manufacturer in which accuracy is as essential as speed. In industry a pattern cutter needs to be able to produce as many accurate patterns a day as possible. No one will want to employ a freelance pattern cutter to labour intensively for days on one pattern, no matter how perfectly it is cut, especially as a self-employed pattern cutter may be the most expensive member of the production team. It is fortunate, therefore, that speed and accuracy can both be assured by taking a structured approach to drafting the pattern.

ORGANIZATION OF THE BOOK

Chapters 1 to 4 follow one approach from design concept to finished pattern. The essential first steps to cutting a successful pattern involve good preparation, and these are explored in the first chapter. Before starting work, the pattern cutter also requires a set of tools, and we will examine these in Chapter 2.

In the third chapter we look at how to draft a block, the next stage of a structured pattern cutting approach, and learn how to draft blocks for a bodice, sleeve, skirt, dress and trousers. The block is a basic garment shape that can be used and adapted to make any pattern. Most pattern cutting studios will have a pre-existing set of blocks cut according to the company's signature style and fit and it is essential to understand the rationale behind the block before starting to work. The existence of such a block, however, will save time and provide an effective and accurate starting point. In Chapter 4 we explore the process of drafting a paper pattern from a block, adding seam allowances and annotations to communicate your pattern cutting and construction directions to the manufacturer, and will also look at the purpose of making and fitting a toile.

Having looked at one approach to the pattern cutting process from the initial stages of the fabric and size selection through to production of a block, paper pattern and toile, the next two chapters in the book look at how to use and adapt the block. In Chapter 5 we look at how to convert the block into different styles, whether it is by adding a collar, moving a seam or eliminating a dart. In Chapter 6 we look at how a creative approach to the art of pattern cutting itself can act as the inspiration for the garment design, and explore a range of techniques, including extension, mirror imaging and repetition, which can be used alongside the foundation of the block. There is also a subtle reminder of how important it is to consider fabrics and their characteristics in order to further creative possibilities.

Finally, in Chapter 7, we look at how technology can be used in the pattern cutting process, simplifying some of the more mundane tasks and allowing for greater speed and accuracy.

Before you begin to cut any pattern, however, it is worth looking in your own wardrobe to see how garments have been cut. Looking around you at people on the street is also a good exercise; as a pattern cutter you can learn a great deal by observing how others dress. Setting aside the prevailing trends, try to look at clothes objectively and ask yourself why you like or dislike a garment. Is it too tight? Does it fit properly? Is it well cut? If so, how is it cut? Where have the darts been placed? What is the fabric? Is it well made? Is it flattering to your figure? Why? What part of this is emphasized by the colour and drape of the fabric? If a certain part of the garment is not well cut or fitted, what could be done to tackle the problem? The aim of this book is to help you find the answers to many of these questions, and gain an understanding of the theory of pattern cutting, as well as its practicalities.

CHAPTER 1
PREPARATION

INTRODUCTION

Common sense is the key to pattern cutting. When trying to make something, whether it is a pillowcase, a cushion cover, a tablecloth, an apron or even a simple quilted case for a personal computer, you need to know four things before beginning:

1. The measurements.

2. The intended material.

3. The techniques that will be used to make it; for example, machine stitching, hand stitching, taping, gluing, overlocking, zipping, buttoning and so on.

4. Finally, and perhaps this is the most important point, whether you want to make more than one. If so, you will need to keep a record.

To translate the above in terms of pattern cutting for the garment industry:

1. Before beginning you need to know the measurements required and the sizing system you need to work to.

2. You need to know the fabric from which the garment will be made because this will affect the method you use to cut the pattern and will also determine how to apply the seam allowances.

3. To be a good pattern cutter, you also need to understand construction. Pattern cutting is not only working out the shape, it is also about engineering the pieces to fit together to form a garment. To understand how to do this you need to be able to sew.

4. To make more than one garment you need to be able to record the shape in a pattern. This is done by perfecting the shape first through a draft pattern then through toiling and alteration. The resulting pattern(s) can be reused many times throughout production.

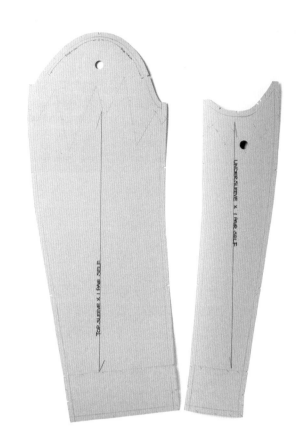

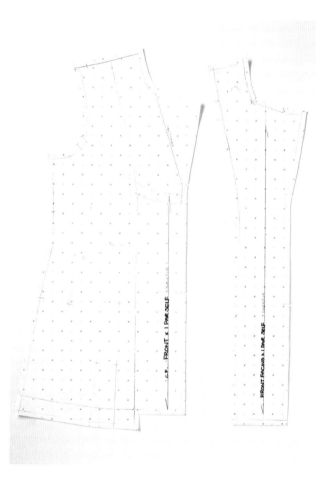

While you will mainly use either pattern card (top) or spot-and-cross paper (right), in practical terms you can use almost any type of paper for pattern cutting. Recycled newspaper, for example, might make an economical and interesting set of paper patterns (opposite page), but only if you can read any marks you might make through the newsprint and the paper does not tear too readily.

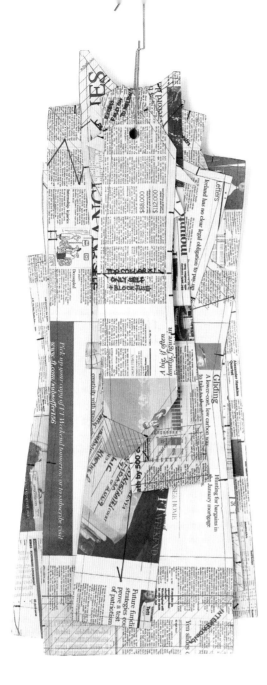
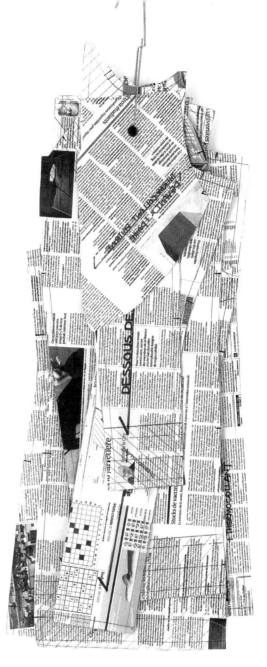

An extremely experienced pattern cutter will be able to draft the pattern directly onto real fabric with chalk from a set of measurements. This needs experience, confidence, practise and a lifetime of dedication to one skill. This method, however, can only really be used in home dressmaking or bespoke tailoring because there is no mass production and therefore no need to make a record. For mass production in the garment industry patterns must be used. These are usually made from plain paper or soft card, card being more durable.

Patterns record the shape of the garment accurately. Each part of the garment is drafted separately: sleeve, collar, front, back, yoke, lapel and so on. Sets of paper patterns should be stored, recorded or even archived systematically so they can be reused throughout production.

Having established the need to record the garment in the form of a pattern, the next stage is usually the creation of a block, which is a basic garment shape from which a pattern for a specific garment can be drafted. You will learn how to draft a block in Chapter 3. Before we begin, however, we will further explore the first two premises listed opposite – measurements and sizing systems and the effect of different fabrics on pattern cutting. There is also a third item a pattern cutter needs before beginning to draft the block or pattern, and that is an idea of the garment they are to create. This comes in the form of a working drawing, which will be explored at the end of the chapter.

MANNEQUINS & MEASUREMENTS

Before you start to cut a block or produce a paper pattern for a garment you must consider the person for whom you are making the garment. Is it:

1. a garment for yourself?
2. a garment for a particular person?
3. a garment for an assignment at college?
4. a garment for a fashion show?
5. a garment made professionally for the industry?

Each of these different scenarios will require a different size chart and the selection of a different mannequin for fitting.

PERSONAL SIZE CHART

When making a garment for yourself or for a specific person you can create a unique size chart containing the following measurements:

Bust
Waist
Hip
Thigh
Inseam
Outseam or waist to ankle
Circumference of the knee
Circumference of the ankle
Waist to hip
Waist to mid hip
Waist to knee
Nape to waist
Shoulder (neck point to shoulder point)
Cross shoulder at front
Cross shoulder at back
Cross front armhole
Cross back armhole
Circumference of the neck
Shoulder neck point to bust level
Shoulder neck point to waist at front
Shoulder neck point to waist at back
Armhole
Sleeve length (shoulder point to wrist)
Elbow (shoulder point to elbow)
Circumference of the wrist

Using a personal size chart will ensure a made-to-measure fit, which is virtually impossible using any other kind of size chart; some people have longer than average arms or a smaller waistline, for example. Tailors, bridalwear designers and the haute couture industry not only produce each garment to the exact measurements of their customers, but also use custom-made dress mannequins sized for some of their most loyal and regular customers; Hardy Amies, for example, had a special mannequin for Queen Elizabeth II, as had Givenchy for Audrey Hepburn.

MANNEQUIN SIZE CHART

Most colleges use a European size 12 mannequin as a standard size, though some are now using a size 10 as the ideal shape slims down on the catwalk. Using a size 10 mannequin is increasingly a better choice in scenario 4 as catwalk models selected for shows rarely have a hip measure above 88cm (35in) and are at least 176cm tall (5ft 9in), unless they are chosen to model underwear or plus sizes.

Metric specifications

Size	Bust	Waist	Hip	BNW
10	82	59	87	40
12	87	64	92	40.5
14	92	69	97	41
16	97	74	102	41.5
18	102	79	107	42
20	108	85	113	42.5
22	114	91	119	42.5

BNW = Centre back of neck to waistline, or nape to waist
(Courtesy Kennett and Lindsell Ltd)

Imperial specifications

Size	Bust	Waist	Hip	BNW
10	32¼	23¼	34¼	15¾
12	34¼	25¼	36¼	16
14	36¼	27¼	38¼	16⅛
16	38¼	29¼	40¼	16¼
18	40¼	31¼	42¼	16½
20	42½	33½	44½	16¾
22	44¾	35¾	46¾	16¾

The above measurements are taken from a Kennett & Lindsell BSD mannequin. Mannequins come in a number of different shapes and sizes because a standard-size dress mannequin is not always satisfactory as each industry (or brand) has its own clientele. A company producing womenswear for the Japanese market will require a mannequin with an overall bust measurement that is smaller and a measurement from waist to hip that is longer than for the European market. A company producing bridal and eveningwear for the American market may require a mannequin with a larger hip measurement. Both of these companies, therefore, need dress mannequins to fit a specific shape according to a specific group of customers. This is common in the garment industry.

Most colleges use dress mannequins for their students to prototype and make garments for assessments and graduate shows. A size chart can be produced by measuring directly from the mannequin, but mannequins may be far from the shape of the human form. Many colleges, therefore, produce their own size charts based on industry practice and the prototyping of garments on real people, thus reminding students that pattern cutting and garment construction is for the human figure and not for mannequins.

Womenswear main size chart at London College of Fashion 2010
Measurements in cm (in)

	Size 10	Size 12	Size 14	Size 16
Height	159.6 (62¾)	162 (63¾)	164.4 (64¾)	166.8 (65¾)
Hip	87 (34¼)	92 (36¼)	97 (38¼)	102 (40¼)
Bust	81 (32)	86 (34)	91 (35¾)	96 (37¾)
Waist	61 (24)	66 (26)	71 (28)	76 (30)
Chest (above bust/corset line)	77.4 (30½)	81 (32)	84.6 (33¼)	88.2 (34¾)
Top hip (1cm below waist)	81 (32)	86 (34)	91 (35¼)	96 (37¾)
Rib cage (under bust, useful for bra size)	66 (26)	71 (28)	76 (30)	81 (32)
Neck	35 (13¾)	36 (14¼)	37 (14½)	38 (15)
Bicep	24.7 (9¾)	26.5 (10½)	28.3 (11)	30.1 (11¾)
Elbow	23.7 (9¼)	25.5 (10)	27.3 (10¾)	29.1 (11½)
Wrist	15.2 (6)	16 (6¼)	16.8 (6½)	17.6 (7)
Thigh	49.8 (19½)	53 (21)	56.2 (22)	59.4 (23¼)
Knee	32.6 (12¾)	34 (13½)	35.4 (14)	36.8 (14½)
Calf	31.6 (12½)	33 (13)	34.4 (13½)	35.8 (14)
Ankle	22.3 (8¾)	23 (9)	23.7 (9¼)	24.4 (9½)
Cross chest (cross front)	29.8 (11¾)	31 (12¼)	32.2 (12¾)	33.4 (13)
Cross back (12cm from nape)	31.8 (12½)	33 (13)	34.2 (13½)	35.6 (14)
Shoulder length	11.7 (4½)	11.9 (4¾)	12.1 (4¾)	12.3 (4¾)
Bust width (between bust points)	17.8 (7)	19 (7½)	20.2 (8)	21.4 (8½)
Nape to bust (halter neck)	32.6 (12¾)	34 (13½)	35.4 (14)	36.8 (14½)
Nape to waist over bust	51.8 (20½)	53 (21)	54.2 (21¼)	55.6 (22)
Nape to waist at centre back	40.4 (16)	41 (16)	41.6 (16¼)	42.2 (16½)
Nape to hip	62.1 (24½)	63 (24¾)	63.9 (25¼)	64.8 (25½)
Nape to knee	97.5 (38½)	99 (39)	100.5 (39½)	102 (40¼)
Nape to floor	137.9 (54¼)	140 (55)	142.1 (56)	144.2 (56¾)
Sleeve length (overarm)	57.1 (22½)	58 (22¾)	58.9 (23¼)	59.8 (23½)
Sleeve length (underarm)	43.1 (17)	43.5 (17)	43.9 (17¼)	44.3 (17½)
Body rise	27.9 (11)	29 (11½)	30.1 (11¾)	31.2 (12¼)
Shoulder angle (degrees)	20.5	20.5	20.5	20.5
Outside leg	100.5 (39½)	102 (40¼)	103.5 (40¾)	105 (41¼)

INDUSTRY SIZE CHARTS

Pattern cutting for industry is easier in some ways and more difficult in others.

It is easier because you have a standard set of measurements for each sector of the market – eveningwear, high-end designer wear, teenage high street or active sportswear, for example – and those measurements remain set over a long period of time.

It is more difficult, however, if you are selling to different markets worldwide because the sizing works differently in at least three different markets: Europe, America and the Far East.

Measurements in cm (in)	K+L dress mannequin (BSD) UK	Japanese	American	London Fashion Week designer
Small/sample/standard size	12	9	8	6 to 8
Bust	87 (34¼)	82 (32¼)	92 (36¼)	86 (34)
Waist	64 (25¼)	62 (24½)	74 (29)	68 (26¾)
Hip	92 (36¼)	88 (34½)	98 (38½)	90 (35½)
Nape to waist/back length	40.5 (16)	37 (14½)	42 (16½)	41 (16⅛)
Sleeve	58 (22¾)	54 (21¼)	60 (23½)	62 (24½)

CHOOSING A SIZE CHART FOR INDUSTRY

Despite the presence of industry-standard size charts, collating a size chart to offer customers a good fit is a collaborative process between designers and pattern cutters. Fitting sessions are very important during the cutting and sampling process and it is out of this process that the size chart will emerge. A 'house model' representing the ideal customer's shape is often employed for fitting sessions. Alternatively samples can be tried on various representatives of the target market. An ideal solution is to try the samples on both a model and on members of staff in the company who are a similar size and shape to the sample and could be said to represent the general public or 'real people'.

THE SAMPLING SIZE, SIZE SMALL OR STANDARD SIZE

Most sampling rooms in industry choose to begin pattern cutting from a small size as a standard version. When the measurements are approved, this standard size is then graded up to larger or down to smaller sizes.

In the UK, a size 12 dress mannequin is favoured as the standard size and the garment could then be offered in sizes 6 to 18 with a 5cm (2in) difference in circumference and a small difference in length from one size to the next, or in larger companies, sizes from 4–24 might be produced. In Japan the standard size is a size 9 while in North America it is a size 8, with measurements in each case being increased or decreased by 4cm (1½in) between sizes.

THE HIGH STREET EFFECT ON SIZING

Competition on the high street is fierce and fashion retailers and manufacturers constantly need to come up with different marketing strategies, some of which include a psychological, feel-good element for the consumer. Over the years it has become the practice to reduce the number of the standard size by one once the garment goes into production; a customer who is actually built closer to a size 12 will consequently end up finding a dress labelled size 10 is a good fit. This 'tempering' of sizes, which has no regulatory control, means that it is very important for pattern cutters to be flexible and work with a given set of measurements, rather than sticking to standard size charts.

The basic rule for all pattern cutters is to consider the person for whom the garment is to be cut before you begin to create the block or pattern. The first step, therefore, should be to acquire an appropriate set of measurements that will then be relevant to the eventual wearer so that the garment is created with the human form in mind. Pattern cutting is the skill of interpreting this human form on paper.

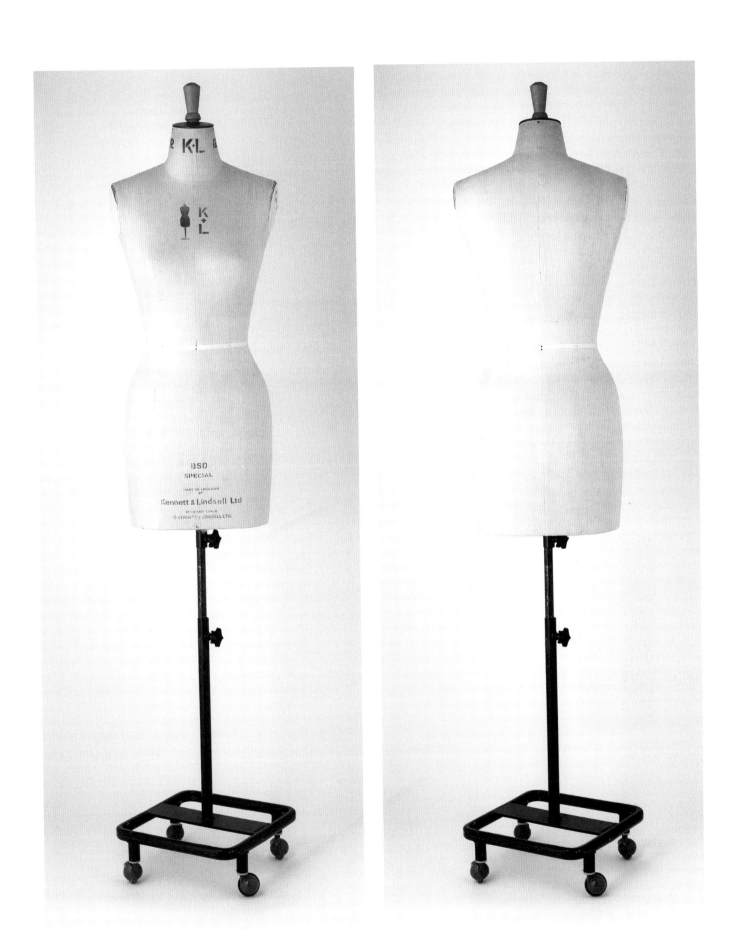

UNDERSTANDING
THE FABRIC

Pattern cutting is a skill through which we are packaging human anatomy, just like designing a package for an object. Many products we purchase nowadays rely on intelligent packaging design for marketing: the iPod, chocolate, shoes, books, perfume and many more. In the same way, designing clothes that fit the human shape well affects marketability, both of the clothes and also of the package within – the wearer.

Imagine you are wrapping a present. Some of the easiest presents to wrap are flat rectangular shapes or cubes, such as CDs, books and diaries. It has always been much more challenging to wrap a gift that is an irregular shape, like a mug or a coffee maker. Under those circumstances, we will automatically go to look for a box. Somehow common sense tells us that a box, large or small, square or rectangular, is a lot more manageable when it comes to wrapping and packaging.

Body packaging has to cope with a basic principle: human anatomy is an irregular three-dimensional shape. We do not have the option of searching for a box. Pattern cutting is about finding ways to cut fabric so that it wraps neatly around the three-dimensional body in the desired shape.

The natural characteristics of the fabric can contribute a great deal towards the way in which it can be shaped and wrapped around the body and consequently the pattern cutting techniques that need to be employed. The first question to ask, therefore, is whether the fabric is woven, stretchy or neither.

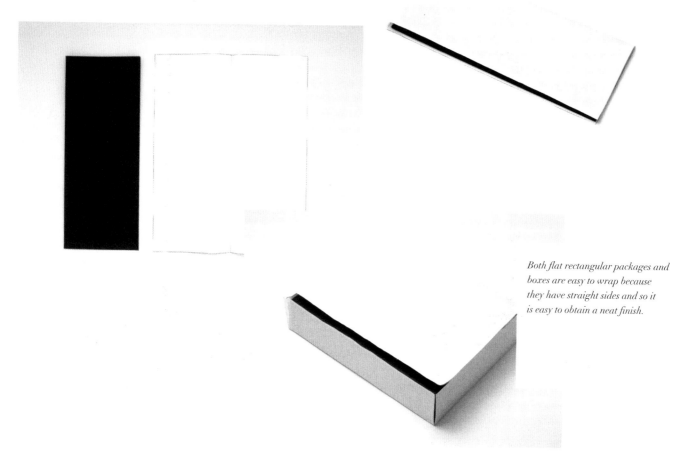

Both flat rectangular packages and boxes are easy to wrap because they have straight sides and so it is easy to obtain a neat finish.

It is much more difficult to wrap a sphere, requiring the paper to be folded into awkward shapes that are very difficult to make neat. Instead, a stretchy fabric, like an orange net, makes a much better presentation.

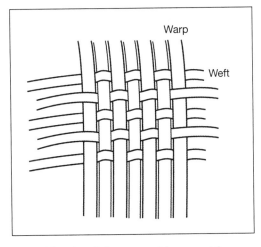

WOVEN VERSUS STRETCH

Woven fabrics consist of intersecting vertical and horizontal yarns, termed respectively warp and weft yarns. The warp yarn is set up on the loom first and is usually the stronger of the two. The weft yarn is then passed horizontally through the warp threads, passing under and over each successive warp thread in turn.

The warp direction is the most stable and if you pull a piece of fabric along the warp, then it should not give. If you pull it along the weft, from selvedge to selvedge, the fabric might, however, give slightly if the weft yarn is less strong. Woven fabrics are sometimes made to stretch in one direction to tackle problems of fit through the introduction of elastic fibres or filaments in the weft.

Knitted fabrics differ from woven fabrics because they are made from one continuous thread that is manipulated into loops, each loop interlinked with the next. This is the principle of a single knit jersey. A more complex construction would consist of more than one yarn or the manipulating of various layers of yarn. Any knitted fabric will give much more than any woven fabric because the

Woven fabrics have little or no stretch because, while the warp and weft threads are interlaced, there is no allowance in the length of the yarn.

interlinked loops are more flexible, rather like a coiled spring that lengthens when it is stretched.

Knitted and woven fabrics can be made from a huge range of natural and manmade yarns using a wide variety of construction methods. In addition, garments can also be made from materials that are neither woven nor knitted, including leather, plastic, metal chains and many more, each of which will have different characteristics affecting the ways in which they can be manipulated.

Pattern cutting and shaping all these fabrics relies on three principles: grainline, gravity and suppression.

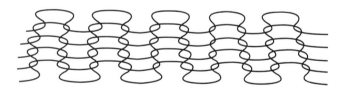

stretch

loops of yarn to be distorted

The interlinked loops of yarn in a knitted fabric are able to stretch easily because the loops can distort without becoming disconnected.

Snagging

Because knitted fabrics are made from one continuous piece of yarn, if the yarn is broken the whole fabric will be jeopardized as the yarn begins to unravel, or 'ladder'. If a yarn in a woven fabric is broken, however, it might just develop a small hole that is easy to repair. To repair a hole in a knitted garment would require a knitting needle or a crochet hook and knowledge of knit construction.

Mastering pattern cutting skills

Pattern cutters working in the fashion industry usually specialize in one of the following fields: woven, jersey, knitwear, leather or tailoring, and each field has its own pattern cutting principles. As a student the key skill to learn is pattern cutting for woven fabrics as these are the most unforgiving of fabrics. This requires precision and includes techniques for ease and stretch, darts and shape manipulation. Many of these techniques can then be transferred when cutting patterns for other fabrics.

Tolerance

In general, woven blocks would include darts; for stretch garment blocks garments are usually without darts because the material has more stretchability. Woven blocks should always include a certain amount of tolerance (a couple of centimetres outside of the body's exact measurements to allow for comfortable fit and movement), but for jersey and stretch blocks the measurements can be even smaller than the body.

GRAINLINE

Any woven or knit fabric has an orderly construction, as we have seen, either of intersecting threads, in the case of a woven fabric, or interlinked loops, in the case of a knitted fabric. The horizontal or vertical construction of either fabric is referred to as the straight or horizontal grainline respectively. In addition there is a third type of grainline, known as the bias.

How you lay your pattern along the grainline will affect the appearance of the garment as the construction of the fabric combined with gravity comes into play. Will the fabric stretch and lengthen and perhaps cling to the body, or will it remain stable? The grainline therefore affects the way that the garment 'hangs' when it is worn.

Straight grain

A garment cut on the straight grain is one where the straight grain of the fabric is parallel to the centre front or centre back. The warp runs down the garment providing stability along its length, while the weft, which runs horizontally, provides a little more give as the fabric is stretched around the body as it is worn. The straight grain of the fabric is, therefore, always parallel to the selvedge.

Many garments are automatically cut on the straight grain, including most skirts, trousers and shirts.

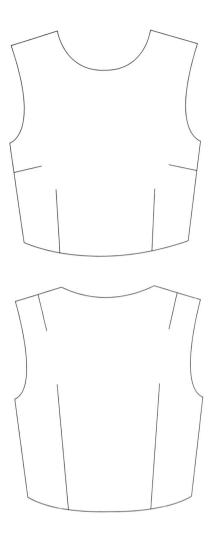

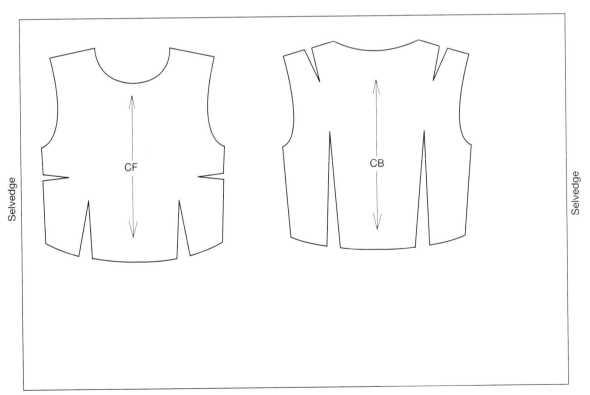

The straight grain runs parallel to the centre back and centre front and runs parallel with the warp.

Horizontal grain

A garment cut on the horizontal grain is one where the grainline of the fabric runs at 90° to the centre front or centre back. It is often difficult to tell when a garment has been cut in this way, but individual pattern pieces are often cut on the horizontal grain to help in the construction of the garment. The cuffs and yokes of shirts, for example, are cut on the horizontal grainline, which means that the warp thread then runs along their length, horizontally across the garment. The strength of the warp means that the fold of the cuff will be sharp and will provide stability where it is joined to the bottom of the sleeve because it will not stretch. Similarly, the warp thread of the yoke will control and strengthen the seam running horizontally across the back of the garment.

Pattern pieces are also cut on the horizontal grain for visual impact – if the garment is made from a striped fabric, for example; shirt pockets are sometimes cut on the horizontal grain.

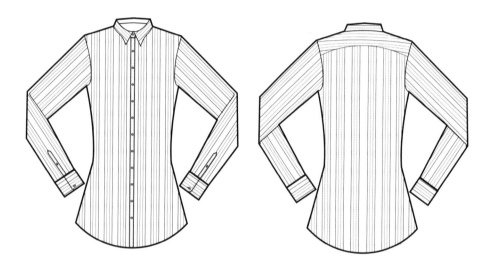

The main bodice and sleeves of the shirt are cut from the straight grain of the fabric, but the cuffs and yoke are cut on the horizontal grain, at 90° to the centre back and front. This helps in the construction of the shirt as the warp now runs horizontally across these pattern pieces, giving extra strength to the seams where the cuff joins the sleeve and across the back of the shirt.

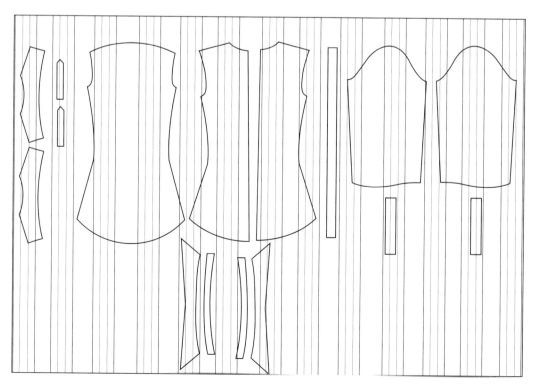

Bias grain

The bias grain runs at 45° to the centre front and centre back. The weight of bias garments, when combined with the effect of gravity, tends to make them relax in length and narrow in width. This gives even woven fabrics a stretch quality that leaves the garment clinging to the body rather than hanging from the shoulder. The bias stretch, however, will also result in wavy seams, which can be corrected slightly if a heavier weight fabric is used.

Pattern cutters should always mark the grainline on the pattern (see page 111). Fabrics should then be cut following the instructions. In addition, on some fabrics the pattern pieces need to be laid out so that the top of each pattern is facing in the same direction, such as those with a pile, like velvet and corduroy, or with an obvious printed or woven pattern. Others, however, with no grain, such as leather and plastic, do not need to be cut on the grainline and here the aim is to lay out the pattern pieces so that as little fabric as possible is wasted.

If the grainline is not followed then, as we have seen, the garment will not hang properly; the seams might not lie flat, the side seams might not hang vertically or the hem might not lie straight. The balance of the garment will also be affected. The human shape is more or less symmetrical and if the grainline is not exactly vertical, horizontal or on the bias then the left-hand side of the garment might not fit as well as the right, or if one piece is not cut exactly on the grain, then the seam joining it to another piece might not hang straight.

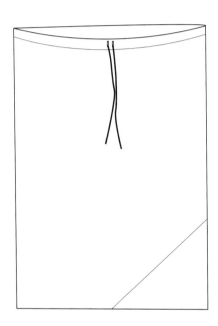
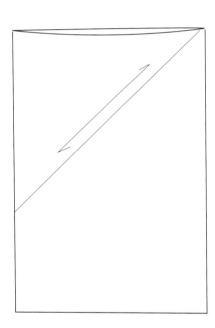

Bias or cross?
Some pattern cutters use the term 'cut on the cross'. This is technically incorrect. The term 'bias' should always be used.

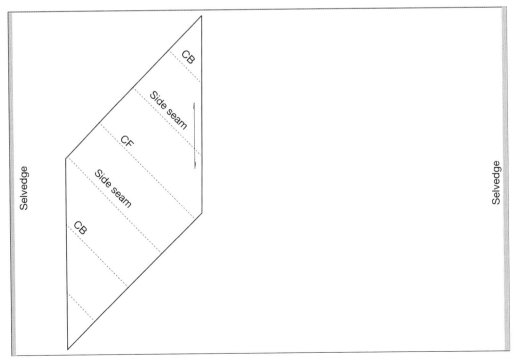

A skirt cut on the bias grain, which runs at 45° to the centre back and front, from one pattern piece will have a natural tendency to relax and cling to the curves of the body.

Pattern cutters must always consider the effect of gravity when drafting patterns; gravity provides the pattern cutter with the second tool for cutting the garment. As human beings we are constantly on the move and gravity affects the way the garment moves with us as we walk. We have already seen how gravity works with the grain and weight of the fabric to affect the hanging appeal of the garment.

The principle of working with gravity in pattern cutting is similar to the practise of architecture. A building cannot float in the air, it must relate and be connected to a structure attached to the ground. In the same way a garment must relate to the body, which has a similar relationship to the ground through the feet. Consequently, garments must be suspended – worn – either on the shoulder, such as a shirt, dress or jacket, or on the waist or the top of the hip; these latter areas being smaller than the circumference of the hip, the largest measurement of the lower part of the body. By suspending the garment from these areas, gravity will work to pull the garment down, but cannot cause it to fall off completely.

A skirt that is well-fitted to the waist will not fall down as it will not be able to pass over the larger circumference of the hips.

A garment can be worn, or suspended, from the shoulder, allowing gravity to play a part in the way that it hangs.

This jacket from John Galliano's Spring/ Summer 2008 collection for Christian Dior has an internal structure that is fitted closely to the body to which the outer 'floating' shell is attached.

Garments can be constructed to seemingly defy gravity, but they need careful engineering. A strapless dress needs an internal corset with vertical boning to hold it up above the waist, but it must be carefully fitted because gravity will act to pull it down until it rests on a larger area, such as the hips. An off-the-shoulder design needs some kind of internal layer that anchors the dress, giving it a place to rest on the body. Any garment that is designed to 'float' is best constructed from a lightweight fabric.

Working with a quarter-size mannequin, an option which is often used to economize on fabric and to create a quick visual reference, can be misleading as the garment created will not have the same weight of fabric. Thus gravity will not be working to the same extent as it would if the garment was full-size.

The completed dress hangs very differently when gravity is allowed full play.

Pinning a dress, or pieces of a dress, to a mannequin gives a false impression of how the garment will eventually hang because gravity is not allowed to work in the same way as it would if the dress was worn by a model.

Working with a mannequin

It is tempting to pin a garment to a mannequin at the shoulder or at the waist or hip, but this gives a false impression of how the garment will hang as it is interfering with the effect of gravity.

A dress made to fit a quarter-size mannequin will not hang in the same way as a full-size version.

SUPPRESSION: DARTS

Suppression is the third tool available to the pattern cutter to fit the garment to the body. The concept of suppression is to remove excess fabric while leaving space to accommodate various parts of the three-dimensional human figure, and eventually to make the garment fit the body: the shape of the shoulders at the back, the shape of the bust, the waist, the curve of the hip and the shape of the elbow. One of the most used forms of suppression is the dart.

Most fashion designers dislike darts because the line of the dart as it cuts through the fabric can look unsightly. When cutting patterns for woven garments they are, however, necessary. If you pin a piece of woven fabric or paper on a dress mannequin, or on the body itself, it will not lie flat; you will need to find ways to take away areas of excess fabric to mould it to the shape of the body and darts are the most commonly used method. For knitted fabrics, their stretchy nature, when combined with the effect of gravity, means that suppression is not usually required.

Finding the position of darts

As a simple experiment, take a piece of paper or calico the same size as the front of a dress mannequin (approximately 35cm/13¾in high x 45cm/17¾in wide). Using masking tape and/or pins secure it at the neckline, shoulder and waist line of the mannequin. To fit the paper or calico to the shape of the mannequin, the obvious method is to fold away the excess material on both sides. Pin the paper/fabric and mark these areas with a pencil. Then remove the fabric and the pins. As you remove the pins you will see the triangular shape of the darts emerge.

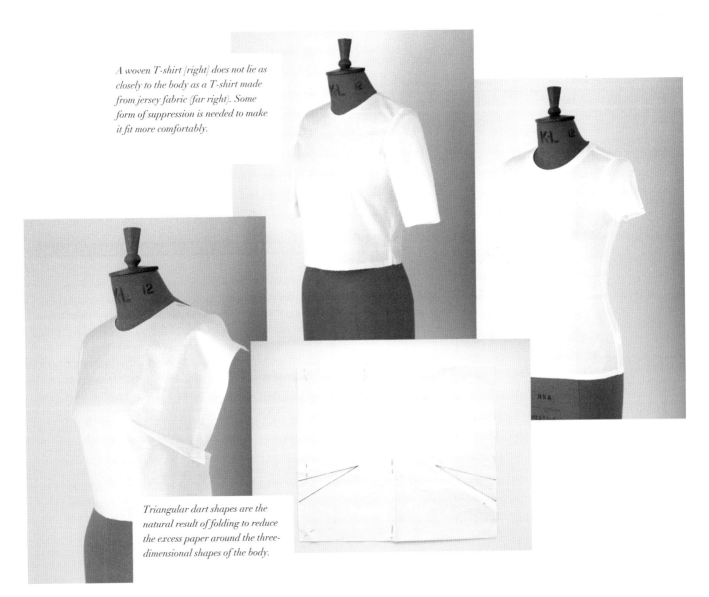

A woven T-shirt [right] does not lie as closely to the body as a T-shirt made from jersey fabric (far right). Some form of suppression is needed to make it fit more comfortably.

Triangular dart shapes are the natural result of folding to reduce the excess paper around the three-dimensional shapes of the body.

A basic dart looks similar to a triangle with an acute angle at one end. In concept it is similar to an ice cream cone, except that it works in the negative, removing shape from a pattern. Unlike an ice cream cone, however, a dart should not reach a defined point (unless the design requires a sharp point) because the human body is curved.

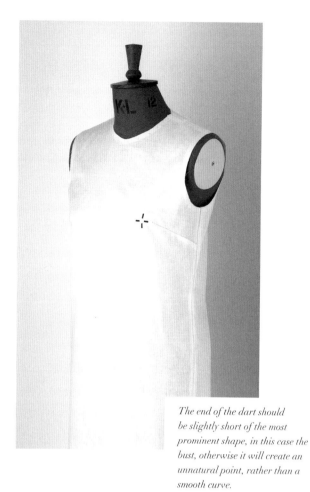

The end of the dart should be slightly short of the most prominent shape, in this case the bust, otherwise it will create an unnatural point, rather than a smooth curve.

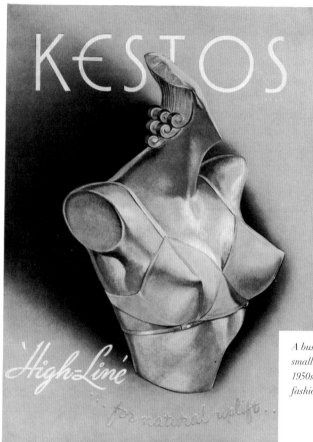

A bust dart can be made larger or smaller to fit the desired shape. In the 1950s a prominent bust shape was fashionable, requiring a larger dart.

COULD A PATTERN WORK IN TWO DIMENSIONS?

With a good knowledge of fabric, we can start to see how some of the basic principles of pattern cutting work if we look at what would happen if we tried to make the pattern in two dimensions, like a child would draw an item of clothing in black outline. Would it work? The answer is yes and no.

YES, if the pattern is drafted with all the relevant components of the human anatomy, such as neckline, armhole, front and back width plus length, and a pair of basic tubes for sleeves in the form of a very basic T-shirt, and that T-shirt is made in jersey or a knitted fabric that will stretch.

A basic shape, such as a T-shirt, will fit comfortably if it is made from jersey because the stretch qualities of the fabric will mould the garment to the body.

YES, if the shape of garment in mind is designed to be quite loose fitting, such as a dressing gown, kaftan or a large smock. Throughout the centuries there have been many examples of costumes based on a similar pattern cutting theory to that of the kimono.

A kaftan, which is loose fitting, is designed to hang from the shoulders.

The pattern for a woven T-shirt looks similar to that for a T-shirt cut from jersey fabric, but it will not fit the figure as well. Suppression and the introduction of darts would be required.

Gravity, together with the effect of the bias cut, will make a skirt cling to the wearer.

NO, if the drafted pattern is used to cut out the garment in a woven fabric because the garment will only materialize as a two-dimensional shell without the right shaped 'spaces' to accommodate various contours of the body, such as the bust and the shoulder blade. If the fabric is not pliable like a knit, or cut on the bias, these spaces are usually formed by the use of a dart or by using suppression. On the other hand, YES this garment can still be worn, but it might not look or feel comfortable to wear because it will not 'fit' with the actual contours of the body shape; the package design will not yet be perfect.

YES, if the garment is cut on the bias grain and made from a delicate fabric such as muslin or chiffon so that, again, it is stretchy.

OBSERVATION, RATIONALE & PRODUCTION OF A WORKING DRAWING

Before you begin to cut a pattern, you first need to understand the required outcome and this can best be done by talking through the design with the designer and making notes: how long is the garment? Does it sit at the waist or on the hip? How does the collar work?

Ideally the designer, or designer working with the pattern cutter together, also needs to produce a working drawing. The working drawing, also known as a technical drawing or flat, is different to a fashion illustration. A fashion illustration provides an impression of a garment and is seldom accurate. A working drawing, on the other hand, is the blueprint for the garment. It is a linear version of the garment showing the silhouette and construction details, and is drawn to the correct proportion. Working drawings are used to communicate details about the garment to both the pattern cutter and the manufacturer. The accuracy of the working drawing is, therefore, paramount to the success of the garment. In some cases the design team will readjust the working drawing after sampling in order to present an accurate drawing when showing a collection to manufacturers and buyers. Even if the garment is a variation on an existing style, a working drawing is still a necessary part of the process that will help save time.

As a pattern cutter you should, therefore, be able to produce a working drawing yourself. The goal is to produce a working drawing with realistic proportions. If it is exaggerated in any way then the test garment will be out of proportion and additional fitting sessions will be required. To produce a realistic working drawing, first take photos of a model's front and back view; it can also be helpful to take poses with the model's arms outstretched. Print the pictures onto A4 paper to use as a template. Placing your photo beneath a sheet of tracing paper, use it as a template to produce your working drawing, which will at least stay true to the real proportions of human anatomy, especially if the model you choose represents your ideal customer in terms of build.

You can also practise drawing garment details by laying a garment flat on a table or on the floor and then drawing from it as accurately as possible. Alternatively, take a photo of the garment, when laid flat, and trace over it. Try not to exaggerate or under represent any part of the garment, or the working drawing will not serve its purpose.

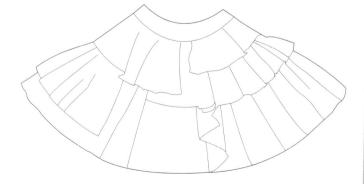

The working drawing of a skirt shows the silhouette and construction details.

This illustration by Sam Parsons reflects the mood of the garment rather than offering an accurate representation of every detail.

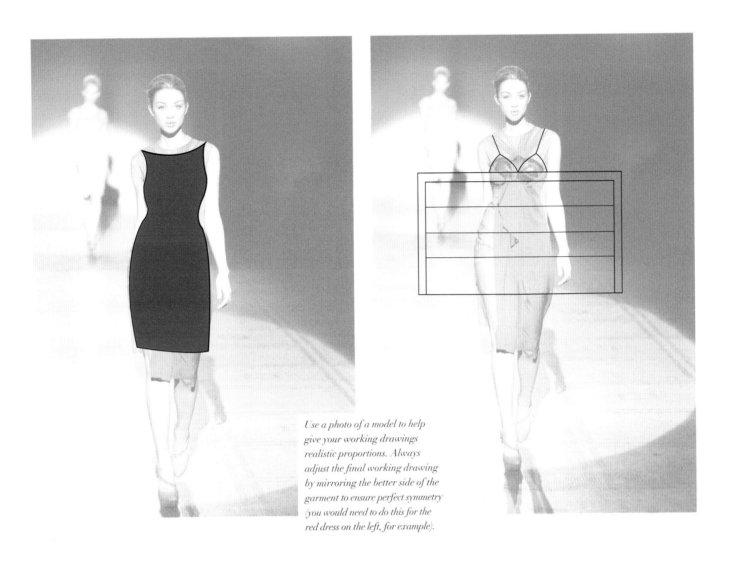

Use a photo of a model to help give your working drawings realistic proportions. Always adjust the final working drawing by mirroring the better side of the garment to ensure perfect symmetry (you would need to do this for the red dress on the left, for example).

To practise drawing garment details, take a photo of your garment and then trace over the outline and construction details.

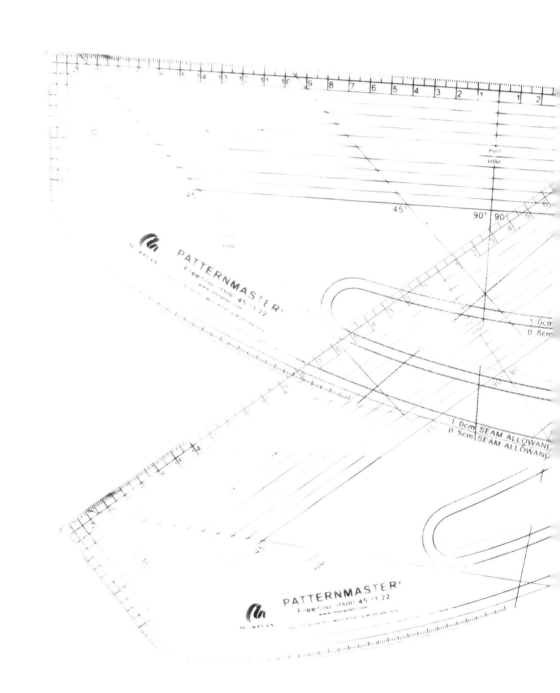

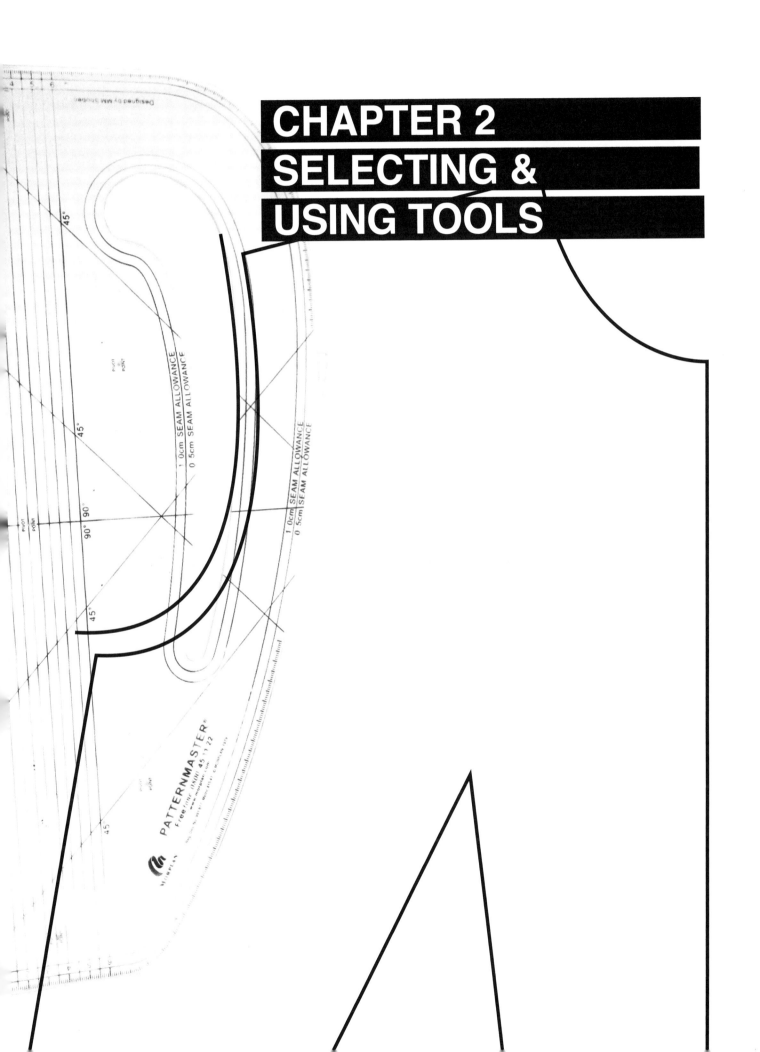

CHAPTER 2
SELECTING &
USING TOOLS

INTRODUCTION

There is an ancient Chinese saying, 'In order to do a good job, one must learn how to sharpen the tools', and the message is that those learning a job should first understand the tools and then learn how to use them to master the skills.

The tools described here form a basic selection with which most pattern cutting techniques can be achieved. The best way to discover which of the many tools available to pattern cutters are most appropriate and how they work is to seek advice from pattern cutters and technicians. Each practitioner will have their own favourite tools, gathered together during a lifetime of experience.

1 Hip curves
2 Armhole ruler x 3
3 Pattern hooks, large and small
4 Cutting mat
5 Glue stick
6 Marker pens in black, blue, green and red and biros in black, blue, green and red
7 Dress pins: long, short, fine, thicker
8 Highlighter pen
9 Scalpel
10 Sellotape, masking tape, Scotch® Magic Tape™, double-sided sticky tape
11 Pattern notcher
12 Pattern hole punch
13 Tape measure: with imperial and metric measurements
14 Metal ruler
15 Metre ruler
16 Pattern master – new version (top) and old version (below)
17 Set squares
18 Grading ruler
19 Unpicker/quick-picker
20 Tracing wheels x 2
21 2H pencils
22 Pencil sharpener and soft eraser
23 Pattern drill with drill parts
24 French curves, as a set
25 Tailor's chalk and chalk dispenser
26 Paper/card scissors
27 Fabric scissors
28 Awls x 3
29 Pattern cutting paper, dot and cross
30 Pattern cutting card

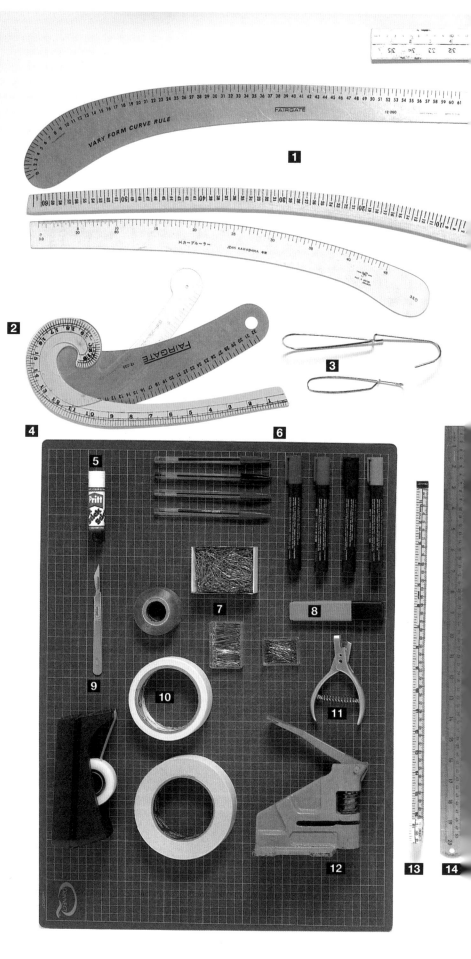

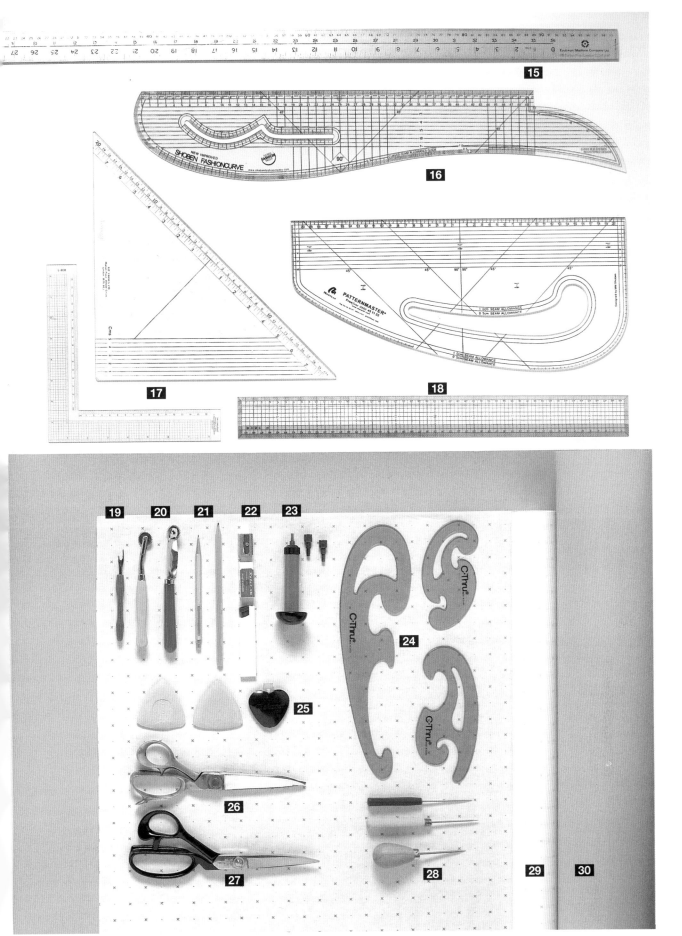

Pattern master

This is an all-in-one, see-through plastic tool consisting of a straight 40cm ruler, a 6cm wide grading ruler marked off in 1cm divisions, 90° and 45° angle indicators, and various curves positioned both inside and outside the tool designed to be used for drawing armholes and necklines. Parallel curves are marked along the inside edge, which are designed to help draft seam allowances.

Metre ruler

Metre rulers are available in both plastic and metal. They are used in industry for measuring fabrics, straightening out fabrics on cutting tables and, of course, measuring long straight lines, especially for dresses and trousers. There is, however, an alternative, and that is to fold the paper in half, using the resulting crease as your straight line.

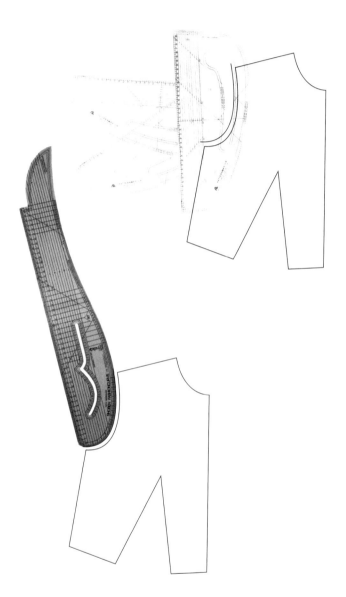

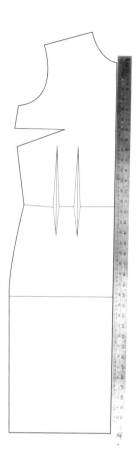

Using a pattern master, however, is not easy for the beginner pattern cutter who is not yet familiar with using the individual tools, such as curves and grading rulers, that it contains. Until the skills of using the individual tools have been mastered, the complexities of the pattern master can make it a frustrating tool to use.

An updated version of the pattern master has been launched recently which is more user friendly. It has a useful curve for drawing armholes and is longer than previous versions, making it a good substitute for the straight ruler.

Grading rulers come in lengths from 40 to 70cm. Obviously, longer versions will have more uses. Usually 6cm wide (although versions 12cm wide are available), this plastic ruler has a graph of lines printed on it marked off in 1cm or 1in squares.

It can be used to draft parallel lines, for example the two sides of a pocket, and can also be used for grading where a right-angled axis is a crucial starting point. The lines can also be used to add seam allowances to paper patterns for both curved and straight seams. It is generally more accurate than using a pattern master.

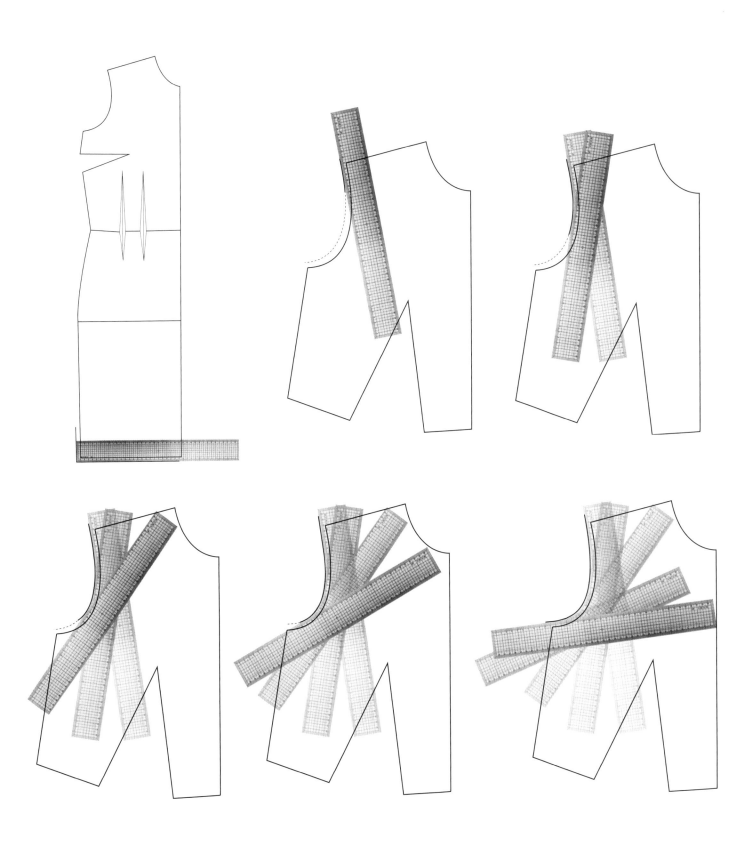

Set square

A set square is used for drafting 90° and 45° angles. Drafting an accurate 90° angle is essential when drafting a pair of trousers, for example; if the centre line of the trouser is not at 90° to the hip and body rise lines, the trouser leg and seam may twist.

An alternative is, again, to fold the piece of paper. First draft a vertical line and then fold the paper in half so that one end of the line meets the other exactly. The crease forms a line exactly perpendicular to the first.

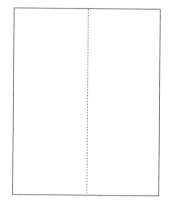

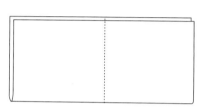

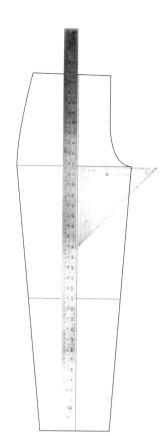

Hip curve

Experienced pattern cutters are able to draft curves freehand as they have experience of the shape of curves required to fit different parts of the body. They know where a curve needs to be shallower or deeper. Curved rulers can, however, be useful to the pattern cutter. The hip curve is used not only for drawing curves for the hip on the side seams of trousers and skirts, but also for developing the curve of the hemline of a circular skirt or a long coat.

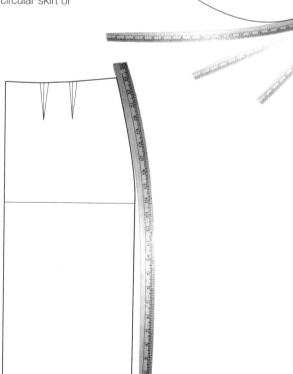

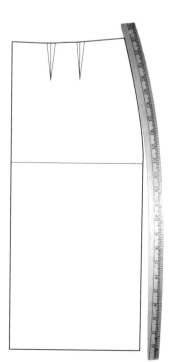

Armhole ruler

The armhole consists of one shallow curve and one deeper curve, the shallower curve being at the back where more fabric is required to allow the arm to move forwards. A curved ruler, like the one shown here, can be used to draft these two different curves.

French curves

These plastic curves are usually purchased in a set of three and used for geometry. The various curves they contain can be used to draft necklines and armholes, but as they were not actually designed for this purpose, they are not an essential piece of pattern cutting equipment.

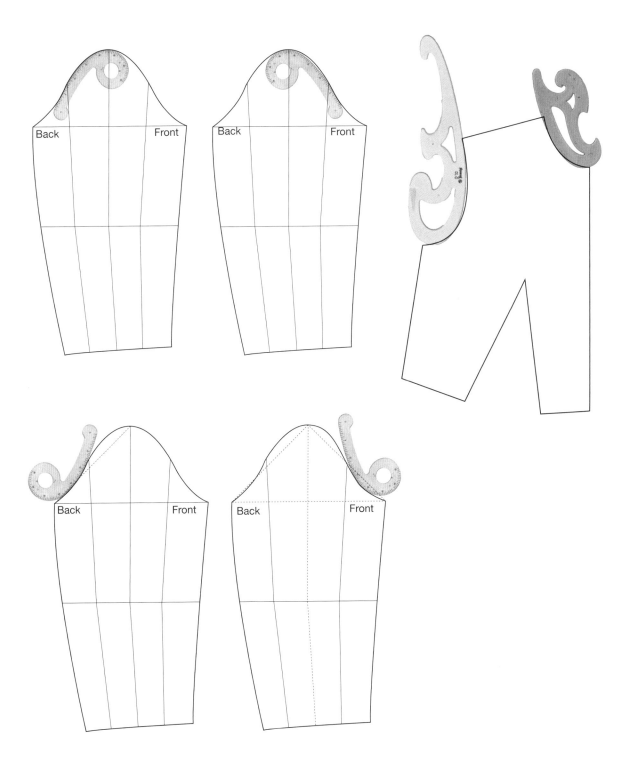

Pencil

For pattern drafting the best pencil is a 2H. This harder pencil will draft the lighter, sharper and thinner lines necessary in pattern cutting where millimetres matter. Also, it will not smudge.

Eraser

A soft eraser is most effective and is less likely to tear the paper.

Marker pens or biros

In the industry, different pattern pieces are marked with four different coloured pens:

Black for the main fabric

Blue for secondary fabrics if the garment is made from more than one type of fabric

Red for interfacing (or interlining)

Green for lining

It is advisable to have marker pens of a medium thickness so that annotations are easy to read by those laying out the patterns on a table. Biros, however, can also be used for marking smaller pattern pieces where a narrower line might be necessary.

Chalk

Tailor's chalk can be purchased in different colours and in versions containing different percentages of wax. Those containing larger quantities of wax are preferable for fabrics that do not take chalk well, such as synthetic polyester and chiffon. Chalk containing less wax is best used for the majority of fabrics as it will not leave a permanent mark.

An alternative is a chalk dispenser, which can either be refilled with specially purchased tailor's chalk or more economically with talcum powder. The latter is more easily rubbed off, but it does give a finer, more accurate line.

Sticky tape

The disadvantage of traditional clear plastic tape is that it hardens and yellows with age, losing its sticky quality, which is not ideal if patterns are to be stored for any length of time. It is also difficult to write on.

Masking tape can be written on, but it is not designed to be permanent and is not readily available in plain white.

Scotch® Magic Tape™ is the most useful sticky tape as it is durable, almost invisible and can be written on.

Parcel or duct tape can be used on the back of card pattern pieces. Double-sided sticky tape, however, is ideal for use on heavier pattern card.

Glue stick

Glue sticks are now rarely used in the industry as they are messy and the glue shrinks the paper.

Pattern hooks

Pattern hooks are used for hanging up sets of patterns. They are available in large and small sizes, but the smaller ones are more difficult to use because they require a special pattern divider to be attached to the wall. In the industry the smaller hooks are used to gather together sub-sets of a pattern (main pieces, lining pieces etc.), which are then hung together on a large hook.

Pattern hole punch

Used to punch holes in patterns so that they can be hung on hooks. This is also called a 'rabbit' because of the shape of its profile. An alternative is to fold over a corner of the pattern and cut out a diamond-shaped hole. The sharp corners of the diamond, however, withstand less weight than the curve of a circular hole, and the pattern can rip.

Pattern notcher

A pattern notcher is an expensive item, but a useful investment. It is used to cut a notch – a small V- or U-shaped indentation – into the edge of the paper pattern to identify where seams should be matched when sewn. The notch should not be wider than half the width of the seam allowance.

Pattern drill

In the industry this is also called a 'mushroom'. Made from metal, or more recently from plastic with tips that screw on, the drill parts are available in 4 and 6mm sizes. It is used to drill small holes through the paper pattern to indicate:

• the corners and position of pockets
• sewing/top-stitching guidelines
• the end of darts
• corners that need to be clipped
• buttons and buttonholes

Awl

Available in different lengths, an awl, or bradawl, can be used to drill a hole through several layers of fabric. The resulting hole makes a temporary mark on the fabric without actually damaging it because the sharp point pushes the yarns of the fabric apart, rather than breaking them. For home dressmaking or one-off pieces, tailor's chalk could be used instead.

An awl can also be used to unpick stitching by inserting the awl under the stitch and applying a little tension to break the thread.

Unpicker/Quick-picker

Used to unpick stitches, the unpicker can be more dangerous to use than an awl because if not used carefully it can slash the fabric, too.

Tracing wheel

Used to trace a line onto another piece of paper or card, the ideal tracing wheel has densely arranged teeth so that it draws a line of closely spaced small holes that is easy to follow and, therefore, more accurate.

Scissors to cut paper & card

Pattern cutters often have two pairs of scissors, one for cutting paper and one for cutting card, because the former are often not strong enough to cut card. An alternative is to use thinner card. You need not, however, purchase expensive scissors for the purpose. As they are used to cut so many other types of materials, such as plastic zips and string, they usually wear out quite quickly and need to be replaced regularly.

Scissors to cut fabric

Patter cutters always have a separate pair of scissors for cutting fabric. This is because a pair of scissors that has been used to cut paper even once will not be as sharp as when they were new. A good pair of scissors will be quite heavy as weight is helpful when cutting along a straight line or around small details. The length of scissors should match the length of the hand holding them. Generally, 25cm (10in) is a good length. The best scissors are made in China or Japan, although the better pattern cutting tools are made in Germany.

Scalpel, metal ruler, cutting mat

A scalpel or blade is useful for cutting straight lines, especially on pattern card, and can be quicker to use than a pair of scissors. It can also be used to score the centre front and centre back of a card pattern, making it easy to fold the pattern in half for layout and tracing onto fabric and to save space when hanging the pattern up on a hook.

A metal ruler should always be used with a scalpel as a plastic ruler would be damaged easily and the scalpel would also be more likely to slip. A cutting mat should also be used to avoid damaging the table beneath.

Pattern cutting paper

There is no one type of paper that is best for pattern cutting, although plain white, slightly transparent paper that can be traced through is ideal. The plain paper used in the industry is available in different widths and most pattern cutters try to create as little wastage as possible for reasons of economy and preservation of the environment.

Paper marked with dots and crosses is slightly more expensive than plain paper and is not essential. It is, however, useful as it provides a grid of 2.5cm (1in) squares that can be used to estimate and check measurements.

Many patterns are traced onto card, which is more durable. Cloth cutters can then trace around the card with tailor's chalk, rather than having to use pins to mark the pattern shape onto the cloth. Patterns that are used frequently, such as blocks, should be made on the most durable card.

Pattern card is available in different weights and in a range of colours that can be used to identify different parts of the pattern, such as the lining. A cheaper alternative to pattern card is Manila card.

Tape measure

Most tape measures are made with a metal cap at both ends. Often this obscures the first and last centimetre or quarter inch of the tape, so care needs to be taken when measuring. While the industry continues to work with both imperial and metric measurements, a tape with one system on each side would be most useful.

Dress pins

Dress pins are available in different lengths, while some are also finer than others. The pin should be chosen according to the fabric and use. On heavier fabrics, a longer pin will be of more use passing through the thicker layers than a heavier one, while on chiffon a medium-sized pin will anchor slippery layers together better than a finer dress pin and will not damage the open weave.

Longer pins should be used when working with a mannequin as they need to pass through several layers of fabric, including the fabric cover of the mannequin itself.

Fine dress pins are best used for securing fabric that is to be machine stitched as the machine needle is less likely to hit the pin and break, while shorter dress pins should be used in difficult to sew areas, such as when attaching the lining at the armhole of a jacket by hand, as they are not as likely to become entangled in the sewing thread.

When an individual garment, such as a sample, is made in the industry, longer pins are faster and easier to use when pinning through the pattern card and the various layers of fabric.

Imperial/US or metric measurements?

While the industry is gradually converting to metric, many professionals use the imperial/US measurement system. Some measurements are easier to remember in metric, such as pocket openings for womenswear, which are usually 16cm wide to allow the hand to pass through (approx 6½in), while the width of the neck is more easily remembered in imperial – as around 6in, rather than as the 'one fifth neck size minus 0.2cm' often quoted in pattern cutting books. Pattern cutters today, therefore, need to be able to be flexible and communicate using both systems.

A quick rule of thumb for approximate conversions is:
1in = 2.5cm and 1cm = $\frac{3}{8}$ in
½in = approximately 1.2cm

Another solution is to use a tape measure with inches on one side and centimetres on the other that can be turned over to find the equivalent measurement.

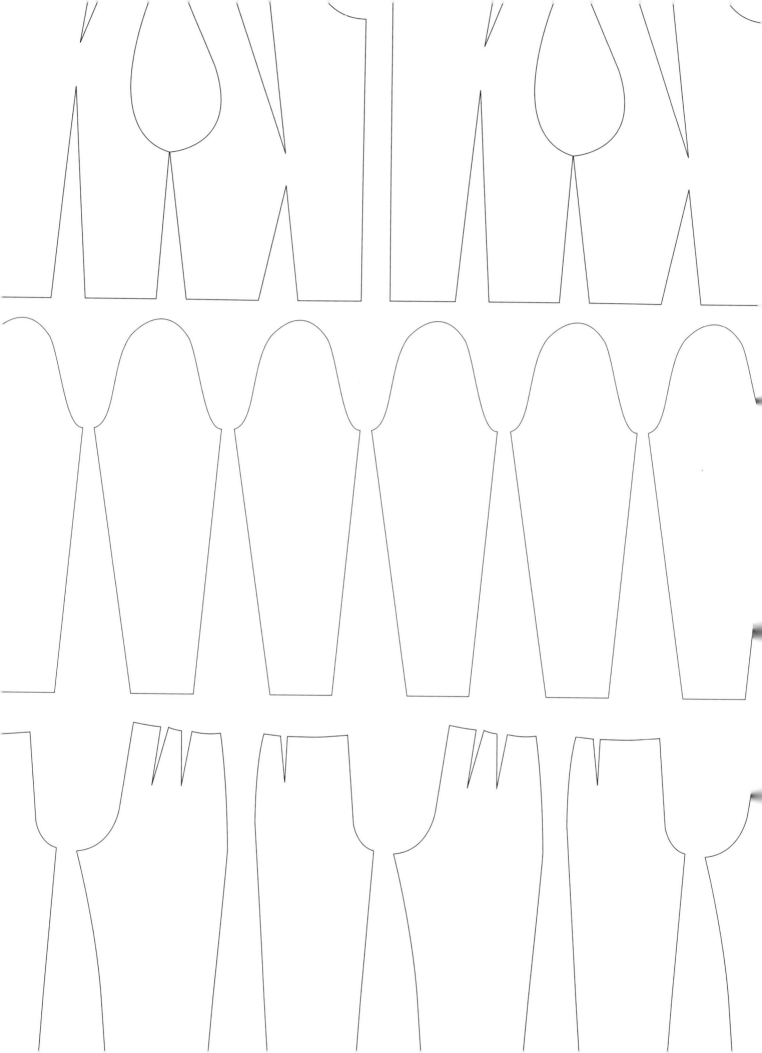

CHAPTER 3
THE BASIC BLOCK

A block is a basic pattern shape that pattern cutters use and adapt to draft patterns, rather than starting from scratch. It is a tool and should not be used without adaptations of detail, fit, length and design, otherwise the garment will be soulless.

A well-organized pattern cutting studio should be equipped with a set of basic pattern blocks in a chosen size; in industry this is usually a size 10 (or a size small) while in the educational environment a size 12 is often used (see pages 12 and 13).

A set of blocks should consist of at least four basic shapes:
• a skirt block
• a trouser block
• a bodice block (which automatically comes with a sleeve block)
• a dress block

These are the basic shapes for the womenswear industry and from this set a pattern cutter could cut most patterns. Of course, the more styles of block that are created, the easier it will be for a pattern cutter to go into a sample room, choose the most sympathetic basic block and then adapt it according to the designer's instructions. Blocks are, therefore, also created in fitted, semi-fitted and loose-fitting shapes. A dress, for example, can be made in a fitted, loose-fitting or oversized style, or a pair of trousers can be cut in a tight-fitting jeans style, a tailored slim-fitted style or loose wide-leg style.

There is no such thing as a perfect block and each company or college will develop their own set of blocks that work for their own vision, silhouette or target market. A block, for example, can convey a 'signature' fit; a fitted jacket by John Galliano will be completely different to one by a high street chain store. This is a matter of style, but also of target market. A high-end designer might cut in tune with an ideal market that is tall and slim, whereas a block destined for the mass market, where wearability and practicality is key, might have a larger waist and hip measurement. The shape of block for the American market will reflect its customer and will also use a different sizing system than one for the Asian market.

Understanding the block you are given is very important. Blocks exist in sample rooms, or in college, and before you begin to use them you should ask the pattern cutter who made the block how it works. You need to know if it is a tight-fitting block or if tolerance has been added, for example. A good way to start is to measure the basic block and establish a vision of how it relates to the measurements from which you are working. Is it too big or too tight? Are the sleeves too small or the collar too wide? Without an exact understanding of the block from the person who made it, however, you are better off making one yourself from scratch, and we will explain how to do this later in this chapter.

A good tip is also to expect the block to be the smallest version of what you are going to make and draft your patterns larger, rather than smaller, than the block. If you understand your block then it can help you cut perfect patterns.

A fitted jacket by Paul Smith (right) is cut with a different signature to that of a high street brand (far right).

MAKING A BASIC BLOCK

In this chapter we will make a block from scratch, using a UK size 12 set of measurements, which can be adapted for any other sizing system for basic block drafting. Please refer to the size chart on page 45 for details of the measurements used throughout this chapter.

TOOLS & MATERIALS

You will need:

- 2H pencil
- eraser
- scissors
- set square
- ruler
- armhole ruler
- hip curve
- measuring tape
- sticky tape
- tracing wheel
- plain paper (for drafting the block)
- pattern card or Manila paper (for making the final block)

Once you have completed your block, trace around each piece onto heavy pattern card. You will keep this as your master draft template. Each time you want to make a paper pattern, trace around this template onto your pattern cutting paper. Then you can modify it according to the design, as we will discuss in Chapter 5.

Basic blocks are used over and over again, so they should be made from a material that will withstand constant use. Many suppliers of pattern cutting materials stock various weights and thicknesses of card, and for a block you should ideally select a heavy pattern cutting card.

Many students find transporting a card block cumbersome and in this case it is acceptable to draft and keep the basic block on a piece of white pattern cutting paper and trace it when required.

Two golden rules for drafting a block

1. Always make the block larger rather than smaller. You can always take in a garment at the fitting stage. It is much more difficult to let one out.

2. To ensure that a block is not too tight, add tolerance (or an extra allowance of fabric, thus creating more room in the garment) for ease of movement, not only for arm, body and leg movements but also to allow the chest to expand when breathing.

These rules are essential for garments to be cut from woven fabrics, but less so for ones to be cut from stretchy fabrics, such as knits.

THE BASIC BODICE BLOCK

The basic bodice block fits the upper torso of the body without sleeves or a collar. If it is cut accurately and fits well, then it can be developed into a shirt, top, jacket, waistcoat or coat simply by shortening, lengthening, widening or tightening the fit in the construction of the paper pattern.

It is also used in many contemporary collections to cut similarly shaped and wearable basic pieces, or can be combined with other blocks to create a variety of garments in a collection.

For this dress from the Autumn/Winter 2008 collection, Yves Saint Laurent combined a basic bodice shape with a skirt cut with a round yoke (see pattern pieces, below right).

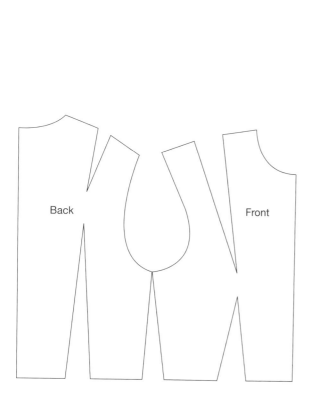

Back

Front

The basic bodice shape consists of a front and back with a shaped neckline and armholes, a seam at the shoulders, darts at the shoulders and waist (suppression to fit the shoulder blade), and a side seam that also incorporates a dart. Two front darts are used to fit the most prominent shape of the front bodice (i.e. the bust).

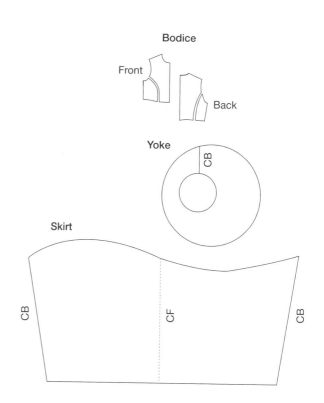

Bodice

Front

Back

Yoke

CB

Skirt

CB

CF

CB

KEY MEASUREMENTS

Nape to waist	41cm (16in)	Actual nape to waist measurement
Bust	96cm (37¾in)	90cm (35½in) + 6cm (2¼in) tolerance
Waist	70cm (27½in)	66.5cm (26in) + *3.5cm (1½in) tolerance
Front cross shoulder	37cm (14½in)	This is exact
Back cross shoulder	38cm (15in)	This is exact
Shoulder length	11.5cm (5in)	From shoulder neck point, exact length
Cross front (armhole)	33.5cm (13¼in)	33cm (13) + 0.5cm (¼in) tolerance
Cross back (armhole)	38cm (15in)	37cm (14⅝in) + 1cm (⅜in) tolerance
Front body length	44cm (17¼in)	This is exact
Back body length	43cm (17in)	This is exact
Neck circumference	38cm (15in)	This is exact (and minimum)
Armhole circumference	42cm (16½in)	38.5cm (15in) + 3.5cm (1½in) tolerance
Armhole depth	17.5cm (6⅞in)	16.5cm (6½in) + 1cm (⅜in) tolerance

*it is recommended to include sufficient bust tolerance at the beginning: 6cm (2¼in) is a starting point

Nape to waist   41cm (16in)

Pattern cutters do sometimes draft the bodice block 1cm (⅜in) shorter than the actual nape to waist measurement. A shorter top bodice looks more pleasing because the wearer will look taller, while a longer top bodice may create excess fabric at the waistline, making the garment look ill-fitting (see page 79).

Bust 90 + 6cm tol. (35½ + 2¼in)   96cm (37¾in)

Tolerance is added to the bust to ensure ease of movement. If the garment is too big, then it is easier to take in the excess on both side seams or across the centre front and back and side seams together.

Waist 66.5 + 3.5cm tol. (26 + 1½in)   70cm (27½in)

Tolerance is also added to this measurement to ensure ease of movement. Excess fabric can be removed in the same way as for the bust.

Front cross shoulder   37cm (14½in)

Using this measurement ensures that the shoulder of the garment sits in the right place by helping to locate the width between both shoulder points, and also to locate the shoulder slants (see Step 5, page 48). There is not, however, an exact place to take the measurement. Fashion trends and designs also influence the position at which this measurement is taken, which will vary according to the desired fit of the bodice.

Back cross shoulder   38cm (15in)

This is measured in the same way as the front cross shoulder. The two do not have to be exactly the same; a wider back cross shoulder indicates that the person has a curved back, while a narrow back cross shoulder indicates that the person stands with an arched back.

Shoulder length   12.5cm (5in)

Each company specifies its own shoulder length measurement as the 'silhouette' or 'signature' of a garment begins with the width of the shoulder. The average measurement for the Western market is 11.5cm (4½in), while 10 to 11cm (4–4¼in) is the average for an Eastern market.

Cross front (armhole) 33 + 0.5cm tol. (13 +¼in)
33.5cm (13¼in)

This is measured 13cm (5in) down from the shoulder neck point (SNP), horizontally across the body between the two front armholes. This measurement assists easy drafting of mid-curve front armhole.

Cross back (armhole) 37 + 1cm tol. (14⅝ + ⅜in)
38cm (15in)

Like the cross front, this is measured 13cm (5in) from the shoulder neck point, horizontally across the body between the two back armholes. Genuine allowance must be added to this measurement to allow adequate material to enable the arms to move forward.

Front body length   44cm (17¼in)

This is measured from the SNP to the bust point and then to waist level. This must be taken into account, especially if the bust size is larger, because the front bodice will then need to be longer than the back bodice to avoid the garment lifting up at the front (see page 55).

Back body length   43cm (17in)

This is measured from the SNP to the shoulder blade and then down to waist level. Again, this measurement should be taken into account, especially if the back is rounded when the measurement might be longer.

Neck circumference   38cm (15in)

A measurement of 38cm (15in) is the minimum that should be allowed. A neckline cannot be too tight. After drafting both the front and back necklines it is important to measure the neck circumference on the pattern to double-check if it is comfortable.

Armhole circ. 38.5 + 3.5cm tol. (15½ + 1½in)   42cm (17in)

This measurement is crucial as armholes that are too small are very uncomfortable and the garment is impossible to wear.

Armhole depth 16.5 + 1cm tol. (6½ + ⅜in)   17.5cm (6⅞in)

An average armhole depth is 16cm (6¼in) and should not be equated to the plastic plate on a mannequin.

DRAFTING THE BASIC BODICE BLOCK

Step 1
The frame

Draw a rectangle 48cm (19in) wide and 43cm (17in) long as a 'frame' for the basic bodice block.

Width = bust measurement ÷ 2 + half the tolerance
= 45cm (17¾in) + 3cm (1¼in)
= 48cm (19in)

Length = Back body length
= 43cm (17in)

Divide the frame in half vertically; the right-hand side is the front of the bodice and the left is the back. Mark the right edge of the frame as the centre front and the left-hand edge as the centre back. The central line is the side seam.

Begin by drafting half the block
As for most blocks for symmetric garments, you will start by drafting half of the bodice. This saves time and makes for greater accuracy. Once the block is complete, you can trace the other half of the pattern.

As you are only drafting half the pattern, you will need to divide all the width measurements and tolerance circumference by half.

Step 2
Depth of armhole

The depth of the armhole is usually half of the width of the front or back bodice block (plus an optional 1 to 1.5cm/⅜ to ½in). In this case the measurement would be 24cm (9⅜in) + 1cm (⅜in). Draw a horizontal line across the block 25cm (9¾in) below the top of the frame. As you can see, you have created a square in relation to the front or back bodice (see shaded square below).

Relative proportions of front and back bodice
There are no rules about whether the front or back bodice should be the same size or whether one should be larger than the other. If the chest is larger, then the front bodice would be larger; but if the back slouches, then the back bodice might be wider.

Step 3
Neck opening

To draft the front neck opening draw a dotted vertical line 7cm (2¾in) from the centre front (which is half the front neck width of 14cm/5½in). Then draw another dotted line 7.5cm (3in) from the centre back of the frame to indicate the width of the back neck opening.

The front neck depth should always be a little more (approx. 0.5cm/⅜in) than the front neck width to achieve an oval shape. For the back neck depth, a suggested measurement is 2.5cm (1in). It can also be the measurement of nape to waist, in this case from waist line it measures 41cm (16in) or the equivalent of 2cm (¾in) from the top edge.

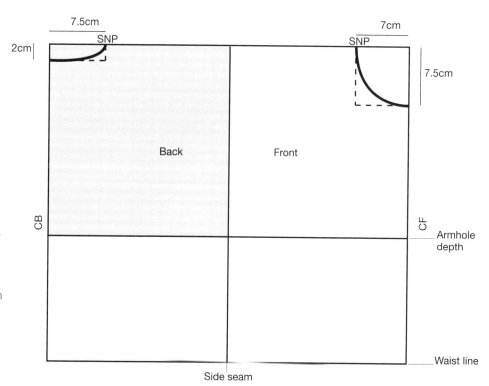

The neckline

The neck is similar to a tube in shape, so it would be logical to suppose that the neckline should be circular. However, the neck sits slightly forward on the body and so the front neckline should scoop downwards (like an oval), taking up the greater part of the neck circumference measurement; imagine how uncomfortable a shirt collar that is worn too high on the neck would be. The neckline of the block should sit below the base of the neck, hence why the centre front of the neckline is called the base of the neck.

The curve of the back neckline, consequently, is shorter.

The back neck opening is also wider than the front. This is because the garment sits closer to the neck here than at the front. A wider opening also creates more room for the neck to move.

Draw the curves for both necklines using an armhole ruler. It is key to draw the front neck like an oval, not a circle, and the back like a 'boat neck'.

Step 4
Bust point
Mark the bust point 27cm (10½in) down from the shoulder neck point and 9.5cm (3¾in) from the centre front line.

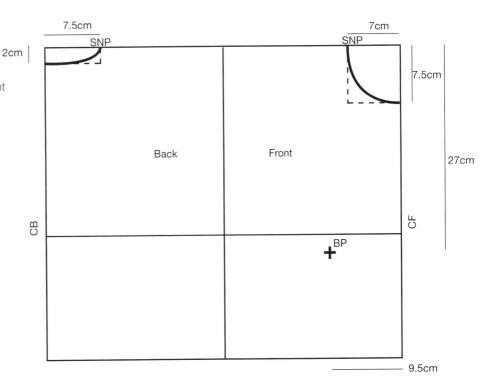

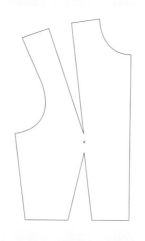

The bust point (BP)
The bust point should always be the highest point of the bust line. As all the front darts are directed towards this point, accurate placement ensures a good fit and good hanging of a garment. The bust points are usually 19 to 20cm (7½ to 8in) apart and located 27cm (10½in) from the shoulder neck points.

Step 5
Shoulder point

Next you will locate the shoulder point (the outer point of the shoulder seam), identifying the shoulder width and slant.

To locate the front shoulder point you need to use the following calculation:

Front cross shoulder ÷ 2
i.e. 37cm (14½in) ÷2
= 18.5cm (7¼in)

The front shoulder slant is 4.5cm (1¾in).

Lightly draw a horizontal line 4.5cm (1¾in) from the top of the frame. From the shoulder neck point, draft a straight dotted line to touch the horizontal line. This is a temporary construction line.

Repeat to locate the back shoulder point. To locate the back shoulder point you need to use the following calculation:

Back cross shoulder ÷ 2
i.e. 38cm (15in) ÷2
= 19cm (7½in)

The back shoulder slant is 4cm (1½in).

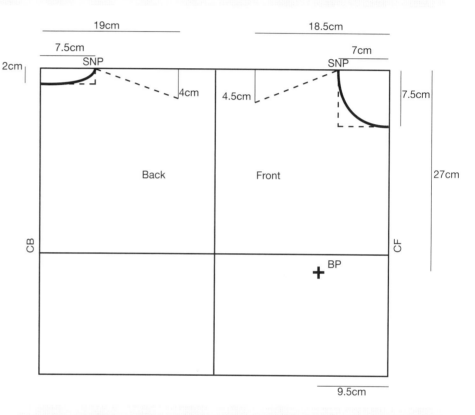

The shoulder slant and the height of the armholes
The shoulder slant is greater at the front than at the back to allow for a shorter front armhole. The back armhole is taller (longer) than the front as it incorporates the curve of the shoulder blade. It is easy to understand the counterbalance of this measurement and why the front armhole level is always lower than the back by looking at the side view of the mannequin on page 55.

There is no specific system for calculating the shoulder slant, which really needs to be adjusted for each individual. The measurements given here are just a starting point. Some size charts will give an average measurement, called the shoulder angle or shoulder slant; on the London College of Fashion size chart (see page 13), for example, it is given as 20.5° to the shoulder neck point.

Step 6
Back shoulder dart

To locate the back shoulder dart, measure 5cm (2in) from the back SNP along the dotted line. Then mark a point a further 1.5cm (½in) along the dotted line as the dart. Mid-way between these two points, draw an 8cm (3in) line at 90° to the dotted line towards the centre back. Create the dart by joining the two points you marked on the dotted line to the end of the 8cm (3in) line.

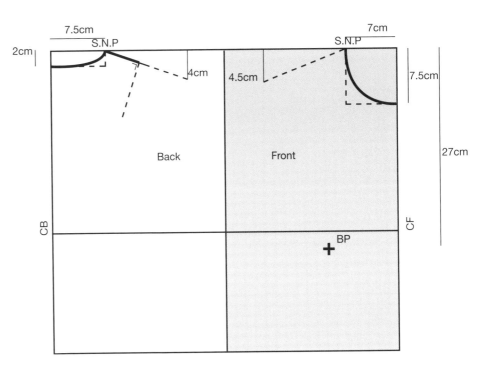

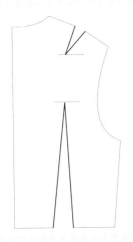

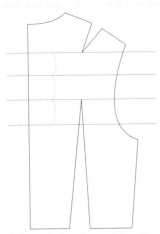

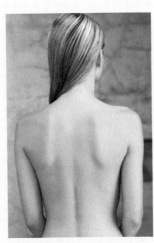

The shoulder blade is a rectangular shape.

Positioning the points of the back darts

The point of a dart should be at the highest point of the underlying shape. For the back bodice, the highest point is the shoulder blade. However, the shoulder blade is not a single point but a rectangular shape. The back bodice, therefore, has two darts, one pointing towards the top of the shoulder blade and one towards the bottom.

To locate the points of the darts, we can divide the depth from the shoulder neck point to the bottom of the armhole curve in three, positioning the point of each dart at either side of the central section, therefore the shoulder dart approximately occupies the highest section, the shoulder blade the central section and the waist dart the lower section.

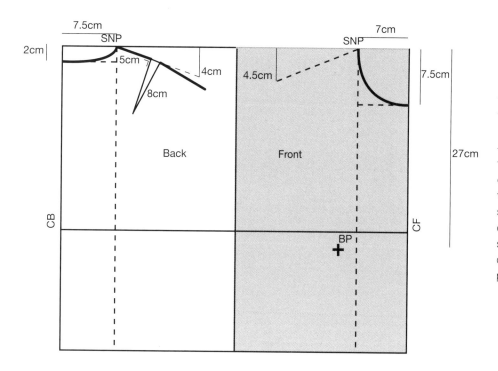

(Back shoulder dart continued)
To draft the back shoulder seam, use sticky tape to close the dart as if it had been sewn on a machine. Using a tracing wheel, draw a straight line from the shoulder neck point to the shoulder point (this line should be 11.5cm/5in – the length of the shoulder seam) to create the shoulder line. Carefully cut through the sticky tape, open out the dart and re-draw the shape of the shoulder line along the line of holes created by the wheel. You will find the shoulder line now has a slight curve down towards the shoulder point (see photos below).

To re-draw a seam line split by dart

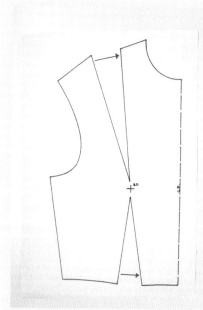

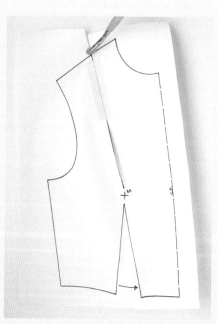

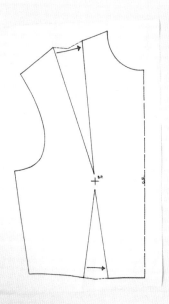

To draft a new seam, use sticky tape to close the dart as if it had been sewn on a machine.

Using a tracing wheel, draw a straight line from one end of the new seam to the other.

Carefully cut through the sticky tape, open out the dart and re-draw the shape of seam along the line of holes created by the wheel.

Suppressing fabric with darts on the back bodice

On the basic bodice block, in order to provide a good distribution of fabric and avoid interfering with the grainline, darts are generally placed at the shoulder and waistlines. However, as long as the darts point towards the shoulder blade points, it does not matter if they start at the shoulder, side seam, waistline, armhole or from the centre back – or even how many darts are used. The key is that each should start from a seam and be positioned to create the desired visual effect on the garment.

Shoulder and waist darts

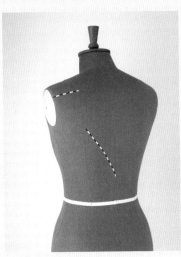

Armhole and centre back darts

Neck and waist darts

The shoulder line

There is no exact position for the shoulder line on the human body and neither is there one on a garment. Some blocks are drafted with the shoulder line slightly towards the back so that it is less visible when the garment is viewed from the front. Other basic blocks position the shoulder line slightly forward; in this case the front neck point would be slightly lower than the back neck point. The garment hangs from the shoulder line when the front and back seams are joined, so the shoulder line is a crucial part of the garment.

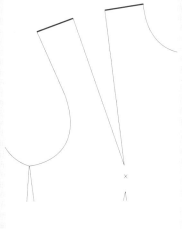

Step 7
Front shoulder dart

To create the front shoulder dart, measure 5cm (2in) from the front shoulder neck point along the dotted line and draft a straight line towards the bust point, but ending 1.5 to 2cm (½ to ¾in) short of the point.

Measure 5cm (2in) further along the dotted line and draw another straight line to meet the first, just short of the bust point.

Positioning front dart at bust point
Front darts should always
end 1.5 to 2cm (½ to ¾in)
short of the bust point.
This is to avoid creating an
exact point where the dart
ends. Darts can also vary in
length for both aesthetic
and practical reasons.

To draft the shoulder seam, use sticky tape to close the dart as if it had been sewn on a machine. Using a tracing wheel, draw a straight line from the shoulder neck point to the shoulder point (again this line should be 11.5cm/4¾in – the length of the shoulder seam) to create the shoulder line. Carefully cut through the sticky tape, open out the dart and re-draw the shape of the shoulder line along the line of holes created by the wheel. You will find the shoulder line now has a slight curve down towards the shoulder point (see photos on page 50).

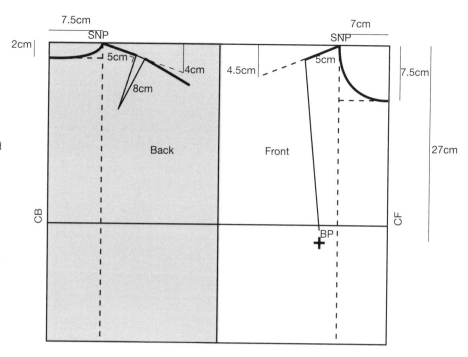

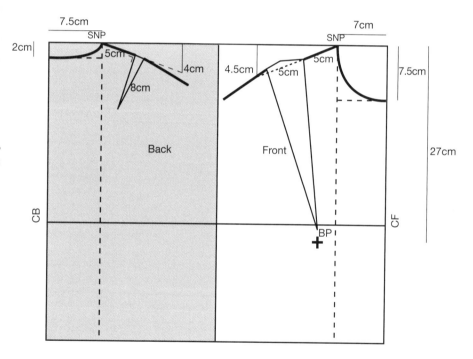

Suppressing fabric with darts on the front bodice

The highest point on the front bodice is the bust point and, therefore, darts on the bodice front should point towards this area. As long as the darts point towards the BP, it does not matter whether they start at the shoulder, side seam or waistline – or even how many darts are used. The key is that each should start from a seam and be positioned to create the desired visual effect on the garment.

On a bodice block, in order to provide a good distribution of fabric and avoid interfering with the grainline, darts are generally placed at the shoulder and waistlines.

Front shoulder and waist darts

Armhole and CF waist darts

Neckline and side seam darts

The cross front (armhole) and cross back (armhole)

The cross front (armhole) is the width between the front armholes, measured at a point halfway down the depth of the armhole, and represents the direction that the front armhole should curve towards. It's important to locate this measurement mid-way down the armholes when drafting the curve of the armholes; if it is too narrow, then the movement of the arms will be restricted. On flat pattern cutting this measurement should be realized when bust darts are folded.

The cross back (armhole) is the width between the back armholes, measured at a point halfway down the depth of the armhole. It, too, represents the approximate half curve point of the back armhole. If it is too narrow, it will also restrict movement of the arms forwards. The width of the cross front and back measurements directly affect how tight or loosely a garment fits.

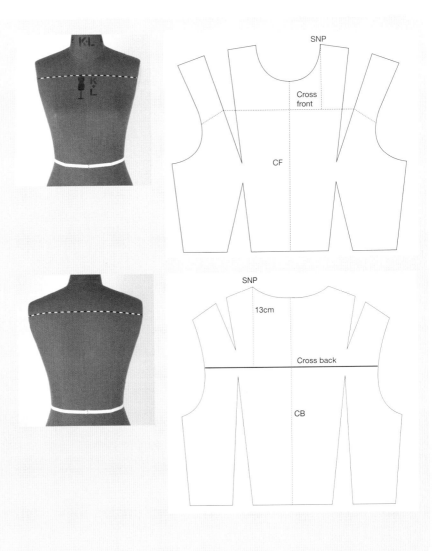

Step 8
Creating the armholes

Now that both the front and back shoulder seams have been established and the armhole depth has also been drawn, the armholes can be created with the help of an armhole ruler and the cross front and cross back measurements.

Starting with the back bodice, first calculate half of the cross back measurement plus half the tolerance: 37cm (14½in) ÷ 2 + 1cm (⅜in) ÷ 2 =19cm (7⅝in)

On the back bodice, from the shoulder neck point, drop a line 13cm (5in) in length parallel to the CB. At the end of this line draft another at a 90° angle from the CB towards the armhole; this line should measure half the cross back measurement, i.e. 19cm (7⅝in).

Then calculate half the cross front measurement plus half the tolerance: 33cm (13in) ÷ 2 + 0.5cm (¼in) ÷ 2 = 16.75cm (6⅝in)

On the front bodice, from the shoulder neck point, again drop a line 13cm (5in) in length, parallel to the CF. At the end of this line draft another at a 90° angle from the CF towards the armhole; this line should measure half the cross front measurement, i.e. 16.75cm (6⅝in). These two points are there to indicate an approximate direction where the armhole curve should be, but not the exact points to intersect or touch.

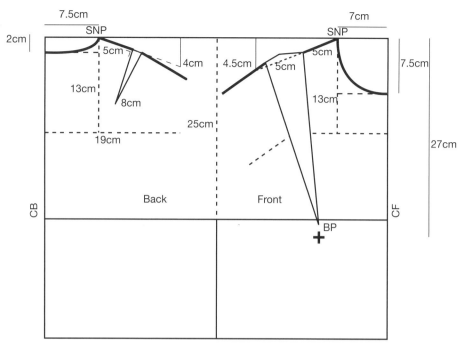

Calculating the cross front if there is a dart

If the bust dart cuts across the cross front measurement, you must fold and close the dart using sticky tape before drafting the straight lines. Once you have established the lines, you can then re-open the block.

Step 9
Drawing the curve of the armholes

To draw the curve of the armholes you will be joining three points – the shoulder point, the end of the cross front/back measurement and the underarm point on the side seam (which is located at the side seam on the line indicating the armhole depth that you drew in Step 2).

You can use an armhole ruler to help draw the curves. Start at a 90° angle at both SNPs. The back armhole should have a slightly straighter curve than the front.

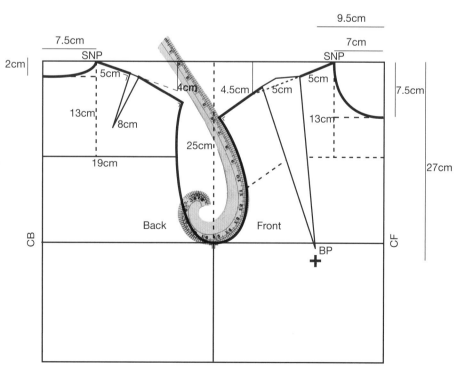

The shape and height of the armholes

The armhole is oval in shape and is cut from the front and back bodice pieces. The front armhole is slightly more curved under the arm than the back armhole. A straighter curve on the back armhole incorporates more fabric, allowing the arm to move forward freely, while the smaller quantity of fabric at the front ensures that there is less excess fabric just in front of the armpit to ruin the line of the bodice.

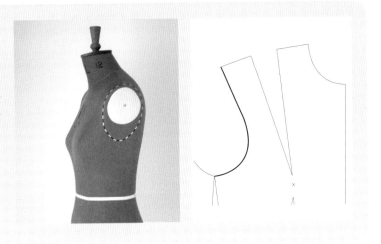

Step 10
Front waist dart

To draft the front waist dart, draw a vertical line from the bust point to the front waistline. At the waistline, measure 2.25 to 2.5cm (⅞ to 1in) each side of this line and from these points draw both sides of the dart, remembering to end the point of the dart 1.5 to 2cm (½ to ¾in) below the bust point. This will create a 4.5 to 5cm (1¾ to 2in) wide dart.

At this point you also need to re-adjust the length of the front bodice block using the actual front body measurement (in this case, 44cm/17¼in from the SNP). If the bust is larger, then this measurement will be longer and hence the front waistline must be lowered (made longer).

Again, close the dart with sticky tape as if it had been sewn and re-draw the line of the waistline before re-opening the dart (see page 50).

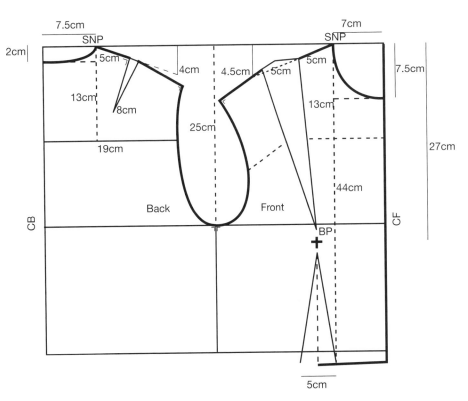

Adjust the front length

You will also notice that height of the front armhole is slightly shorter than the back. This is caused by the difference in shoulder slant (see Step 5). The shape of the bust means that most womenswear garments tend to be lifted up and move towards the back. By increasing the length of the bodice front, this potential imbalance can be addressed.

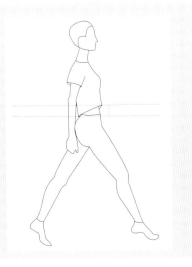

Step 11
Back waist dart

To draft the back waist dart, draw a light vertical line from the end of the shoulder dart created in step 6. At the waistline, measure 2cm (¾in) each side of this line (to make a dart 4cm/1½in wide).

To find the end of the dart, divide the distance between the end of the shoulder dart and underarm point vertically into three equal parts (see page 49). The top of the third section indicates the end of the back dart.

Draw the dart from the two points you located at the waistline, positioning the point at the lower edge of the central section.

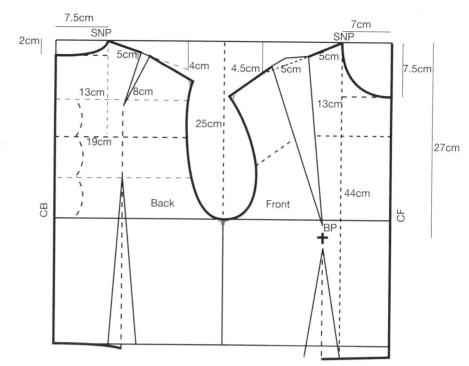

Step 12
Side seam dart

To complete the waistline and position the side seams we need to calculate the width of the waist, and remove any excess measurement from the block as darts in the side seams. This can be done as a simple calculation. If we look at the block:

Half of the bust + tolerance = Half of waist + tolerance + waist darts.

48cm (19in) = 35cm (14in) + 13cm (5in)

To remove 13cm (5in) from the waistline of the block we have already removed 5cm (2in) at the front waist plus 4cm (1½in) at the back waist (= 9cm/3½in), leaving 4cm (1½in) still to be removed from the waist, which can done by drawing a small dart 2cm (¾in) either side of the side seam at the waistline and drawing two lines to meet at the underarm point, thus creating the side seam.

To complete the waistline, close all the waist and side seams darts with sticky tape and use a tracing wheel and hip curve to draw a smooth curve.

Carefully cut through the sticky tape, open out the dart and re-draw the shape of the waistline along the line of holes created by

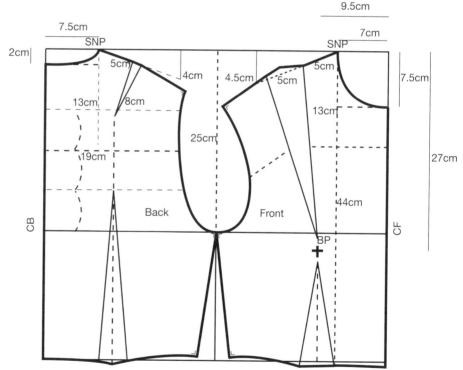

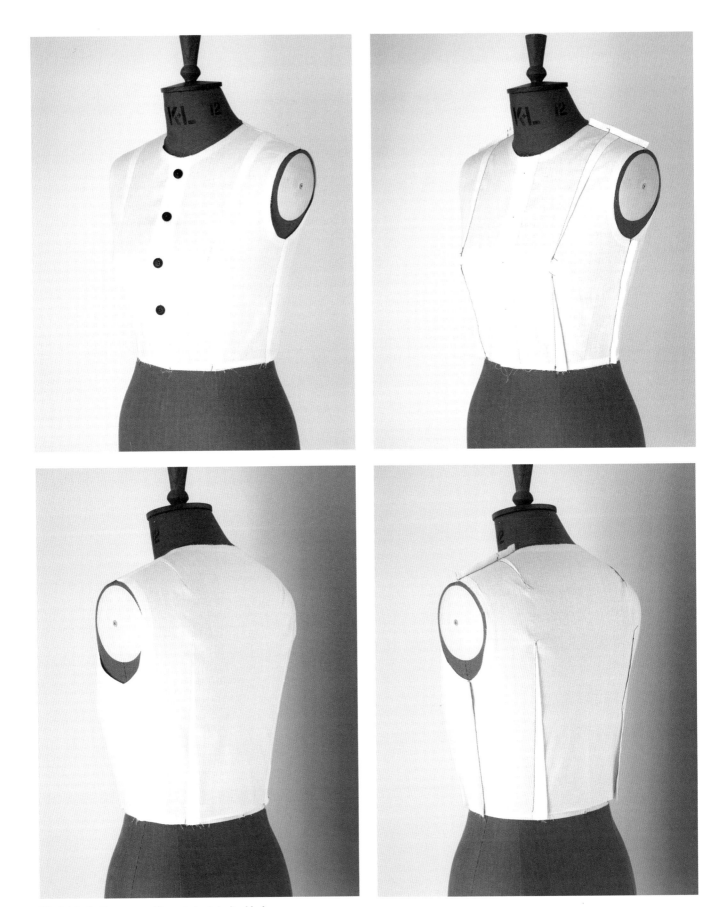

The finished toile constructed from the basic bodice block.

THE BASIC SLEEVE BLOCK

The basic bodice block is usually accompanied by a sleeve block, and often by more than one version. Sleeve blocks can, for example, be made for one-piece sleeves or two-piece sleeves, with or without ease.

As for any type of block, it is essential that the pattern cutter understands the block, questioning the original person who drafted the block about the concept behind the way in which it was drawn up.

The basic premise behind the sleeve is that it should fit the armhole, in the same way that a lid fits a jar. A designer may, however, create a sleeve that is larger than the armhole, adding in sleeve head ease, and the excess fabric may be compressed in gathers, darts or pleats. A sleeve could even be designed to be smaller than the armhole, leaving part of the upper arms or shoulders exposed.

In order to understand how to draft a sleeve it is first necessary to understand how a sleeve works and particularly how it works in relation to the movement of the arms. There are five measurements any pattern cutter needs in order to draft a sleeve, and each has an effect on the way the sleeve moves: the height of the crown, the width and length and the positioning of the elbow and the width of the wrist.

Sleeve Head Ease

Ease is an extra allowance of fabric that can be added to a sleeve head (the top of the sleeve) to allow it to fit over the curve at the top of the shoulder. This extra fabric is then 'eased' into the top of the armhole either by a line of gathers or small pleats. The amount of ease you add depends on the type of sleeve and the fabric you are using. A pair of tailored sleeves fit quite closely to the arm and so need extra ease to accommodate the shape of the top of the shoulder. A T-shirt sleeve needs little or no ease because it doesn't fit as closely and the material is usually stretchy.

Sleeve head ease

Sleeve without head ease

Ease, or an extra allowance of fabric, can be added to the sleeve head to create a full sleeve-head roll on a pair of tailored sleeves.

A sleeve head without ease is more suited to a casual shirt.

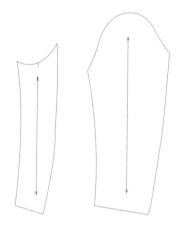

A one-piece sleeve fits inside the armhole of the basic bodice. The grainline runs down the centre of the sleeve and it has one seam under the arm.

A two-piece sleeve also fits into the armhole of the basic bodice. It has two seams, which allow for more shaping.

Sleeve crown

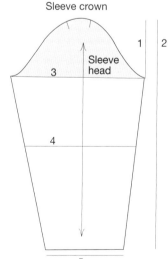

1) Crown height
2) Sleeve length
3) Sleeve width
4) Elbow
5) Wrist

There are five basic measurements that you require before drafting a sleeve, and each is dependent upon the other.

SLEEVE CROWN

The sleeve crown is the upper part of the sleeve above the sleeve width. Its height is not necessarily exactly the same as the depth of the armhole. It depends on the desired crown height, which will in turn create a different fit and appearance.

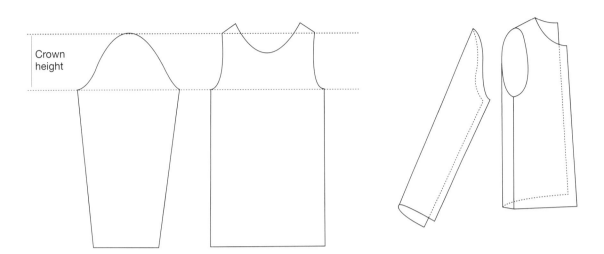

To estimate the height of the crown, lay a garment flat and observe the lift of the sleeve, or how high the arm can be raised before the side seam is lifted and the garment is disturbed. Draw lines at 90° to the fold of sleeve, or top of the armhole seam, and to the point at which the sleeve meets the armpit.

The height of the crown has both aesthetic and practical considerations.

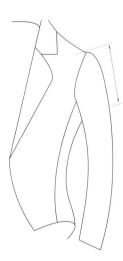

A fitted, tailored garment usually has a high crown.

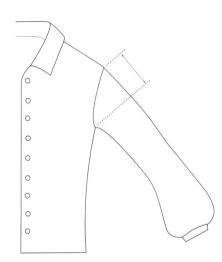

A semi-fitted garment, such as a shirt or a dress, has a medium-height crown.

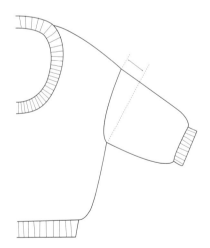

A loose-fitting, casual garment often has a low crown.

High sleeve crown

Aesthetic considerations: a high sleeve crown gives a very tidy appearance to the garment as there is no excess fabric around the underarm. The sleeve is constructed almost exactly to fit the shape of the arm when the arms are hanging down naturally and is usually used for tailored jackets and coats.

Working drawings

When making a flat or working drawing, it is vital to draw the sleeve accurately so that the pattern cutter can identify how high the crown should be.

Practical considerations: a high sleeve crown combined with a tightly fitting sleeve restricts the movement of the arms in an upward direction. As the arm moves up, the side seam of the garment follows in the same direction and on a jacket or coat with a fitted sleeve, unless it is unbuttoned, movement is awkward. As aesthetically pleasing as a beautifully tailored pair of sleeves may be, they are not very practical for wear on some occasions.

Medium sleeve crown

Aesthetic considerations: a medium sleeve crown results in a small amount of excess fabric at the underarm, consequently garments with a medium crown need to be made from a lighter fabric than a tailored garment. A medium crown height is, therefore, used for garments that are less tightly fitted, such as dresses and non-tailored outerwear such as shirts.

Practical considerations: a garment with a medium crown is more comfortable than one with a high crown. A small amount of excess fabric at the underarm means that the arm can be raised higher before the side seam is lifted.

Low sleeve crown

Aesthetic considerations: garments with a low sleeve crown have the largest allowance of excess fabric beneath the underarm in direct contrast to the tailored look of a high sleeve crown. This results in a more casual appearance, more suited to sportswear.

Practical considerations: the excess fabric beneath the underarm of a garment with a low crown allows much greater freedom of movement before the side seam begins to rise.

Calculating sleeve crown height

Sleeve crown height needs to be calculated to allow some flexibility for movement, and may also need to be adjusted according to the design of a fitted, semi-fitted or casual style. One method of calculating the crown height is to divide the armhole measurement by four for a medium crown height and then to add a further 4 to 6cm (1½ to 2¼in) for a higher crown or to subtract 4 to 6cm (1½ to 2¼in) for a lower crown height:

Total arm measurement	= 45cm (17¾in)
Higher sleeve crown height	= 15 to 17cm (6 to 6¾in)
	[11.25cm (4½in) + 4 to 6cm (1½ to 2¼in)]
Medium sleeve crown height	= 11.25cm (4½in)
	[45cm (17¾in) ÷ 4]
Lower sleeve crown height	= 5 to 7cm (2 to 2¾in)
	[11.25cm (4½in) − 4 to 6cm (1½ to 2¼in)]

This is the method of calculation that will be used in this chapter.

SLEEVE WIDTH

The width of the sleeve is directly connected to the height of the crown and the width of the bicep.

The height of the crown

The general rule is that 'the higher the crown, the narrower the sleeve width'. If, for example, the front and back armhole are both 20cm (8in) in length, and the sleeve head is consequently also 20cm (8in) in length at both back and front so that the two fit together like a lid on a jar, then a high sleeve crown will result in a narrow sleeve and a low crown will result in a wider sleeve.

Bicep measurement

The bicep measurement gives the minimum width of the sleeve. This measurement, therefore, directly affects the height of the sleeve crown as the sleeve width can be larger than the bicep, but not smaller. With the bicep and sleeve head measurement we can estimate the height of the highest sleeve crown, while lowering the crown height will then create a sleeve wider than the bicep measurement.

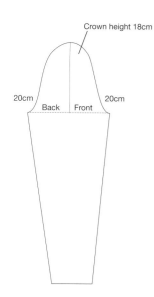

Crown height 18cm

20cm   20cm

Back   Front

The crown height on this sleeve is 18cm (7in), while the sleeve head measures 40cm (15¾in), resulting in a high crown.

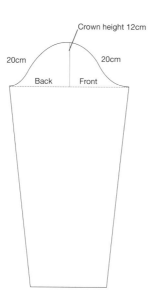

Crown height 12cm

20cm   20cm

Back   Front

The crown height here is 12cm (4¾in), while the sleeve head still measures 40cm (15¾in), resulting in a medium crown.

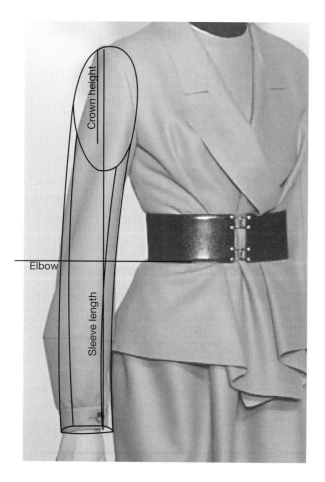

Crown height 8cm

20cm   20cm

Back   Front

Here the crown height is 8cm (3in), and the 40cm (15¾in) sleeve head results in a low crown.

Checking the crown height on the block

Checking the height of the crown on the block is advisable before starting work. You will then know whether you need to re-draft the sleeve or select a different block.

ELBOW

Elbow measurement is from shoulder point to elbow. Calculations also exist for finding the position of the elbow. As a general rule, if you divide the underarm seam in two, the elbow is usually positioned 1.5 to 2cm (½ to ¾in) above the halfway point.

It is more necessary to know the position of the elbow when making a two-piece sleeve as the sleeve is shaped to accommodate the arm swing forwards from the line of the elbow downwards.

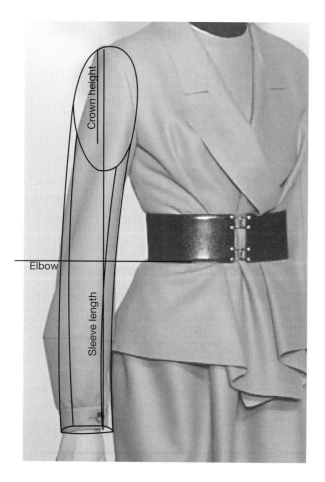

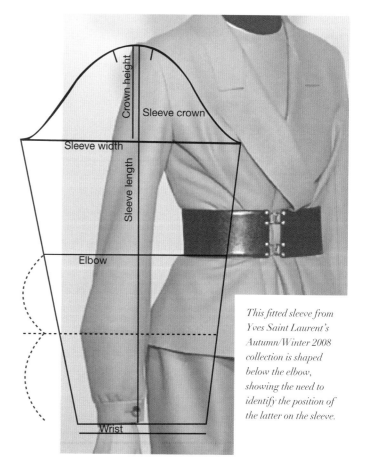

This fitted sleeve from Yves Saint Laurent's Autumn/Winter 2008 collection is shaped below the elbow, showing the need to identify the position of the latter on the sleeve.

Human anatomy and the sleeve

When our arms hang down in a
relaxed position, they are not
perfectly straight, but tend
to bend forwards at the elbow —
our arms are naturally designed
to swing forwards from the
elbow down.

A one-piece sleeve is
essentially a straight tube of
fabric with a single straight
seam. If it is at all tight,
it will consequently tend
to crease at the elbow. The
solution to the problem is a
two-piece sleeve, which has two
seams, one at each side of the
tube, that can be shaped at the
elbow. A fitted garment, such as
a tailored jacket, will usually
have a two-piece sleeve.

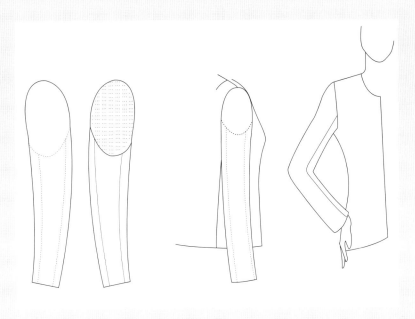

WRIST

The sleeve ends at the wrist, which, in the industry, is called the
sleeve opening. On most blocks it is drawn as a straight line,
parallel to the sleeve width and can be as wide as the block itself.
The actual wrist measurement will, however, be much smaller and
a method must be found to reduce the sleeve opening so that it
fits around the wrist.

One method would be to reduce the sleeve width by narrowing
the side seams towards the cuff. This should not be done too
drastically, however, because the side seams would be on the
bias and would be difficult to sew. Also, this would reduce the
width of the whole sleeve without any consideration of other
measurements, such as the elbow. Instead, there are several
ways of reducing the sleeve opening.

The underarm seams can be reduced by 1 to 2cm (⅜ to ¾in) on
both sides and a small dart taken at the back of the sleeve. This is
achieved by adding a dart into the back side seam, at elbow level,
thus reducing the sleeve width at the cuff. The effect is similar to
the shaping of the two-piece sleeve.

Calculating the sleeve opening

The wrist is narrower than the circumference
of the hand, which is usually 20 to 22cm (8
to 8¾in) for most adults, and so the sleeve
opening must be wide enough to allow the hand
to pass through, or be made to open in some
way, such as by the addition of a cuff and an
opening in the seam at wrist level.

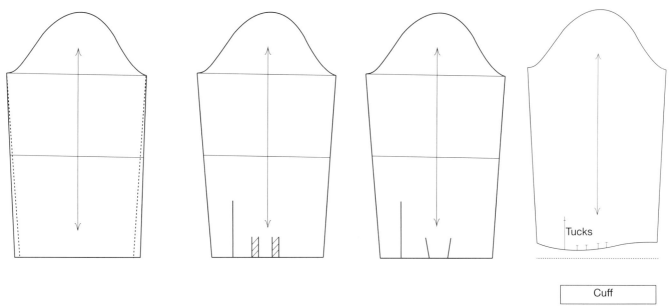

Tucks

Cuff

A cuff can be created and the excess fabric pleated into a seam. The illustration on the far right demonstrates shortening the sleeve length to coincide with the cuff depth + 2cm (¾in). This allows the sleeve to hang on top of the cuff more naturally. The back of the sleeve can also be curved further down to enhance the sleeve's 'puff'.

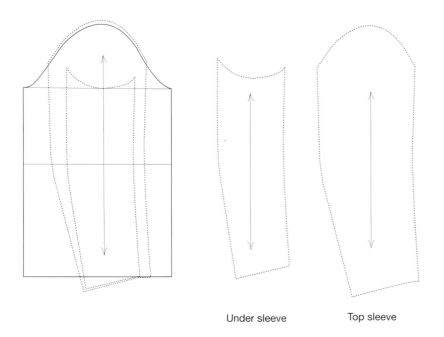

Under sleeve

Top sleeve

The sleeve can be translated into a two-piece sleeve and the excess fabric removed in the additional seams created.

CENTRE LINE OF THE SLEEVE

A vertical line from the shoulder point to the wrist bone divides the front of the sleeve from the back. It is helpful to locate this line to check the proportion and balance of the sleeve.

For a one-piece sleeve this line usually acts as a first draft construction or grainline and as a guideline for a set-square.

On a two-piece sleeve, however, this line swings forward 1.5 to 2cm (½ to ¾in) from the shoulder point to the wrist, depending on the swing of the arm.

With an understanding of how a sleeve works, it should be possible to select the most appropriate sleeve block and adapt it according to the sleeve width, crown height and the type of garment – tailored, semi-fitted or casual.

Many pattern cutters, however, choose to make the pattern for the bodice first, make a toile, and then construct a sleeve from scratch using the front and back armhole measurements. In this chapter we will learn how to construct a sleeve in 12 steps using just these measurements.

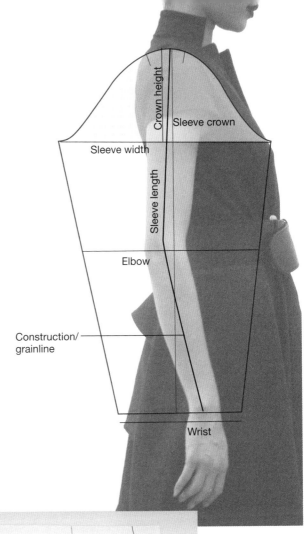

DRAFTING THE BASIC SLEEVE BLOCK

Step 1
Measure the front and back armhole

Measure the front and back armholes. For this example we will assume the following:

Front armhole = 22cm (8¾in)
Back armhole = 23cm (9in)
Total armhole measurement = 45cm
(17¾in)

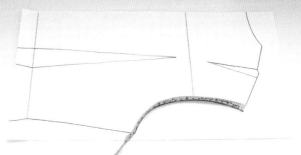

To measure around a curve, use a tape measure held upright.

Step 2
Calculate the sleeve crown height

Calculate the sleeve crown height according to the desired design, appearance and level of comfort using the following equation:

$$\frac{\text{Armhole}}{4} + \text{ or } - (4 \text{ to } 6\text{cm})/(1\frac{1}{2} \text{ to } 2\frac{1}{2}\text{in})$$

+ = a tall crown
− = a low crown

For a sleeve for a fitted jacket with a high sleeve crown the calculation would be as follows:

$$\frac{\text{Armhole (45 cm/17¾in)}}{4} = 11.25\text{cm (4½in)}$$

$$+ 5\text{cm (2in)} = 16.25\text{cm (6½in)}$$

Step 3
Establish the position of the sleeve width

Take a piece of paper (approximately 100 x 50cm/40 x 20in) and, using a long ruler, draw a vertical line of approximately 60 to 70cm (24 to 28in) down the centre. Alternatively, you can fold the paper in half and then make a small mark at the top of the fold to indicate the top of the sleeve. Measure the crown height (16.5cm) from the top of the line, or mark, and then, using a set square, draw a horizontal line at 90° for the sleeve width.

Drafting the sleeve in one piece
As the sleeve is not symmetrical, the sleeve block is drafted as one piece, rather than in half.

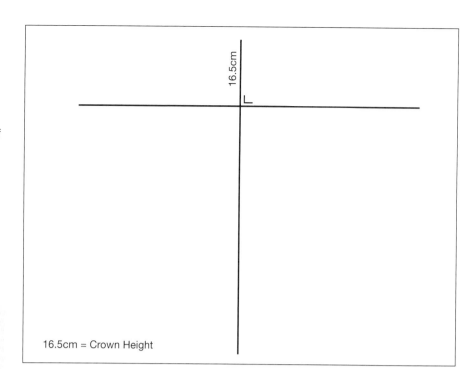

16.5cm

16.5cm = Crown Height

Step 4
Indicate the top of the crown

At the top of the line, draw a short 10cm (4in) line at 90° to indicate the top of the crown. This will help you draft a smooth line at the top of the sleeve and avoid a sharp peak. At this stage you should also decide which side is the front and which the back of the sleeve (there is no rule about which should be which).

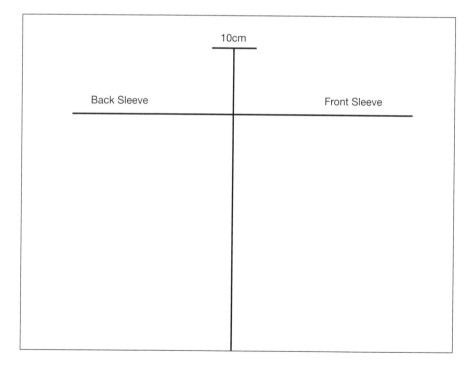

10cm

Back Sleeve

Front Sleeve

Step 5
Establish the width of the sleeve

From the top of the sleeve, draw a straight line the same length as the front armhole less 1cm (³⁄₈in) [22cm (8¾in) – 1cm (³⁄₈in)] until it touches the line indicating the sleeve width. The 1cm (³⁄₈in) adjustment is to compensate for the lengthening of the line when it is curved later (see Step 8). A curved line will always be longer than a straight line when covering the same distance from one point to another.

Draft a straight line [23cm (9in) – 1cm (³⁄₈in)] for the back of the sleeve in the same way.

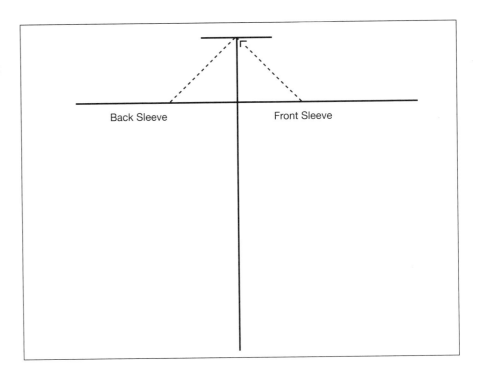

Back Sleeve   Front Sleeve

Step 6
Check the sleeve width

Now measure the sleeve width, which is the distance between the ends of the two lines you have just drawn. Check this against the bicep measurement on your size chart. If it is too wide raise the crown height to make the sleeve narrower; if it is too narrow, then lower the crown height to widen the sleeve.

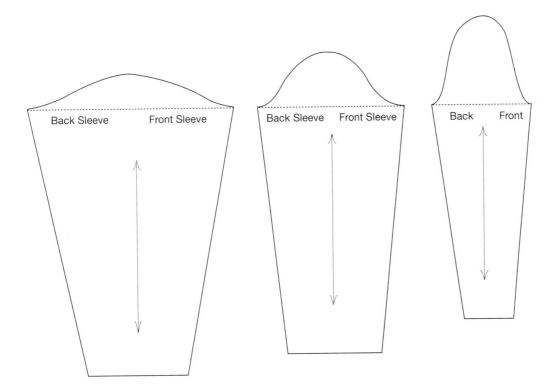

Back Sleeve   Front Sleeve   Back Sleeve   Front Sleeve   Back   Front

Step 7
Begin to shape the armhole

Mark a point halfway down each of the two lines to indicate the reverse of the sleeve curve. This is not an exact point, however, and the line of the final armhole does not have to touch these two points.

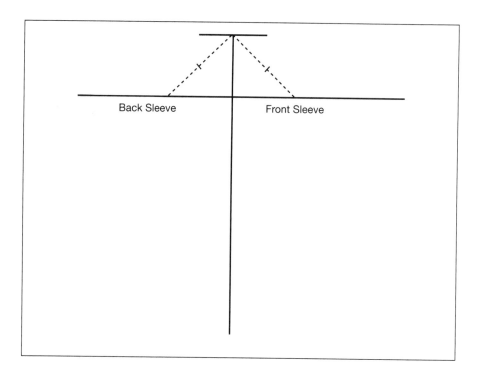

Step 8
Draft the front armhole curve

Using a curved ruler, ideally an armhole ruler, draft a smooth curve for the front of the sleeve, reversing the curve at the mid-way point to finish. The top of the curve should be wider (straighter) to accommodate the shape of the top of the arm, while the reverse of the curve should be deeper (curvier) so that there is less fabric under the arm.

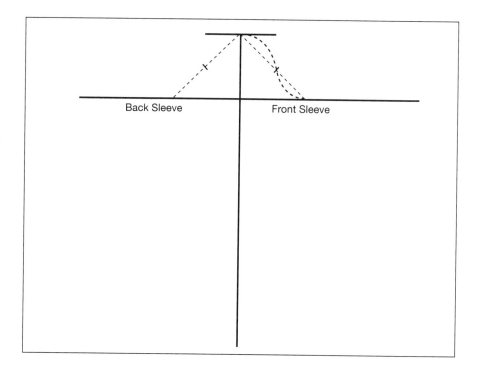

Step 9

Draft the back armhole curve

In the same way, draw a smooth curve for the back of the sleeve. The top of this curve is wider (straighter) while the reverse of the curve is shallower as more fabric is required here to allow the arm to move forward.

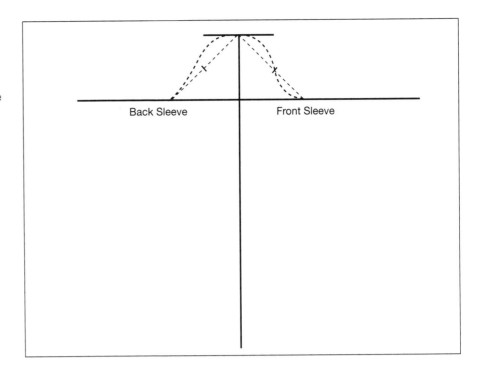

Back Sleeve   Front Sleeve

Step 10

Check & adjust the length
of the armhole

Now check the length of the finished curves on both the back and front of the sleeves using a tape measure held upright. The measurements should coincide with the measurements of the front and back armholes. If there is a difference of under 1 to 1.5cm (³⁄₈ to ½in) you can increase or decrease the sleeve width accordingly. If the difference is greater, then try to adjust the curves. If this is unsuccessful, then you need to start again and re-work your calculations from Steps 2–5. Often the crown height will need to be re-evaluated.

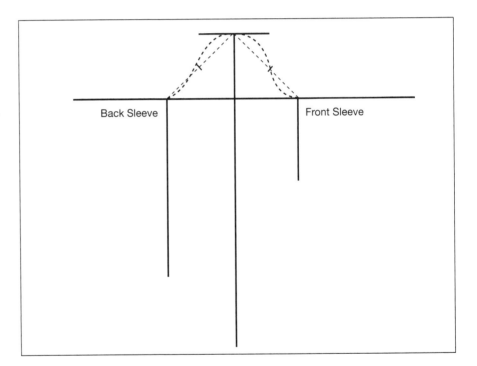

Back Sleeve   Front Sleeve

Step 11
Draft the remainder of the sleeve

Check the sleeve length on your size chart and measure this distance from the top of the sleeve. Make a mark at the end of this line to indicate the position of the wrist or sleeve opening. Now draw a line at 90° at this point, parallel to the sleeve width.

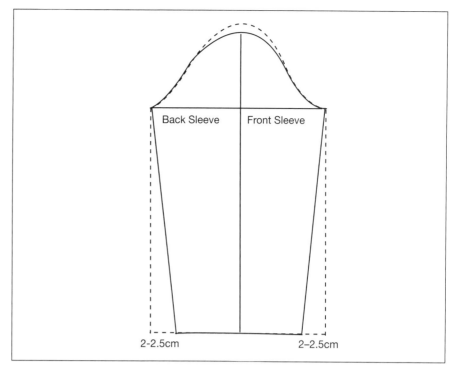

Step 12
Add sleeve head ease

If you need to add sleeve head ease – for a full sleeve head roll on a tailored jacket, for example – simply raise the armhole line to increase the measurement. At this point you have a simple one-piece sleeve block with no sleeve head ease.

In contrast, if you need to decrease the sleeve head measurement, simply lower the crown height and redraft the line. You can do this to quickly amend small discrepancies.

Always tolerate a small amount of excess material by the back armhole as this allows arm movement towards the front.

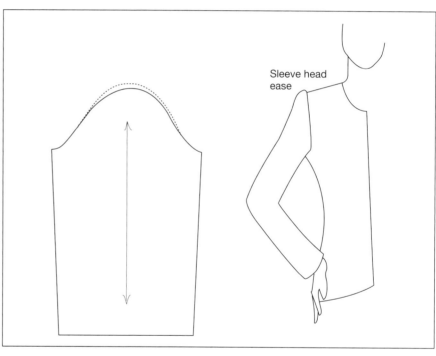

Making a toile
You should always make a toile of the garment to check the crown height.

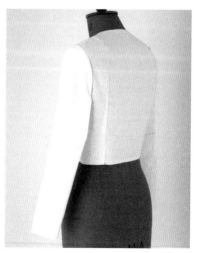

The finished toile constructed from the basic sleeve block.

THE BASIC SKIRT BLOCK

A skirt is essentially a tube of fabric that is wrapped around the body. In order for it to stay up it needs to be suspended from the waist or at least from above the hip line. Skirts can be described as high-waisted, on the waist, or below the waist, and the latter can also be described as above the hip and sitting on the middle of the hip. If the circumference of the top the skirt is larger than the hip then it will fall down, unless it is suspended from the shoulders, for example.

In the same way that you draped a piece of fabric around a mannequin to understand the shape of the bodice, you can drape a piece of paper around the figure to understand how a skirt works. The paper will fit around the hips and then will have to be pleated to manipulate the shape closer to the waist (an exercise in suppression). These pleats will represent the darts when you start to draft your block. It is, therefore, more important to fit the skirt on the hip line than below, where the skirt can be straight, tapered or flared.

Here we will draft a basic skirt block for a straight skirt. Like any block, the basic skirt block can then be manipulated into any shape you wish. A pattern cutter using a previously constructed skirt block should always check that they understand how it was made before starting to use it.

A skirt must be suspended from an area smaller than the circumference of the hips, or it will fall down. Skirts can therefore be high-waisted, or sit on the actual waist or at hip level.

KEY MEASUREMENTS

Waist	69cm (27in)	66.5cm + 2.5cm tolerance (26in + 1in)
Hip	96cm (37¾in)	92cm + 4cm tolerance (36¼in + 1½in)
Length of garment	58cm (23in)	A shorter length to avoid making the wearer appear to look short

Waist 66.5 + 2.5cm tol. (26 + 1in)　　　　　　69cm (27in)

Tolerance should be added to the waist measurement for garments to be made from woven fabric to give room for movement. It is also always easier to take in a garment that is slightly too big than to let out one that is too small.

Hip 92 + 4cm tol. (36¼ +1½in)　　　　　　56cm (37¾in)

Again, tolerance should be added if the skirt is to be constructed from a woven fabric. An additional measure of tolerance should also be added to the hip measurement as it will expand when the person is sitting down. Try tying a tape measure around your hips and then sit down; the measure will feel tighter than when you are standing up. This is also a good way to gauge tolerance.

Length　　　　　　　　　　　　　　　58cm (23in)

This is literally the length of the finished skirt from the position at which it will sit at the waist or on the hips to the bottom of the hem. It is measured down the centre back or side seam – this can be decided by the team when compiling the size chart.

Specifying the skirt length

Designers often specify certain lengths for a skirt, usually dictated by the trend or their preferred visual effect. A knee-length skirt, for example, might just touch the top of the knee or instead the crease at the back of the knee. If there is no specified length, many experienced pattern cutters would draft such a skirt 61cm (24in) long.

DRAFTING THE BASIC SKIRT BLOCK

Step 1
The frame

Draw a frame the length and half the width of the skirt. In this case the length is 58cm (23in) and the width is 48cm (19in), or half the width of the widest part of the skirt, i.e. the hip.

Begin by drafting half the block

As with all symmetrical blocks, you should draft half the width of the garment and then trace off the other half when the block is complete.

48cm

58cm

Step 2
Identify the widest part of the skirt

To pinpoint the widest part of the skirt, draft a horizontal line 20.5cm (8in) below the top edge of the box. This is equivalent to the hip length on the size charts (see pages 12-13). Then a dotted line is drawn half way from the waist line to the hip line 10.25cm (7¾in) below the top edge of the box. This is equivalent to the mid-hip length. The top edge of the box is the waistline, this second (dotted) line is the mid-hip line and the third line is the hip line. The bottom line is the hemline.

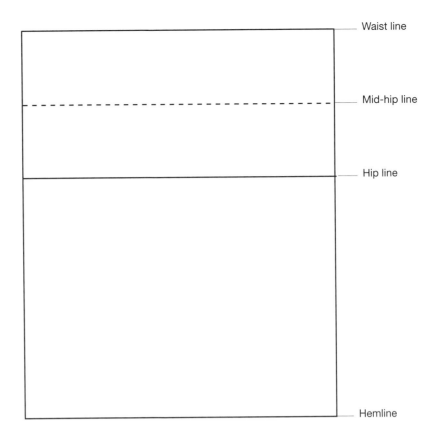

Waist line

Mid-hip line

Hip line

Hemline

Step 3
Identifying the front & back of the skirt

Divide the box in half vertically and decide which is the front and which is the back. Like the bodice block, there is no rule about which should be which. Here the left will be the back and the right the front. The central vertical line is the side seam, the left edge of the frame is the centre back and the right the centre front.

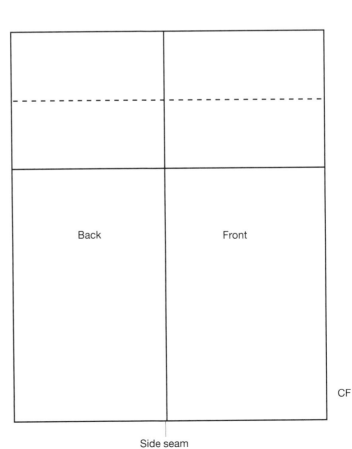

Back

Front

CB

CF

Side seam

Step 4
Calculating the darts

The aim of the darts is to reduce the fabric from the hip width to the waist measurement. You can start with a simple calculation:

Hip – Waist = total measurement of the darts (i.e. the amount of fabric that needs to be taken away)

96cm – 69cm = 27cm
(37¾in – 27in = 10¾in)

We then need to divide this measurement in half as we are only working on half the skirt:
27cm (10¾in) ÷ 2 = 13.5cm (5¼in)

On the basic skirt block one dart is usually used at the front, two at the back and both side seam curves from waist to hip naturally form a fourth dart. Darts are usually measured as shown in the table shown below.

Width of front and back of the skirt

From an aesthetic point of view, some pattern cutters move the side seam slightly towards the back so it is less visible from the front. The front of this skirt could be drafted 1 to 1.5cm (⅜ to ½in) larger than the back. However, anatomically the back of the hip is usually larger than the front of the hip. This is why the decision should be made from an aesthetic viewpoint.

For simplicity, however, we will draft the front and back half of the pattern equally here. The exact aesthetic position of the side seam is difficult to pinpoint, and it could be easier to adjust the pattern at the fitting stage.

Front dart	2.5cm (1in) maximum	A dart any larger will create a very rounded shape over the abdomen that will not be flattering to wear, unless it's specifically required – e.g. for maternity wear.
First back dart near to centre back	1.5 to 2cm (½ to ¾in)	The back darts together create a fuller shape to accommodate the buttocks.
Second back dart nearer to the side seam	2.5 to 3cm (1in)	
Side seam darts	6cm (2½in) in total (the excess on this particular block once the above darts have been taken into consideration) Front side seam = 3.5cm (1¼in) Back side seam = 2.5cm (1in)	Excess fabric is normally taken in at the side seam, however the size of these darts should be in proportion to the other darts on the skirt. The size of the dart at the back side seam is normally smaller than the dart at the front because the back of the skirt is already more rounded in shape and so the side seam needs to be less curved. Here we will distribute 3.5cm (1½in) for the front and 2.5cm (1in) for the back.

Step 5
Side seam darts

The most direct darts (suppressions) are at the side seams, which have been decided at step 4 (3.5cm/1½in at the front and 2.5cm/1in at the back).

To curve both side seams use the hip curve. When drafting near hip level, the line must go as close to the vertical side seam as possible to ensure sufficient hip measurement is allowed for.

Step 6
Front dart

Different companies have different aesthetic and practical considerations for their market demographic, so the design team need to decide whether to include one or two darts on the front or back.

Here, one dart is included: divide the remaining top edge by half. From this point draft a 2.5cm (1in) dart towards the side seam along the top edge in order to position the dart a little closer to the side seam (for aesthetic reasons).

In the middle of this dart, draft a perpendicular vertical line from the top edge to approximately 2cm (¾in) past the mid-hip line, then finish the dart.

Whether to include a front dart
Most skirts do not have front darts as the ideal female shape has a flat abdomen. However, the need for a front dart depends on the target market. Skirts designed for a younger market might not need darts, while those for a more mature market will. The block, however, should be drafted with a front dart, which can easily be removed later if necessary.

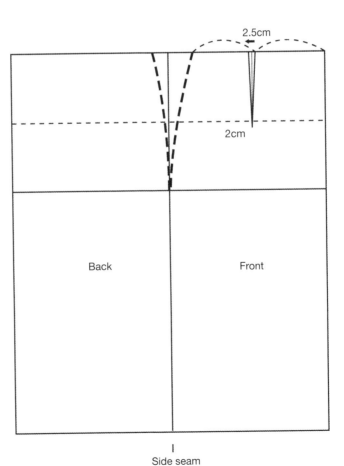

Step 7
Position of back skirt darts

Since the back of the hip should be wider than the front, it is decided to include two darts to accommodate the buttocks: this will distribute suppression more evenly as the back of the skirt needs a substantial three-dimensional shape.

Looking at the shape of the buttocks, they are more prominent towards the side seams and less so near the centre back seam. Therefore, a larger dart is positioned near the side seam (3.5cm/1½in) and a smaller one (2.5cm/1in) near the centre back seam.

To position the first dart near the side seam, mark 5cm from the back side seam. To position the second dart near the centre back seam: after the first back dart, divide the remaining back waist line by two and draft this point towards the side seam.

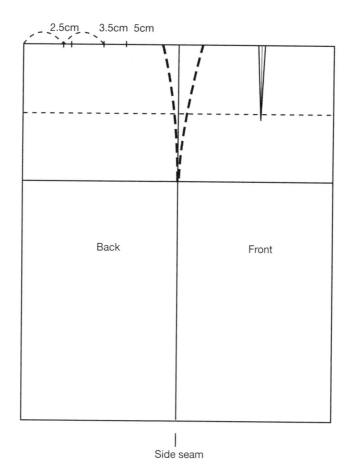

Step 8
Length & direction of back darts

From the large dart near to the side seam, draft a vertical line from the middle of the dart to the mid-hip line. For aesthetic reasons and for creating a three-dimensional shape, the end of the dart could be moved approximately 0.5cm (¼in) towards the side seam.

From the small dart near the centre back seam draft a vertical line from the middle of the dart and stop at approximately 5 to 6cm (2 to 2¼in) above the hip line. Then complete both darts.

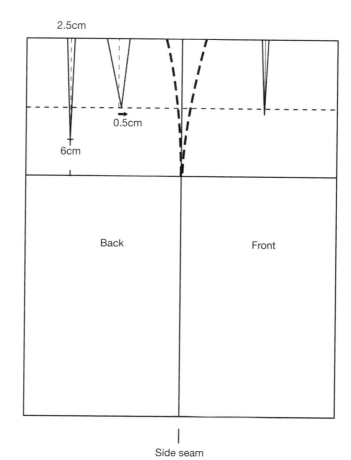

Step 9
Raise side seam to true corner & finish the darts

To finish off a pattern, all corners of the set of patterns must be trued.

In order to achieve a trued corner, we must raise the side seam to get a straight squared corner. Starting with the front side seam, only a small amount is needed, usually about 0.5cm (¼in) and no more than 1cm (½in). Close the dart with sticky tape and redraft the top of the dart with a tracing wheel (see pictures on page 50). Readjust the whole of the top edge from the side seam to the CF line. Open the paper to readjust the curves and complete the front top waist line.

As both side seams must be identical in length in order to be sewn together, you only need to measure the front side seam from hip to the top edge. Achieve the same measurement by raising the back side seam then readjust the dart and top edge as before.

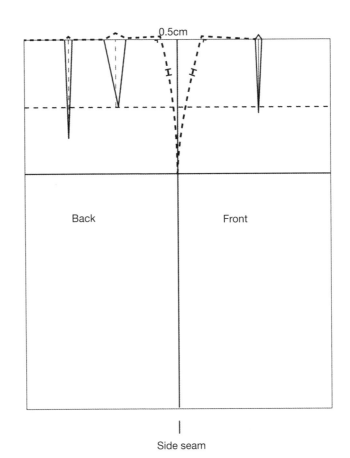

Back

Front

Side seam

Lengthening the side seams

Curved lines are usually longer than straight lines. The side seams should, therefore, be slightly longer than the centre front and centre back seams, usually by 0.5 to 0.7cm (¼in), depending on the curve of the hip and the narrowness of the waist.

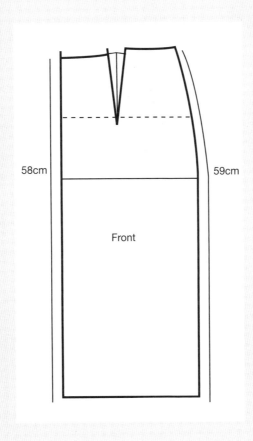

58cm

59cm

Front

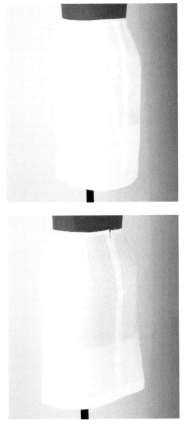

The finished toile constructed from the basic skirt block.

THE BASIC DRESS BLOCK

In the womenswear industry, dresses are an important component of any collection and come in many styles: classic, corseted dresses for eveningwear, looser, summer dresses for hot weather, the little black dress for a minimal, timeless look, and the wedding dress, the ultimate fairytale dress.

At its most basic, a dress is an elongated top or shirt. When the bodice is well cut and fitted, the rest of the dress is basically a skirt. The skirt section can be flared, tapered or straight, whether there is a seam at the waistline joining the bodice section to the skirt section or not.

There are two methods for drafting the dress block:

1. combining an existing bodice and skirt block.
2. using on an existing bodice block and drafting the skirt section using body measurements.

This knee-length summer dress by Hervé Leger from the Spring/Summer collection 2009 has a centre front zip.

A corseted evening dress by Gianfranco Ferré from the 2009 Spring/Summer collection with an internal corset, cut with rectangular panels sewn into the side seams.

Yohji Yamomoto's wedding dress from his Spring/Summer 2009 collection is cut along deceptively simple lines and is worn with a crinoline.

Margaret Howell's black dress from her Spring/Summer 2009 collection is cut on simple, classic lines based on a loose-fitting vest shape.

Bodice part

Nape to waist	40.5cm (15⅞in)	0.5–1cm (¼–⅜in) shorter than bodice block
Bust	96cm (37¼in)	Same as basic bodice block
Waist	70cm (27½in)	Same as basic bodice block
Front cross shoulder	37cm (14½in)	Same as basic bodice block
Back cross shoulder	38cm (15in)	Same as basic bodice block
Shoulder length	11.5cm (4¾in)	Same as basic bodice block
Cross front (armhole)	33.5cm (13¼in)	Same as basic bodice block
Cross back (armhole)	38cm (15in)	Same as basic bodice block
Front body length	43.5cm (17in)	0.5 to 1cm (¼ to ⅜in) shorter than bodice block
Back body length	42.5cm (16¾in)	0.5 to 1cm (¼ to ⅜in) shorter than bodice block
Neck circumference	38cm (15in)	Same as basic bodice block
Armhole circumference	42cm (16½in)	Same as basic bodice block
Armhole depth	17.5cm (7in)	Same as basic bodice block

Skirt part

Waist	70cm (27½in)	Skirt block + 1cm (⅜in) to match bodice
Hip	96cm (37¾in)	Same as basic skirt block
Length of skirt part	58cm (22¾in)	Same as basic skirt block

Nape to waist 41 – 0.5 to 1cm (16⅛ – ¼ to ⅜in)
40.5cm (15⅞in)

Although most size charts include a nape to waist measurement, it is an average measurement. Body length also varies from one person to the next; a tall person does not necessarily have a long body nor does a shorter person necessarily have a shorter body. Many pattern cutters, therefore, reduce the nape to waist measurement for bodices, tops, jackets and dresses by 1cm (⅜in). This means the bodice will fit someone with a shorter body and if the wearer has a longer body, the garment will still fit and even look better as the lower body will look longer and taller.

This dress fits from the nape to waist exactly.

On a person with a longer body, the same dress is lifted up from the exact waistline, but still fits well.

A dress with a long nape to waist measurement, however, will bunch up on the hips if the wearer has a shorter body.

Bust 90 + 6cm tol. (35½ + 2¼in)　　　　　　**96cm (37¾in)**

Even though in this case we are using the bodice block to construct the top of the dress, it is important to check that the bust is not too tight. The dress hangs from the shoulders, and if the bust is too tight it will affect the fit of the shoulders, neckline and armhole because the dress will become 'stuck' at the bust level.

Waist 66.5 + 3.5cm tol. (26 + 1½in)　　　　　**70cm (27½in)**

The same rules apply for the waist measurement as for the skirt measurement. The waist measurement of the bodice block is, therefore, 1cm (⅜in) larger than that of the skirt block. As the golden rule of pattern cutting is to create a pattern that is larger, rather than smaller, we should use the larger measurement of the two when creating the dress block.

Hip 92 + 4cm tol. (36¼ + 1½in)　　　　　　**96cm (37¾in)**

The same rules apply here as to the hip measurement of the skirt block. The hip measurement should always be generous to avoid the skirt pulling across the hips. It is particularly important in the case of a dress as a hip measurement that is too narrow will cause the skirt to rest on the hips so that the bodice of the dress bunches at the waistline or rises up to the narrower circumference of the waist. This effect can in part be counteracted by shortening the nape to waist measurement (see above).

Front body length 44 – 0.5 to 1cm (17¼ – ¼ to ⅜in)

　　　　　　　　　　　　　　　　　　43.5cm (17in)

If the nape to waist measurement is shortened by 0.5 to 1cm (¼ to ⅜in), then the front body length measurement should be shortened by the same amount.

Back body length 43 – 0.5 to 1cm (17 – ¼ to ⅜in)

　　　　　　　　　　　　　　　　　　42.5cm (16¾in)

The back body length should also be shortened in the same way as the nape to waist measurement.

Constructing a tightly fitted dress

If the dress is designed to be very tightly fitted, a corset might need to be constructed inside the bodice of the dress to avoid horizontal pull marks.

With an internal corset, the dress fits across the bust (top). Without a foundation, the dress pulls across the bust (above).

DRAFTING A BASIC DRESS BLOCK COMBINING EXISTING BODICE & SKIRT BLOCKS

Step 1
The frame & the bodice sections

Draw two vertical lines parallel to each other and approximately 50cm (20in) apart, which should be wide enough to fit both the front and back bodice blocks. The length of the lines should be equivalent to the sum of the bodice and skirt length, in this case approximately 105cm (41in).

Designating the left-hand line as the centre back and the right as the centre front, trace (or draft from scratch) the front and back bodice block, matching the centre front and backs, to both sides of the frame.

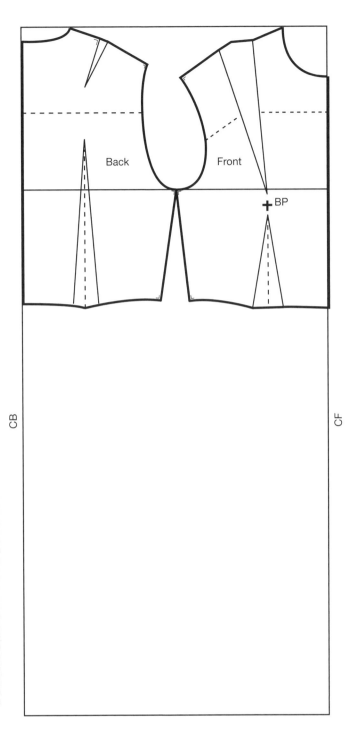

Position of the side seams

As we did for the bodice and skirt blocks, we will draft the dress block with equal front and back sections. The front bodice and skirt can be made smaller and the back larger to move the side towards the back for aesthetic reasons at the fitting stage.

Remember to adjust the back and front bodice sections

Always try to remember to shorten the front and back bodice sections; they can be adjusted at the fitting stage later, but it is easier if you follow the suggestions outlined below and shorten them at this stage.

Step 2
Shorten the front & back bodice sections

Shorten the front and back bodice sections by
0.5cm (¼in) at the waistline.

Step 3
The skirt sections

Trace the basic skirt block (or draft from
scratch) matching the centre front and centre
backs and lining up the waistlines of the two
sections so that they touch at the centre front
and centre back (the side seams can overlap
at the waist).

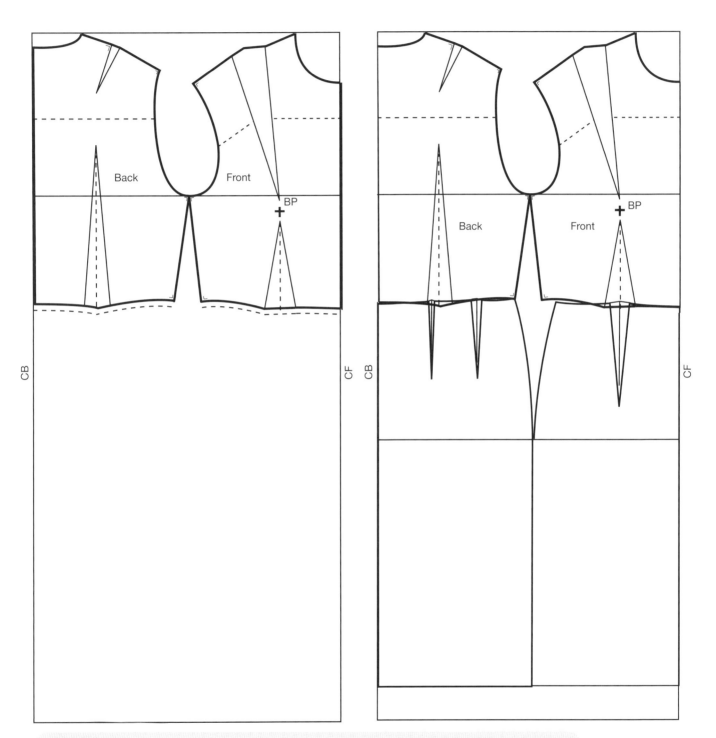

Back   **Front**   BP

CB   CF   CB   **Back**   **Front**   BP   CF

Reduction in the bodice length
Although the result of joining the bodice and skirt in this way looks as if
the bodice will be shorter than the skirt, it will in fact contribute to the
principle that the bodice should be reduced by 0.5 to 1cm (¼ to ⅜in).

Step 4
Adjust the darts

On the back of the dress, extend the back bodice dart downwards, ending the dart approximately halfway between the original two darts on the skirt block. Redraft the shape of the dart to make it as smooth as possible to coincide with the shape of the body.

On the front of the dress, extend the front bodice dart downwards, combining it with the existing dart. Again, redraft the shape to make it smooth. The new dart is based on the smaller skirt dart as a smaller suppression compensates for the discrepancy at the side seam.

Step 5
Smooth out the side seams

Finally, smooth out both the side seams, checking that they are exactly the same length. You might need to check the measurement using a tape measure held upright.

Finally, use a tape measure to double check that the bust, waist and hip measurements are correct and include sufficient tolerance.

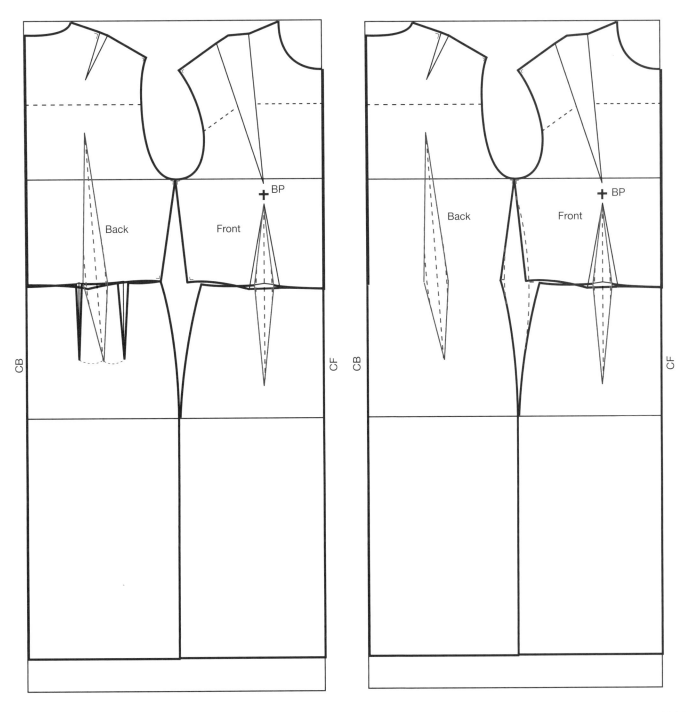

Darts on one & two piece dresses

For the bodice and skirt blocks the darts were placed to fit the garment as closely as possible to the figure. In creating this one-piece dress we need to line up the front and back darts at the waistline. This creates some fit problems because, initially, we have darts of different sizes and numbers on the bodice and skirt. In joining the two together we can, therefore, only aim to reduce the excess fabric, rather than fit the dress exactly to the shape of the figure: without a waistline different darts cannot be incorporated. A closely fitting dress, instead, must have a horizontal seam at the waist into which darts can be added as required without the need to line them up.

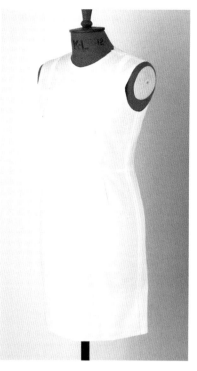
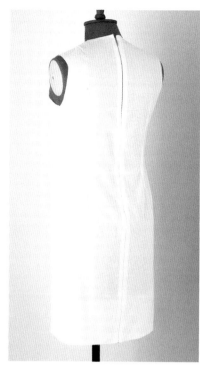

The finished toile constructed from the basic block made using an existing skirt and bodice block.

KEY MEASUREMENTS: USING AN EXISTING BODICE BLOCK & CONSTRUCTING THE SKIRT FROM ACTUAL BODY MEASUREMENTS

Bodice part

Nape to waist	40.5cm (15⅞in)	0.5 to 1cm (¼ to ⅜in) shorter than b. block
Bust	96cm (37¼in)	Same as basic bodice block
Waist	73cm (28¾in)	Bodice block + further 3cm (1¼in)
Front cross shoulder	37cm (14½in)	Same as basic bodice block
Back cross shoulder	38cm (15in)	Same as basic bodice block
Shoulder length	11.5cm (4½in)	Same as basic bodice block
Cross front (armhole)	33.5cm (13¼in)	Same as basic bodice block
Cross back (armhole)	38cm (15in)	Same as basic bodice block
Front body length	43.5cm (17in)	0.5 to 1cm (¼ to ⅜in) shorter than b. block
Back body length	42.5cm (16¾in)	0.5 to 1cm (¼ to ⅜in) shorter than b. block
Neck circumference	38cm (15in)	Same as basic bodice block
Armhole circumference	42cm (16½in)	Same as basic bodice block
Armhole depth	17.5cm (7in)	Same as basic bodice block

Skirt part

Waist	73cm (28½in)	Skirt block + 4cm (1½in) to match bodice
Hip	100cm (39¼in)	Skirt block + further 4cm (1½in)
Length of hip (from waist to hip)	20cm (8in)	This is very important to justify fit
Length of skirt part	55.5cm (21¾in)	Measured at CB
Total garment length	96cm (37¾in)	CB nape to waist + CB skirt length

Waist 66.5 + 6.5cm tol. (26 + 2½in)   **73cm (28½in)**

This is a simpler method of drafting a dress block and, therefore, it is less fitted. The front bust dart is reduced by 1cm (³⁄₈in) to loosen the front waist measurement and reduce the definition of the bust shape.

Hip 96 + 4cm (37¾ + 1½in)   **100cm (39¼in)**

Again, the hip measurement is wider for this loosely fitted dress. It could even be increased further and adjusted once the toile is made.

Length of hip   **20cm (8in)**

This is measured from the waistline. It indicates the widest part of the skirt below the waistline, the hip line. It also indicates the most appropriate level to position the opening of a garment; in the case of the dress block, a centre back opening from the nape to the hip line is usually recommended.

Total garment length   **96cm (37¾in)**

There is no standard dress length. Usually the length of the dress is measured from the nape vertically to the back of the knee; at the front the hem of the dress will 'touch' the middle of the knee. Most industry size charts suggest a length of approximately 98 to 99cm (38½ to 39in). For the block in this book the hem will sit slightly above the knee.

DRAFTING A BASIC DRESS BLOCK USING AN EXISTING BODICE BLOCK & CONSTRUCTING THE SKIRT FROM ACTUAL BODY MEASUREMENTS

Step 1
The frame & the bodice sections

Draw two vertical parallel lines 50cm (19½in) apart (to fit both the front and back of the basic bodice block). The length of both lines should at least be equivalent to the total garment length – in this case 100cm (39¼in).

Designating the left-hand line as the centre back and the right as the centre front, trace (or draft from scratch) the front and back bodice block, matching the centre front and backs to both sides of the frame.

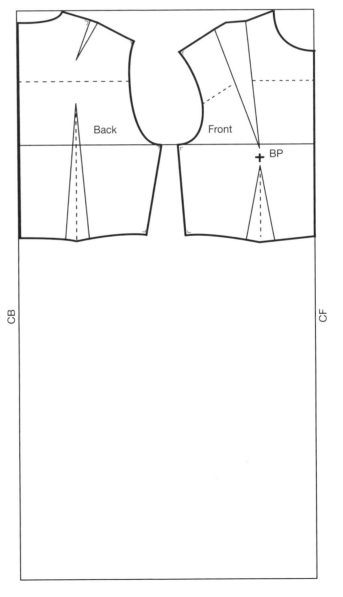

Shorten the front & back bodice sections

At the centre back, shorten the length of the bodice by 0.5cm (¼in).

Step 3

Create a new waistline

Draft a line at 90° to the centre back to divide the bodice from the skirt and create a new waistline. Do the same at the centre front.

From the new waistline, measure down 20cm (8in) and draft one line parallel to the waistline for the front and one for the back representing the hip lines. These lines should each measure one quarter of the hip width measurement (measured from the centre front and centre back) – in this case 25cm (9¾in).

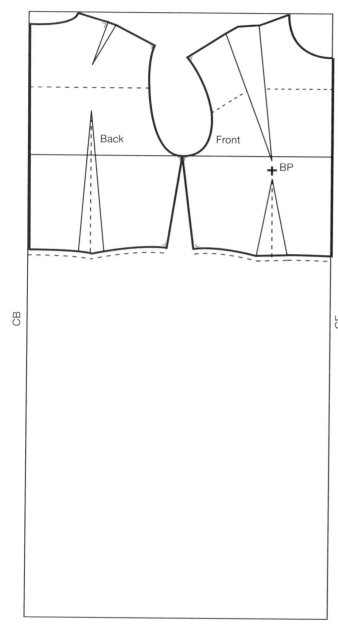

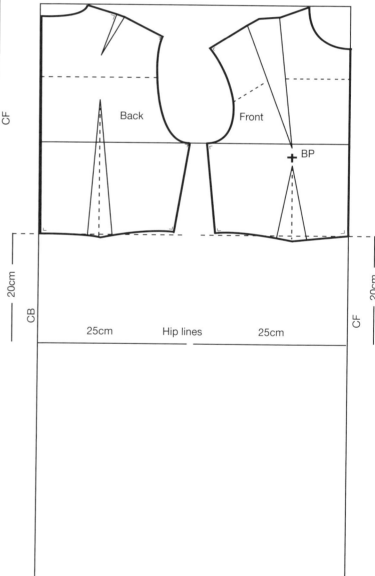

Position of the side seams

As we did for the bodice and skirt blocks, we will draft the dress block with equal front and back sections. The front bodice and skirt can be made smaller and the back larger to move the side towards the back for aesthetic reasons at the fitting stage.

Step 4
Adjust the darts

Extend the back bodice dart downwards, ending the dart approximately 6cm (2¼in) above the hip line. Then redraft the dart to make it as smooth as possible.

Since this is a loose-fitting dress with less definition to the bust, we will aim to reduce the width of the front dart by 1cm (⅜in) at the waist. To do this, reduce the front bodice bust dart by 0.5cm (¼in) at each side at the waistline and re-draw the dart, extending it downwards so that it ends approximately 5cm (2in) above the hip line.

Step 5
Calculate the back skirt length

Calculate the total length of the dress:

Nape to waist 40.5cm (16in) + waist to hem 55.5cm (21¾in) = 96cm (37¾in)

Measure this length from the nape, extending the centre back line downwards. At the foot of the line, draw a line at right angles to mark the hemline. The width of this line should be at least one quarter of the total hip measurement (in this case 25cm/9¾in).

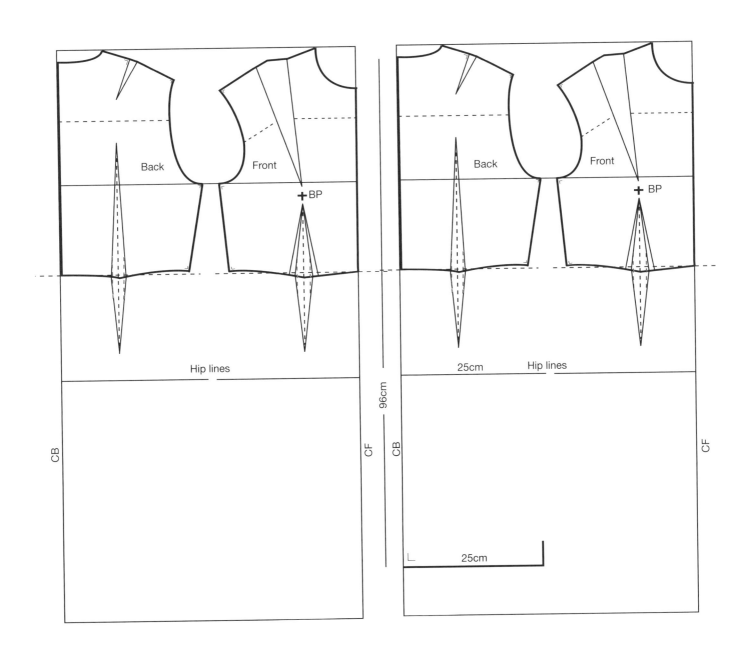

Complete the back skirt section

Complete the skirt by drafting the side seam. Draw a line from the hemline to the hip line. Then join this line to the waistline with the help of a hip curve. Finally, smooth out the side seam where it meets the bodice at the waistline.

Circumference of the hem

For A-line and flared skirts the circumference of the hem should be wide enough to allow the wearer to walk or climb stairs comfortably. Narrower silhouettes, for example dresses with pencil skirts, might be too narrow around the knee and will require a centre back vent or opening in the side seams.

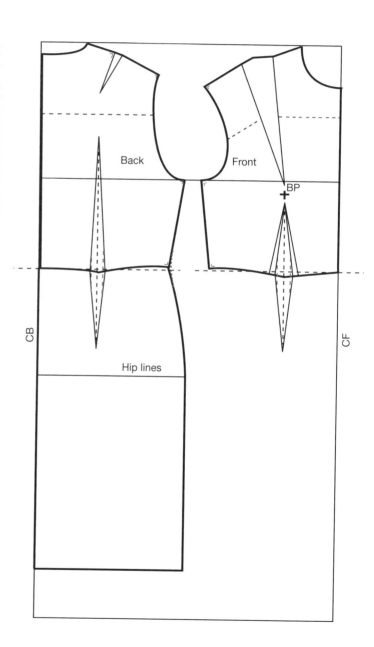

Step 7
Calculate & complete the front skirt section

Even though the front and back bodice are slightly different lengths, we can still complete the front skirt section in exactly the same way as the back (see Steps 5 and 6).

When both skirt sections are complete, measure the side seams. Since the front bodice is usually longer than the back by approximately 1 to 2cm (⅜ to ¾in), decide whether to shorten the back or front skirt side seam by the same amount.

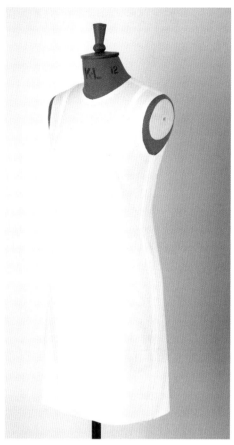

The finished toile constructed from the basic block made using an existing bodice block and actual measurements for the skirt. This will create a less body-hugging dress.

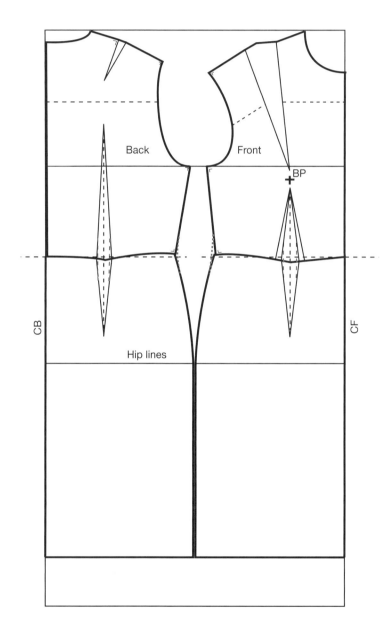

Back   Front

BP

CB

CF

Hip lines

THE BASIC TROUSER BLOCK

From the waist to the hips, the trouser block is similar in shape to that of the skirt block – a single tube. Trousers, however, have the addition of two separate tubes covering both legs – trousers are, therefore, constructed from three tube shapes.

The body is a three-dimensional object and when wrapping it we have to consider not only height and width, but also depth. In the case of the trouser block, we need to consider how to create a shape that will wrap around the waist and hip (the top-most tube) and also around the legs (the lower tube) without creating a horizontal seam at the line of the crotch to join the two. The trouser block accomplishes this by essentially creating two tubes of fabric, joined at the centre front and centre back from the waist to the hip with an additional allowance of fabric, or extension, to wrap around the legs that is then joined from the crotch to the ankle along the inside leg seam, or inseam.

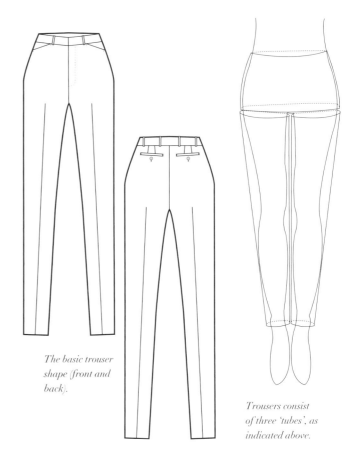

The basic trouser shape (front and back).

Trousers consist of three 'tubes', as indicated above.

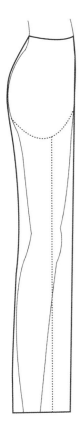

The side view of the trouser shows how the trouser leg is wrapped around the body and is joined at the crotch and inseam.

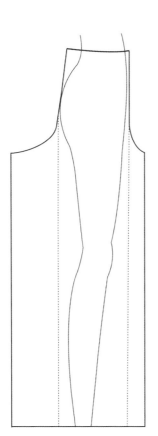

When the trouser leg is opened out it is possible to see the shape required to wrap the three-dimensional body from the waist to the ankle.

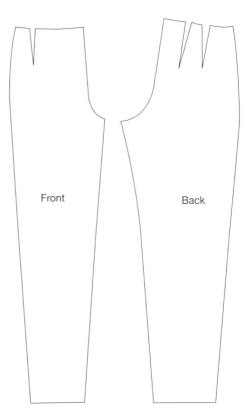

Front   Back

The actual trouser block consists of two pieces – a front and a back section joined at the side seam – which, like all blocks, can be duplicated to cut a pair.

Recently, the fashion has been for garments to be tightly fitted. Cutting a block for a pair of skinny jeans or tightly fitting trousers is relatively simple as there is less need to create curves and include darts. However, such trousers must be made from fabrics that will withstand wear and tear and preferably ones that offer a degree of stretch, such as knit fabrics. Denim is strong enough to withstand constant friction and now manufacturers have also begun to mix elastane with cotton to produce a denim fabric with a slight amount of stretch that offers both comfort and fit.

A loose and fluid trouser from Neil Barrett, Autumn/ Winter 07/08.

Skinny fit trouser from the high street fashion chain Warehouse.

KEY MEASUREMENTS

Waist	68cm (26¾in)	66.5cm (26¼in) + 1.5cm (½in) tolerance
Hip	99cm (39in)	92cm (36¼in) + 7cm (2¾in) tolerance
Length	108cm (42½in)	Total length of garment
Hip length	20cm (8in)	From waist down to widest point
Mid hip	10cm (4in)	half of hip length
Body rise	27cm (10½in)	Depth of crotch
Length of total crotch	68cm (26¾in)	Sum of CF & CB rise
Top of thigh	64cm (25in)	60cm (23½in) + 4cm (1½in) tolerance
*Thigh	53cm (21in)	52cm (20⅜in) + 1cm (⅜in) tolerance
*Knee	47cm (18½in)	34cm (13½in) + 13cm (5in) tolerance
*Calf	42cm (16½in)	33cm (13in) + 9cm (3½in) tolerance
*Ankle	37cm (14½in)	23cm (9in) + 14cm (5½in) tolerance

*Thigh, knee, calf and ankle are four measurements that help us judge whether the leg will fit and hang comfortably, rather than the exact measurements to use, as trouser legs are not usually 'contoured', unless for performance sports.

Waist 66.5 + 1.5cm tol. (26 +½in)   **68cm (26¾in)**

As for most measurements, tolerance is added here for ease of movement.

Hip 92 + 7cm tol. (36¼ + 2¾in)   **99cm (39in)**

Again tolerance should be added if the trousers are to be constructed from a woven fabric. An additional measure of tolerance should also be added to the hip measurement as it will expand when the person is sitting down. Try tying a tape measure around your hips and then sit down; the measure will feel tighter than when you are standing up.

Length   **108cm (42½in)**

This measurement is usually taken down the outside seam, or outseam, of the trousers.

Mid hip   **10cm (4in)**

This measurement is mid-way down the hip length, which itself is 20cm (8in). The measurement is used to double-check the final measurement of the block and to locate the ends of the darts.

Body rise   **approximately 27cm (10½in)**

This is taken when a person is sitting down on a flat surface and is measured from the waist to the flat surface down the outside of the body. It is used as a guideline to work out the depth of the trouser crotch. If the crotch is too shallow, the trousers will be uncomfortable to wear. A deeper crotch, however, can be used for wider trousers or a more casual look (see photo, page 91).

Total length of crotch approximately 65cm (25½in) + 3cm (1¼in) [or 1.5cm (½in) tolerance at front and back]   **68cm (26¾in)**

This is measured from the centre front to the centre back waistline. By taking the body rise measurement and the length of the front and of the back crotch, we can work out the shape of the front and back crotch seams. The front crotch seam, for example, might be almost perpendicular to the horizontal construction lines, whereas the back crotch seam might be much more curved in shape.

Trouser length

There is no standard length for trousers. Many designers designate certain lengths, for example the hem of a knee-length pair of trousers might just touch the top of the knee or the crease at the back of the knee. Experienced pattern cutters might use a standard measurement of 61cm (24in). Mid-calf trousers might be cut with a standard length of 92cm (36in).

Full-length trousers are usually cut longer rather than shorter, as it is always possible to shorten trousers but less easy to lengthen them. This is why some trousers in shops are left with an overlocked hem without further finishing.

Most manufacturers working for the high street use a standard measurement of 112cm (44in). It is important, however, to consider your market; trousers destined for the Asian market might be shorter than those destined for the German or Dutch markets, for example.

We should also take into account the fact that the back crotch seam, like the hip, will expand and lengthen when the wearer sits down. Try using a tape measure to measure along the crotch standing up. When sitting down you will feel how the measure becomes tighter and the back of the waistline has a tendency to be pulled down.

Top of thigh approximately 59–60cm + 4cm tol. (23–23½in + 1½in)   64cm (25in)

This measurement does not always appear in size charts. It is, however, useful for gauging the depth of the crotch extension. This measurement is taken around the top of the thigh level with the crotch (see below, point 'A' on the leg diagram).

Thigh 52 + 1cm tol. (20⅝ + ⅜in)   53cm (21in)

This is the circumference of the thigh measured mid-way between the crotch level and the knee.

Knee 34 + 13cm tol. (13½ + 5in)   47cm (18½in)

This is the circumference of the knee. It is unlikely, however, that you will use this exact measurement when drafting the block. Trousers are tapered from the hip to the ankle in a smooth line. It is wise to check the circumference of the knee on your block, however, as additional tolerance is needed at this point to allow the knee to move. If the trouser block is too narrow at this point, it would be necessary to widen the leg.

Calf 33 + 9cm tol. (13 + 3½in)   42cm (16½in)

This is the circumference of the calf measured mid-way between the knee and the ankle. The same rules for using and checking this measurement apply here as to the measurement of the knee, as stated above.

Ankle 23 + 14cm tol. (9 + 5½in)   37cm (14½in)

The actual circumference of the ankle (23cm/9in) does not equate to the trouser hem opening as sufficient tolerance needs to be added to allow the wearer to pull on and take off the trousers over the foot. It would only work as an exact measurement if the design allowed for an opening, either fastened or unfastened, at the bottom of the trouser leg.

Instead of measuring the circumference of the ankle it is better to measure the girth of the foot from the bottom of the heel to the top of the ankle (37cm/14½in). This measurement would then include 14cm (5½in) tolerance to allow the trouser to be pulled on over the foot (see diagram below right).

The thigh, knee, calf and ankle measurements given here are for reference only, since the block is drafted with a smooth, tapering line from the hip to the ankle. Different styles of trouser will have different leg measurements. Wider or flared trousers, for example, will have a different shape requiring greater amounts of tolerance compared to tightly fitting trousers, which might have little or no tolerance except at the ankle or trouser hem opening.

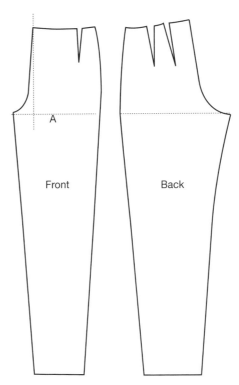

Front   Back

Measured around the top of the thigh, level with the crotch, the top of thigh measurement A (below) should be similar to the measurement of width of both front and back trouser measured at the crotch level (left).

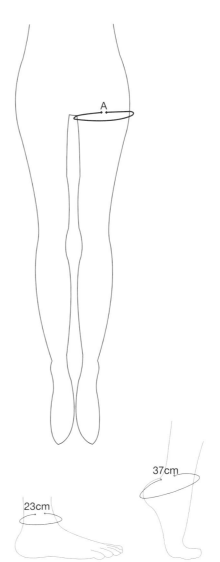

The circumference of the ankle itself is much narrower than the circumference of the foot measured from the heel to the top of the ankle. This latter measurement is the minimum required for the foot to pass through the trouser opening.

DRAFTING THE BASIC TROUSER BLOCK

Step 1
The frames

For this block the front and back trouser legs are drafted in separate frames drawn alongside each other with a gap of 15cm (6in) – this being the total crotch depth. The frame on the left-hand side is the back and the frame on the right is the front. The outside edge of each frame is the side seam. The top of the inside edges are the centre front and centre back of hips respectively. The length of each frame is equivalent to the length of the trousers from waist to hem, 108cm (42½in) here.

To calculate the width of the frame, divide the widest measurement – the hip – in half: 99cm (39in) ÷ 2 = 49.5cm (19½in)

Since the back of the trouser is always larger than the front, generally by 2 to 2.5cm (¾ to 1in), divide the hip measurement in half again, and re-distribute the allowance between the front and the back:

49.5 (19½in) ÷ 2 = 24.75cm (9¾in)
24.75 (9¾) + 1.25 (½) = 26cm (10¼in)
  = back trouser leg
24.75 (9¾) − 1.25 (½) = 23.5cm (9¼in)
  = front trouser leg

Then draw the right-hand (front) trouser leg frame 108cm (42½in) long and 23.5cm (9¼in) wide. Draw the left-hand (back) trouser leg frame 108cm (42½in) long and 26cm (10¼in) wide.

Step 2
Draw in the construction lines

Draw in the following construction lines horizontally across both frames:

Waistline – this is the top of the frame
Mid-hip line – measured 10cm (4in) below the waistline
Hip line – measured 20cm (8in) below the waistline
Body rise – measured 27cm (10½in) below the waistline
Knee level – measured 62cm (24½in) below the waistline
Total length of trouser hemline – this is the lower edge of the frame – 108cm (42½in) below the waistline

Waist line

Mid-hip line

Hip line

Body rise

Back   Front

Knee level

Side seam   Side seam

Total length of
trouser hemline

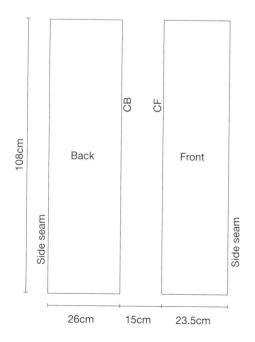

CB   CF

108cm

Back   Front

Side seam   Side seam

26cm   15cm   23.5cm

Step 3
Depth of the crotch

The total measurement of the depth of the crotch – or width of the front and back extensions which wrap around the inside of the leg – is generally 15 to 16cm (6 to 6¼in).

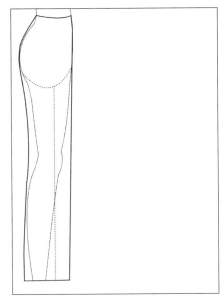

As the back of the trouser is always larger than the front, the back crotch depth will also be longer – usually double the depth of the front. In this case the front crotch depth is 5cm (2in) measured along the body rise and the back is 10cm (4in).

Along body rise line between the front and back frames make a mark to indicate 5cm (2in) for front crotch depth and 10cm (4in) for back crotch depth.

Step 4
Draft the centre or crease lines

For the front trouser, divide the body rise line, including the crotch extension, in half and draw a vertical line down the frame. This is the central line of the front trouser leg.

For the back trouser, again divide the body rise line in half, but this time move the vertical line 1.5cm (½in) towards the side seam to compensate for the wider crotch extension at the back of the trouser. This is the central line of the back trouser leg.

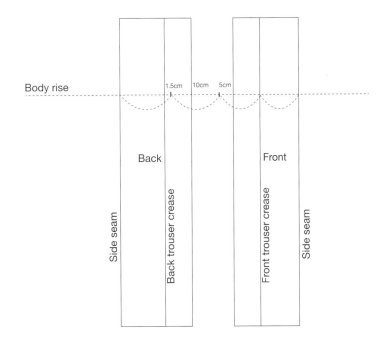

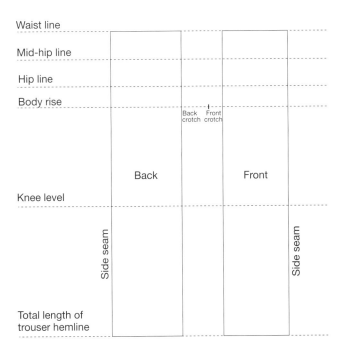

Adjusting the front and back crotch length

If you are drafting a block for a pair of skinny jeans you might shorten the front crotch depth, but in this case you must lengthen the back crotch depth by the same amount.

Step 5
Identify shaping of the side seams, centre front & centre back

Here we will begin to apply some shaping to the seams. Additional shaping will be made using darts later.

Side seams – measure in 2cm (¾in) from the front side seam and 1cm (⅜in) from the back side seam. The back of the trouser will have two darts, thus reducing the waistline by a larger amount than the single dart at the front. Therefore a smaller dart is included at the back side seam.

Centre front seam – measure in 1cm (¾in) from the centre front. This dart is kept to a minimum as the front of the trousers will look better if they are flat. For tight-fitting trousers the centre front is kept completely flat as no shaping is needed.

Centre back seam – measure in 3cm (1¼in) from the centre back. This larger dart helps to shape the back of the trouser around the buttocks.

The centre and crease lines

These two lines are very important. They are the central vertical axis around which the measurements are distributed equally for the circumferences of the thigh, knee and hem openings. If these measurements are not distributed evenly then the side seam and inseam will not sit straight together and the trouser leg will twist when worn. This can be rectified at the fitting stage.

These are the lines around which tailored trousers are creased when ironing and fitting.

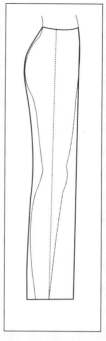 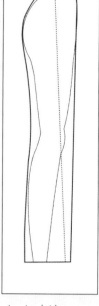

A straight side seam *A twisted side seam*

Step 6
Shape the side seams, centre front and centre back

Draw in smooth curves for the front and back side seams from the waistline to the hip line. At the same time, raise the side seams 5mm (¼in) above the original waistline to add extra length.

Draw the centre front with a straight line from the waistline to the hip line, then, using a hip curve, curve the line out to the end of the crotch extension where it meets the body rise. Measure and record the length of the front crotch, which should be approximately 30cm (12in), using a tape measure held upright.

Before drafting the centre back line, we need to identify the position of the back hip line. On the front of the trouser the hip line was straight, but on the back of the trouser the hip line is curved to accommodate the shape of the buttocks. When the pattern is laid flat the hip line,

therefore, needs to curve up towards the centre back by approximately 2.5cm (1in). Since the back hip line will be curved, it should be longer than the front, usually by 2.5cm (1in). In this case, since the front hip width is 23.5cm (9¼in), the back should be 26.5cm (10½in).

Using a hip curve, draw in the back hip line as a smooth curved line measuring 26.5cm (10½in) from the original position of the hip line 20cm (8in) down the back side seam to the centre back.

Now draw a straight line for the centre back from the waistline to the hip line, then, using an armhole ruler, curve the line towards the end of the back crotch extension where it meets the body rise line, but keeping the end of the line (approximately 4cm/1½in) straight.

Finally, raise the centre back line so that the centre front and centre back crotch lengths equal the total crotch length (68cm/26¾in). Since the centre front crotch was approximately 30cm (12in) in length, the centre back needs to be raised at the waistline so that the back crotch length is 38cm (15in).

Step 7
Calculate the darts

Re-measure the waistline. In this case the unfinished waistline should be approximately 41cm (16in), this being half the total front and back measurement.

For this block we are working with a total waist measurement of 68cm (26¾in) and, therefore, half the waist will be 34cm (13¼in).

The allowance for darts is, therefore:

41cm (16in) – 34cm (13¼in) = 7cm (2¾in)

We can distribute this as follows:

Front dart = 2cm (¾in)
Back darts = 2.5cm (1in) each

Lengthening the side seams
Curved lines are usually longer than straight lines. The side seams should, therefore, be slightly longer than the centre front and centre back measurement to compensate for the curve of the hip. This also enables the trueing of corners.

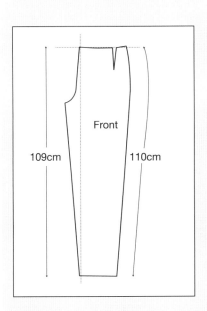

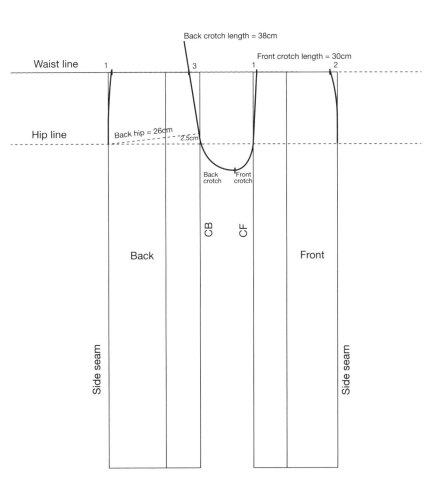

Front dart

Most trousers do not have front darts as the ideal female shape has a flat abdomen. However, the need for a front dart depends on the target market. Trousers designed for a younger market might not need darts, while those for a more mature market will. The block should be drafted with a front dart, which can easily be removed later if necessary.

Back darts

Two darts are usually used on either side at the back of the trousers to accommodate the curve of the buttocks; a single dart on each side can be too large and create an unwanted peak at the back of the trousers that could be unflattering.

Step 8
Drafting the darts

Along the front trouser centre line on the waistline evenly distribute a 2cm (¾in) dart on both sides of this line. If this is cut for tailored trousers, the dart will be 'disappeared' with the ironed crease line.

On the back, draw a line 7cm (2¾in) up from the hip line. Measure the back waistline and divide it into three sections to find the centre of both darts. Also position the ends of both darts equally along the line 7cm (2¾in) above the hip. Position the opening of the darts 1.25cm (½in) either side of the centre of the darts and draw in the darts, ending each 7cm (2¾in) above the hip line.

Finally, close the darts using sticky tape and then re-draw the waistline using a hip curve and tracing wheel. Carefully cut through the sticky tape, open out the darts and re-draw the waistline along the line of holes created by the wheel.

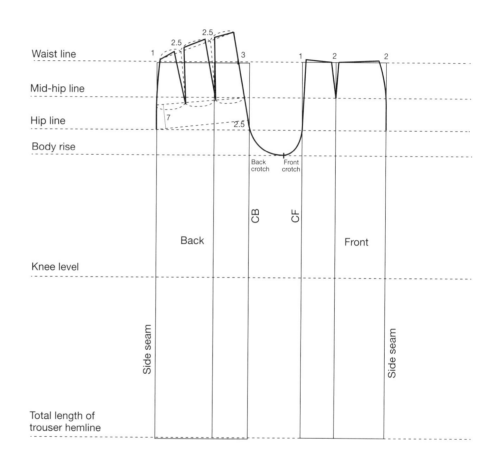

Positioning the front dart

The front dart can be located on the front trouser centre or crease line. Often, alternatively, darts on a flat-fronted pair of trousers are located nearer to the side seam over the highest point, the hip bone, which is approximately 4 to 5cm (1½ to 2in) from the side seam.

Positioning the two back darts

The back darts can be located at equal distances along the back waistline with the darts ending approximately 7cm (2¾in) above the hip line, to coincide with the highest peak of the buttocks. Usually, however, the darts are positioned nearer to the centre back than to the side seams.

Step 9
Draft the trouser legs

Halve the measurements of the thigh circumference (53cm/21in), knee (47cm/18½in), calf (42cm/16½in) and ankle or trouser opening (37cm/14½in). As the back of the trouser leg is larger than the front, re-distribute 5cm (2in) to the back:

	Front of trouser leg: cm (in)	Back of trouser leg: cm (in)
Thigh	26.5 (10½) – 2.5 (1) = 24cm (9½in)	26.5cm (10½) + 2.5 (1) = 29cm (11½ in)
Knee	23.5 (9¼) – 2.5 (1) = 21cm (8½in)	23.5 (9¼) + 2.5 (1) = 26cm (10¼in)
Calf	21 (8¼) – 2.5 (1) = 18.5cm (7¼in)	21 (18¼) + 2.5 (1) = 23.5cm (9¼in)
Ankle	18.5 (7¼) – 2.5 (1) = 16cm (6¼in)	18.5 (7¼) + 2.5 (1) = 21cm (8¼in)

Locate the position of the thigh measurement (mid-way between the crotch and the knee) and the calf measurement (mid-way between the knee level and the hem of the trousers) on your block (the knee and ankle are already located on your block).

We now need to distribute the measurements equally either side of the centre line, or crease line, or the trouser leg will twist, so we need to divide the measurements in half again.

On the front trouser leg, at the thigh level, measure 12cm (4¾in) either side of the centre line. At knee level, measure 9.25cm (3½in) either side of the centre line, and so on down the trouser leg.

On the back trouser leg, at the thigh level, measure 14.5cm (5¾in) either side of the centre line, and so on down the trouser leg.

These measurements are guidelines only.

Now draft the outside leg or outseam by drawing a straight line from the hip line to the ankle on both the front and back legs.

On the front trouser leg, draft the inseam by drawing a straight line from the end of the crotch extension to the ankle.

On the back trouser leg, with the help of a hip curve, draft a smoothly curved line for the inseam from the end of the crotch extension to the knee level and then continue with a straight line from the knee to the ankle. The curve accommodates the extra width of the back crotch extension. In case of a discrepancy in the inseam length, always shorten the back inseam.

Now look at the guidelines you drew at the thigh, knee and calf levels. If you find the inseam or outseam fall within the guidelines, the trouser leg will be too tight and you will need to adjust the seams.

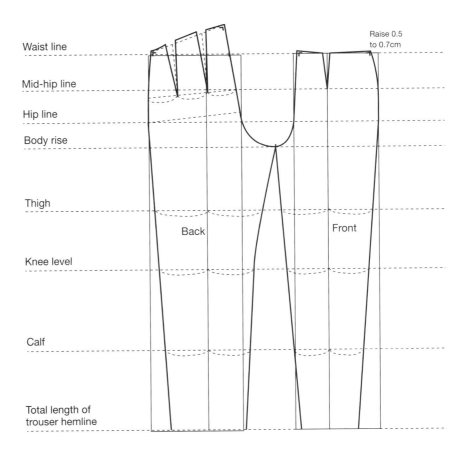

Waist line
Mid-hip line
Hip line
Body rise
Thigh
Back
Front
Knee level
Calf
Total length of trouser hemline
Raise 0.5 to 0.7cm

The finished toile constructed from the basic trouser block.

PATTERN CUTTER'S AIDE MEMOIRE

As a pattern cutter, you will encounter sets of measurements every day, and as you start to use them on a continuing basis, you will begin to memorize them. In the process you'll develop an inbuilt sense of whether a pattern will fit or not just by knowing the rough measurements you would expect to find.

The following list of measurements is offered as a starting point for building up that knowledge bank. It is based on a small size 12 for the commercial European market for use with woven fabrics.

THE 'BIG THREE' MEASUREMENTS

BUST = 90cm (35½in)

WAIST = 68cm (approx. 27in)

HIP = 92cm (36¼in)

BODY/BODICE MEASUREMENTS & KEY POINTS

Head circumference = 58cm (23in) (this is very useful for neck opening and top fastening, especially for millinery industry)

Nape to waist = 40cm (16in); although 41cm (16in) on chart, garment with shorter nape to waist will fit more people

Neck circumference = 36cm (14in)

Front body length = 44cm (17¼in)

Back body length = 43cm (17in)

Shoulder = 11.5cm (4¾in)

Cross front/mid front armhole = 33cm (13in)

Cross back/mid back armhole = 37cm (14½in)

Length of shoulder dart = 8cm (3in)

Position of shoulder dart = 5cm (2in) from SNP (both front and back)

Bust point position (BP) = 27cm (10½in) below SNP

Distance between two BPs = 19cm (7½in)

Armhole = 40cm (16in) (38cm/15in would be the absolute minimum)

All darts should be 1.5 to 2cm (½ to ¾in) away from BP

Size of back shoulder dart = maximum 1.5cm (½in)

Size of back waist dart = approx. 3.5 to 4cm (1¼ to 1½in)

Size of front shoulder dart = 5cm (2in)

Size of front waist dart = 4 to 5cm (1½ to 2in)

Position/direction of back shoulder dart = perpendicular to shoulder line 5cm (2in) from SNP

Position/direction of back waist dart = vertically central to the end of the shoulder dart. Dart ends one third of the distance from the underarm line to the end of the shoulder dart

Direction of front bust darts = directly towards BP; ends of darts 1.5 to 2cm (½ to ¾in) away

Depth of armhole = drafting a square on half of the half block, i.e. after locating a quarter of the bust measurement of block. Approx. 18cm (7in) from shoulder point

Width of neck = 8cm (3in) for half, i.e. 16cm (6¼in) for whole

Depth of front neck = 0.5 to 1cm (¼ to ⅜in) deeper than front neck width

Depth of back neck = 1.5 to 2cm (½ to ¾in) with collar, but no strict rule for collarless garment. Or use direct nape to waist measurement

Front shoulder slant = 4.5cm (1¾in)

Back shoulder slant = 4cm (1½in)

Back armhole shoulder point = 1.5 to 2cm (½ to ¾in) higher than front armhole SP

Side seam shape/side seam dart = both front and back should only be maximum 2.5 to 3cm (1 to 1¼in)

SLEEVE MEASUREMENTS & KEY POINTS

Armhole = 40cm (16in) (38cm would be the absolute minimum)

Sleeve length = Approx. 55cm (21½in) unless specified

Shoulder to elbow = 32cm (12½in)

Bicep = 26cm (10¼in)

Elbow = 27cm (10½in)

Wrist = 16cm (6¼in) (pocket opening is also 16cm/6¼in)

Low sleeve crown = 0 to 5cm (0 to 2in)

Medium sleeve crown = below and around 10cm (4in)

High sleeve crown = approx. 15cm (6in) and above

SKIRT MEASUREMENTS & KEY POINTS

Front dart position = approx. one third division on waistline from side seam, then start dart towards side seam

Front dart end = approx. 2cm longer than mid-hip line

Maximum size of front dart = 2.5cm (1in)

Maximum size of side seam curve (side seam dart) = 3.5cm (1¼in) on front and 2.5cm (1in) on back

Back darts positions = first dart 5cm from the side seam; second dart near centre back – divide the remaining back waistline by two then start the dart towards the side seam

Sizes of back darts = this relies on calculation of difference between hip and waist minus front and side seam darts. Then the leftover measurement will be divided into two back darts; the dart closer to CB is larger than the dart near side seam

Back dart end = first dart ends at mid hip; second dart 5 to 6cm (2in) above the hip line

Hip length = 20cm (8in) (other European systems use 18.5cm/7¼in, which simply means skirt is bigger and fits more people)

Waist to knee length
= 62cm (24½in)

Waist to calf length = 92cm (36in) (same as hip)

Difference of front & back skirt piece = usually 1.5cm (½in) on half block, i.e. 3cm (1¼in) larger/wider on front skirt piece. It is also acceptable to have front and back as equal halves

Raise on side seam points above waistline = approx. 0.5 to 0.7cm (¼in)

TROUSER MEASUREMENTS & KEY POINTS

Minimum pocket opening = 16cm (6¼in)

Approx. total length (depth) of crotch = 15 to 16cm (6 to 6¼in), i.e. 5cm (2in) for front and rest for back trouser

Total crotch curve length, front and back = 68cm (27in) (this is very useful)

Body rise = 27cm (10½in)

Top of thigh = 60cm (23½in)

Mid thigh = 53cm (21in) (this is useful for drafting patterns for shorts)

Inseam = 82cm (32¼in)

Outseam = 112cm (44in)

Waist to mid-calf length = 92cm (36in)

Waist to ankle length = 112cm (44in)

Knee girth = 35cm (14in)

Ankle girth = 25cm (10in)

Trouser hem = 32cm (12½in) (this must be considered, unless there is an opening for the foot to pass through)

Front trouser vertical crease line/central line = equally divide the whole of horizontal body rise line

Back trouser vertical crease line/central line = same as above, then move the whole line approx. 1.5cm (½in) towards side seam

Side seam dart (shape) = 2cm (¾in) on front side seam and 1cm (⅜in) on back side seam

Raise on side seam points above waistline = approx. 0.5 to 0.7cm (¼in) Remember to take a small amount of measurement (dart) from centre front line on waist. This will help minimize front and back dart as CF and CB should also bear a certain amount of evenly placed darts. In this case, approx. 0.5 to 1cm (⅜in)

CB shape (dart) on waistline = 3cm 1¼in)

Maximum front trouser dart = 2cm (¾in)

Approx. back trouser darts = 2.5 to 3cm (1 to 1¼in). Base this on a calculation of the discrepancy in waist to hip measurement. Should not be too big or more darts should be added

Position of front dart along front crease

Length of front trouser dart = no longer than mid hip

Length of back trouser dart = approx. 7cm (2¾in) above hip line

Positions of back trouser darts = dart near side seam is at mid hip; dart

near centre back is 5 to 6cm (2in) above hip line

Thigh/Knee/Calf/Ankle/Hem opening = all these measurements must be placed equally on both sides of centre lines for both front and back trouser legs

Always draft back trouser leg 5cm (2in) larger than front

DRESS MEASUREMENTS & KEY POINTS

Nape to waist = 39.5 to 40cm (15½ to16in) (better shorter than longer)

Total length from nape
= 99cm (39in), i.e. top of knee length
= 132cm (52in), i.e. mid-calf length
= 152cm (60in), i.e. ankle length

Hem circumference
We must consider the practicality of walking; minimum measurements below are for reference only, the ideal would be including a split or vent opening:

Knee length	= 86cm (34in)
Mid calf	= 117cm (46in)
Ankle length	= 132cm (52in)

Centre back opening = from CB nape to pass hip line, or until wherever reaches circumference measurement of minimum of 92cm (36¼in) (hip)

Side seam opening = 32cm (13in) from 2.5cm (1in) underarm point

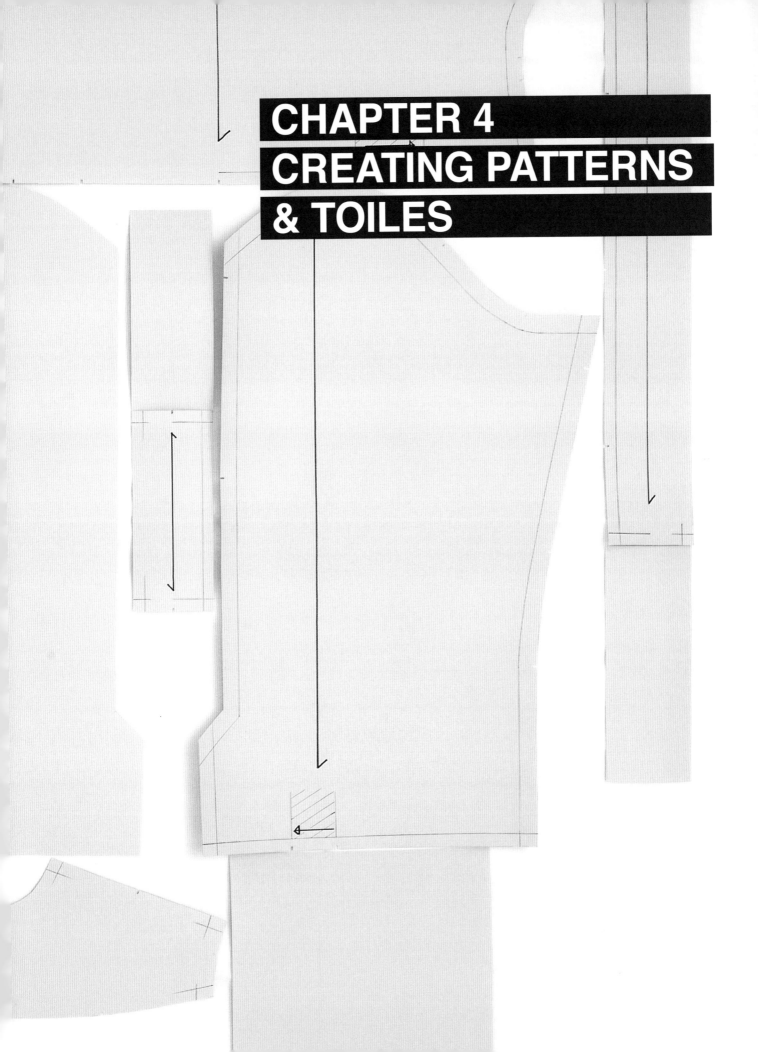

CHAPTER 4
CREATING PATTERNS
& TOILES

Once you have traced your finished block onto heavy pattern card, you are now ready to use it to create the paper pattern. A pattern cutter uses the block as a master draft pattern and traces off the most appropriate block for the pattern they are creating onto pattern cutting paper. They then manipulate the draft pattern according to the style shown in the working drawing (which is usually produced by the design team), and we will look at some of the techniques used to do this in Chapter 5. Before we do that, we will continue to look at the pattern cutting process so that the techniques of drafting the pattern will become familiar.

As each pattern is completed, it needs to be prepared for the technician or manufacturer who will be cutting the fabric and constructing the garment. The pattern cutter first decides whether to present a half pattern to the manufacturer, or whether the full pattern is needed. Then seam allowances must be added, notches and drill holes marked, and annotation written on the pattern. These will convey the pattern cutter's intentions about how to cut the pattern from the fabric and how to construct the garment. Once the pattern is complete the next step is to test it by making up a toile (test garment).

It is advisable not to labour too long developing each individual pattern. The process can be speeded up considerably if the pattern cutter works quickly to cut the pattern, then tests it in the form of a toile. At this stage the pattern can be refined and errors that might not have been easy to pick up at the flat pattern cutting stage can easily be spotted and rectified. For this reason, it is perhaps best to accept that the pattern will not always be correct first time, and to build this fact into the process. Mistakes might even lead you down an alternative and interesting route.

FOLDING THE PAPER PATTERN

When a garment is designed symmetrically, half of the paper pattern is usually drafted first, as we have seen when creating a block (see Chapter 3). Often the word 'fold' is written along the centre line, which is then placed along the fold of a piece of fabric before cutting to create the full pattern piece (see photo below). This method has its limitations. Some materials, such as silk chiffon, are difficult to fold and so there is a risk that the garment cannot be cut accurately because the centre front or centre back lines cannot be placed exactly on the grain of the fabric. Heavier fabrics can be folded more easily, but the thickness of the fold means that, again, the cut fabric will be inaccurate because the thickness of the fabric means that up to an extra 5mm (¼in) or more may be incorporated along the fold line.

Nor does this method work in the industry, where multiple copies of the pattern pieces, in different sizes, are cut from the fabric at the same time. Depending on the thickness of the fabric, from five to fifty lengths are laid one on top of the other. The paper pattern pieces are then laid on the top of the pile in the most economical layout plan before cutting. Consequently there is no opportunity to cut the pattern piece on a fold, and also the need to lay out the pieces as economically as possible means that the manufacturer requires the full pattern (see photo on opposite page). If half the pattern piece is supplied the manufacturer either has to create the other half, or send it back to the customer who then has to re-supply the whole pattern piece, either scenario wasting time.

Using half the pattern only really works when one copy of the garment is required, such as for home dressmaking.

In the industry, the need to cut
multiple copies of the fabric
means that the full pattern piece
is required.

Half a symmetrical pattern
piece can be placed along the
fold of a length of fabric.

To create a symmetrical pattern for cutting out more than one copy of the garment, first draft one half on one side of a piece of paper. Fold the paper along the centre front or centre back line. Then, using fine pins, or staples if you are using card, secure the pattern along this centre line.

Cut around the pattern using scissors. Drill pattern holes using a pattern drill and create notches with a pair of notchers (see below). Then remove the pins and open out the complete pattern.

Draw half the pattern on one side of a piece of paper.

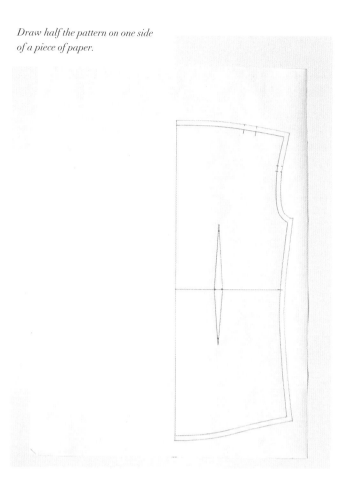

Fold a piece of paper in half along the CF or CB line and pin. Use a pattern notcher and pattern drill to transfer marks from one side of the paper to the other.

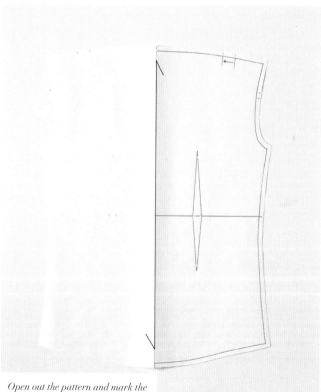

Open out the pattern and mark the grain line.

ADDING THE SEAM ALLOWANCES, NOTCHES & DRILL HOLES

The pattern cutter needs to add an allowance around each paper pattern piece to enable the pieces to be stitched together or to attach components of the garment such as zips, collars and cuffs. Generally an allowance of 1cm (³⁄₈in) is added to the seams. In addition, an allowance is also added to the outer edges of the garment, such as the hem.

A 1cm (³⁄₈in) seam allowance is the standard used within the industry. (Before the wide acceptance of the metric system, the standard was ³⁄₈in). Such a standardized allowance saves on the cost of fabric. If the inclusion of a 1cm seam allowance on the pattern is accepted, then the pattern cutter does not need to indicate the seam allowance on the pattern itself, except at the hem where it might be wider. When working outside the industry, however, seam allowances should always be marked.

A larger allowance is usually added to the hem of a garment than to the seam.

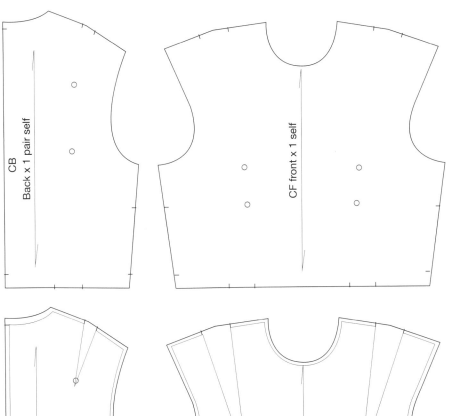

Paper patterns used in the industry do not have marks for the seam allowances, except at the hem, where notches are marked.

On this paper pattern all the seam allowances have been marked and specified.

For high-end fashion, however, which allows for a more expensive manufacturing process, different seam allowance widths are used on different areas of the garment. This is because different types of fabric, different parts of the garment, design details and finishings all require different allowances to coincide with their function and method of construction within the garment.

A 1cm (⅜in) seam allowance would not work on loosely woven or delicate fabrics, for example, because these fabrics tend to fray when handled; a larger allowance is needed to counteract the effect and ensure that the seams are stable.

Sometimes a smaller allowance is needed when constructing garment details, such as a jetted pocket. The depth of such a finished pocket opening is usually 0.5cm (¼in) and so the seam allowance needs to be the same depth.

Adding a 1cm (⅜in) seam allowance to the paper pattern is, therefore, a good starting point, but consideration should be taken of the fabric and method of construction in case the allowance should be increased or decreased. Finalizing the seam allowance can be done as part of the process of making and adjusting the toile when, if the toile is made in as close a fabric to the final garment as possible, it should become apparent where a wider or narrower allowance is needed. The following table shows some areas where the width of the allowance should be considered.

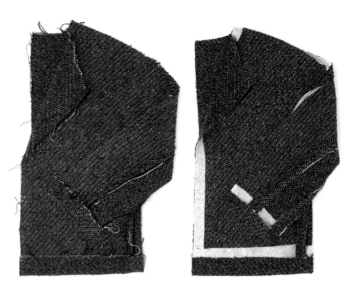

When stretched in the course of wear, the seam of a tweed jacket will easily become unstable. In this case the solution would be to tape the seam allowances with fusible light weight Vilene tape and to increase their width to 1.5cm (½in).

A double-jetted pocket requires a seam allowance of approx. 0.5cm (¼in).

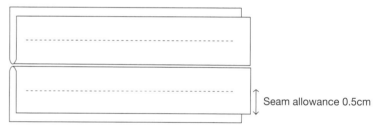

Seam allowance 0.5cm

Chiffon/muslin/fine & delicate fabrics	1.5cm (½in)	These fabrics have a tendency to fray and so require a wider seam allowance. It is also a good idea to overlock the seam allowances of such delicate fabrics or use a French seam (which would require a 1.5cm (½in) seam allowance).
Thick wool/bouclé/loose woven fabrics	1.5cm (½in)	The looser weave of these fabrics means that the seams are easily pulled apart when worn. In this case a wider seam is recommended, together with the application of iron-on tape prior to sewing the seams.
Heavy thick fabrics/padded fabrics	1.5cm (½in)	Heavier fabrics need a wider seam because the two sides of a narrower seam allowance will not lie down flat when pressed.
Curved seams	0.5cm (¼in)	A curved seam is difficult to sew, especially when the outside of the curve matches the inside of the curve. This is because the inside of the curve shortens while the outside lengthens when seam allowance is added. A smaller seam allowance will mean that the difference between the two will not be so obvious. It is also easier to sew a narrower seam allowance on a curve.
Centre back seam on trousers (menswear) near waistband	3.5cm (1½in)	This means 3.5cm (1½in) at the top attached to the waistband then gradually goes back to 1cm (½in) along the centre back crotch seam. A wider seam allowance is often used at the centre back of men's tailored trousers so that they can be let out, if necessary, over time, thus ensuring the longevity of the garment.
Armhole or neckline or edges that are finished with bias binding	No seam allowance	Armholes and necklines finished with bias binding will not need an additional seam allowance. However, if the bias binding is to be stitched down on the inside of the garment and invisible on the outside, then an allowance of 0.5cm (¼in) should be added.

NOTCHES

Notches are used to show where two sides of a seam are aligned and sewn together. They are particularly useful when marked along curved seams. They are also used to mark construction points, such as at the hip line or knee level on trousers, and can be used to distinguish between the front and back of an armhole, where one notch is usually placed on the front curve and two on the back. Notches can also be used at the beginning of a dart or to mark the position of pleats and tucks.

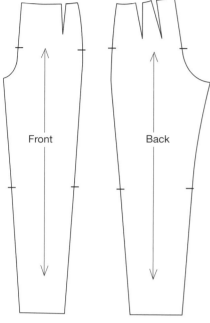

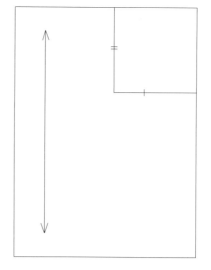

By marking one notch on one side of a square and two on the other, the pattern cutter is able to remove the shape, add seam allowances, and then the technician will know which side of the square should be attached to which seam so that the grainline will run in the same direction on both pieces of fabric.

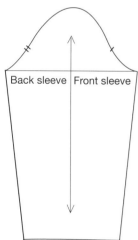

Notches can be used to mark the position of construction lines and also to distinguish between the front and back of an armhole seam.

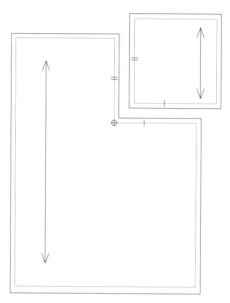

DRILL HOLES

Drill holes can also be used to mark the position of:
- the corners and position of pockets
- sewing/top-stitching guidelines
- the end of darts
- corners that need to be clipped
- buttons and buttonholes

Drill holes are often used with notches. Notches, for example, are usually used to mark the beginning of the dart, while a drill hole is usually placed 2cm (¾in) from the end of the dart. When the dart is sewn from the notches at the beginning towards the end, the stitching continues 2cm (¾in) beyond the drill hole and is then back tacked to finish the sewing line. This ensures that the marked drill hole will be invisible on the right side of the fabric.

Drill holes can also be used to locate the exact point where stitching should end, the point at which the pattern should be cut open, or where stitching should pivot. A drill hole, for example, is used at the end of a godet insertion.

Notches can also be used to distinguish between shapes that are very similar. For example a four-piece bra cup.

Notches are usually marked halfway along a seam, and on a very long seam, such as on the seam of an evening dress with a long train, additional notches should be placed 70cm (28in) apart, for example.

SPEAKING THE PATTERN CUTTER'S LANGUAGE

Specialists in many professions use a unique system of communicating with each other; pianists use music, architects use technical drawings. In the fashion industry, the pattern cutter uses a set of symbols, colour codes and technical terms that are added to the pattern. This language is called annotation.

It is important for every pattern cutter to use this language when creating patterns and to use it accurately. The pattern cutter may not be in the same part of the building as the technician cutting the fabric, or even in the same country as the manufacturer; questions cannot always be asked directly. Using a set of symbols and technical terms understood by everyone, therefore, saves time and money.

Grainline

The grainline, which as we have seen is usually parallel to the centre back or centre front line (see page 19), is marked on the pattern with a straight line. The technician cutting the fabric then knows how to lay the pattern piece on the fabric with the straight grainline parallel to the selvedge.

The straight line is also marked with an arrow at one or both ends.

An arrow at both ends means that, as long as the line is parallel to the selvedge, the pattern piece can be arranged either way up to save fabric on the layout plan.

A line with an arrow at one end pointing up means that all the pattern pieces must be placed with the top of the pattern pieces facing in the direction of the arrow. This usually applies to fabrics with printed patterns; a designer of a floral print, for example, may not want the roses apparently growing down the fabric.

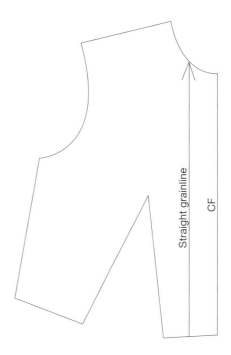

A line with an arrow at one end pointing down is usually used on patterns that will be cut from a fabric with a pile, such as corduroy or velvet. The technician then knows to place all the pattern pieces so that the pile runs down the garment. This applies particularly to fur where our instinct is to stroke downwards.

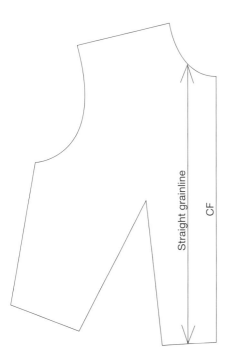

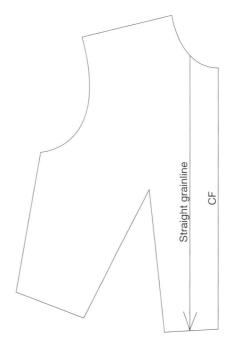

Grainline and written annotation

All annotations are written along the straight grainline on the paper pattern. This ensures that when two people are standing on either side of a table, with the fabric unrolled between them with the selvedges running along the table, at least one of them can see the annotation without having to crane their neck.

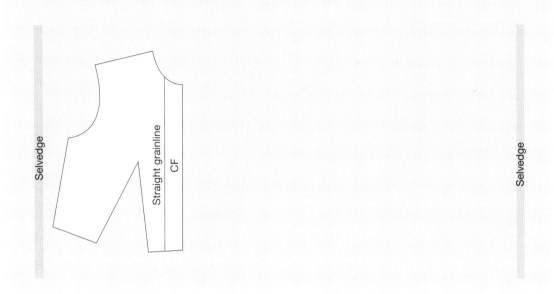

Style name

The name of the style is written along the grainline.

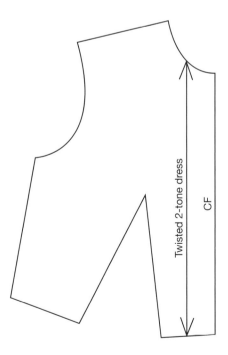

Pattern number/style number/reference number

Each style in a collection should be coded with a unique number that is used for identification between the designer, manufacturer and buyer. The number usually records the season, style in the collection, and in some cases also records the name. 'Spring Summer 2012/a tuxedo jacket/made in silk satin organza/this is the 6th jacket style in the season' would be coded as SS12/TX/SSO/06. If a different version of the same style is introduced, for example with a longer sleeve, then a new style number is created.

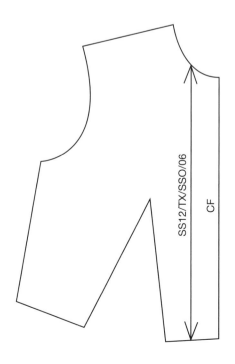

Name of the pattern piece

The name of each component of the pattern is marked on the pattern piece – sleeve, collar, etc. By matching the named pattern pieces to the technical drawing, the manufacturer should be able to construct the garment.

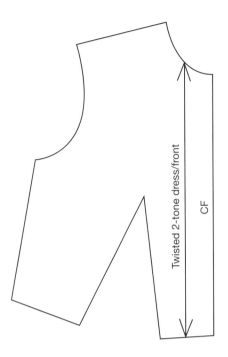

Including or not including seam allowance on the pattern

When working in the industry the seam allowance should be added to all patterns so that the manufacturer does not have to take the responsibility of adding it. It is, therefore, unacceptable just to write 'include seam allowance' or 'no seam allowance' on the pattern. It does not, however, always have to be marked.

The only time when it is acceptable to leave off the seam allowance altogether is on a set of basic blocks which will then be used be used to create many different styles.

Seams and seam allowance

As we have seen, the seam allowance on all patterns is usually 1cm (⅜in) (see page 107). To avoid confusion, and if time allows, draw the seam allowance on the edge of each piece of the paper pattern. Alternatively, just mark the allowance at each end of the seam line. Some pattern cutters use a pair of notches to mark the seam allowance, but this can cause the pattern to tear.

If there is no need for a seam allowance, such as on a hem, this should still be marked clearly. You can do this by using a highlighter pen to draw along the edges of the pattern, or write 'no seam allowance' along the line.

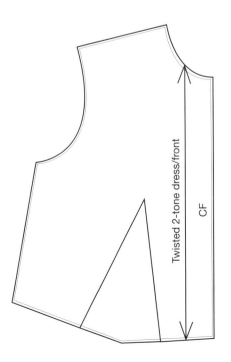

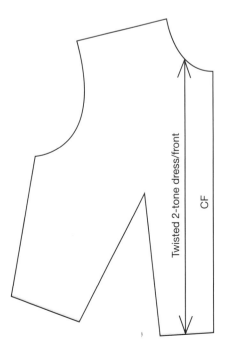

Pairs

A pair of pattern pieces is not always the same as two identical pieces, since one half of the pair will mirror the other – a left sleeve cannot be worn on the right arm, for example, yet both will be made from identically shaped pattern pieces.

The number of pattern pieces to be cut

Usually we cut out a pair of each pattern piece, one for each side of the body. Some pattern cutters write the word 'cut' to indicate the number of pieces required, and some use an 'x' symbol: 'Top Collar cut 1 only' or 'Top Collar x 1 only'.

Colour coding for different fabrics

The pattern cutter also needs to specify from which fabric each pattern piece should be cut. A garment might consist of a main fabric, usually called 'self', a lining and interfacing, for example. The manufacturer and pattern cutter usually agree on a system of colours to indicate each fabric. The instructions written along the grainline are then written in these colours according to the fabric to be used. There is no standard industry coding system, but generally the following colours are used:

- Pencil or black biro to indicate self (the main fabric)
- Blue pencil or biro to indicate a second fabric within the same garment
- Red pencil or biro to indicate the interfacing (or interlining)
- Green pencil or biro to indicate a lining

If a pattern piece is to be cut from both the main fabric and from interfacing, then black would be used to write the style name, the name of the pattern piece and the number to be cut, while red would be used to write the type of interfacing to be used.

Centre front/centre back/centre lines

We have seen that symmetrical pattern pieces for industry are not usually supplied in half with 'fold' written down the centre front or centre back line, but are supplied as complete pieces (see pages 104 and 105). It can be useful, however, to mark the centre line on the pattern, especially if it is to be reused or adapted for a different style, allowing the pattern cutter to locate the principal line of the pattern easily.

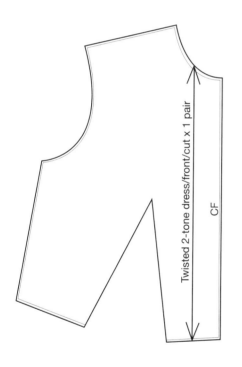

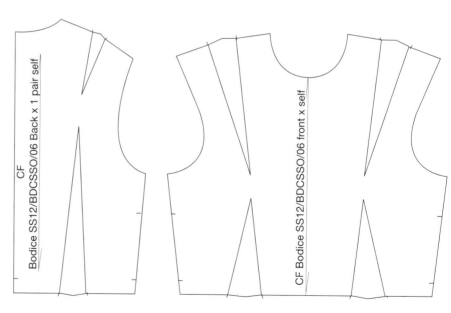

Notches

Notches, also known as balance marks, are used to show where two seams should be joined together. The paper pattern or card is clipped along the seam allowance, usually using a pair of pattern notchers. The notches themselves should not be wider than half the seam allowance; on a pattern with a 1cm (³⁄₈in) seam allowance, the notches should be no longer than 0.5cm (¼in). When the cloth is cut, the position of the notches is then transferred by clipping the fabric with a pair of scissors.

Drill holes

Drill holes are marked on the pattern using a pattern drill (see page 38). While notches are used to mark the beginning of the dart, drill holes are used to mark 1.5 to 2cm (¾in) near the end.

The position of the drill hole can be transferred to the fabric using an awl or bradawl, which can be pushed through several layers of fabric; with tailor's chalk or pencil (though care must be taken if the marks appear on the right side of the fabric); or by hand tacking, the preferred method of bespoke tailors.

To ensure the holes are easy to see on the paper pattern or card, they can be circled in red biro. In some cases the pattern cutter should also mark whether the drill holes should be marked on the right or wrong side of the fabric; drill holes might need to be marked on the right side of the fabric to show where a pocket should be attached, for example, while the position of the end of a dart would need to be marked on the wrong side.

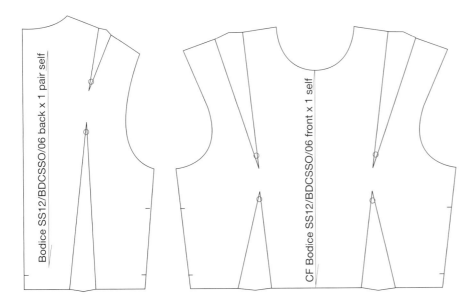

Pleats and tucks

Pleats and tucks are marked with notches on the seam allowance. The pattern cutter also needs to mark the direction in which the pleat or tuck should be folded. This is done by drafting diagonal lines within the area of the pleat or tuck with the highest point of the line indicating the start of the fold and the lowest the finish.

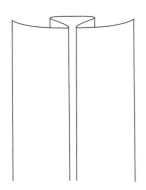

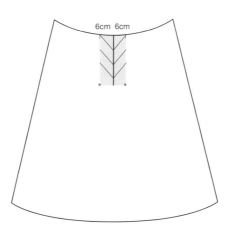

This skirt has a 6cm (2½in) deep box pleat, which is 10cm (4in) in length. The top of the pleat is marked with notches, the end with a drill hole, and the direction of the pleat is marked with diagonal lines slanted from high to low to show the direction in which the pleat should be folded.

Gathers

The start and end of a section of gathering can be marked with a notch. Within the area a wavy line should be marked along the position of the gathers and the word 'gathering' should also be written in the area. A short instruction should also be written, such as 'gathering – to be gathered to 9.5cm (3½in) and attached to yoke seam'.

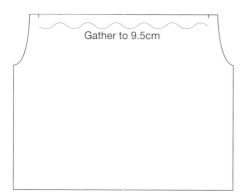

Gather to 9.5cm

Date

The date is often written on the pattern to avoid confusion when different variations of the same pattern are drafted on different days. This date can be written in smaller print and it is sufficient to write it as a simple DD.MM.YY.

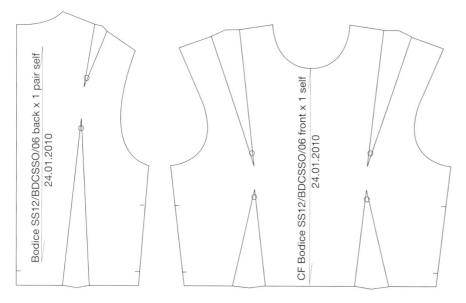

Right side up

Fabrics have a right and wrong side and all pattern pieces should be drafted to be cut with the right side up. This should be marked in red biro on the pattern piece as 'right side up' or 'RSU'.

For asymmetric designs, such as women's trousers where the front of the right and left legs are different, we also need to indicate which is which. The back would be annotated 'Back x 1 pair self', but the front right trouser leg would be marked as 'Front x 1 only self right-hand side RSU.' and the left would be marked 'Front x 1 only self left-hand side RSU'.

Size

The size of each pattern piece should be clearly marked. Samples are usually made in a size 10, but when the pattern is ready for production it is graded from size 8 to size 16, for example, and in some cases from sizes XS to XL.

It is necessary to include the size because, in order to save fabric, more than one size might be cut from the same length. If each piece were not clearly marked, this would be impossible because the different sizes could easily become muddled.

To find the size at a glance, the number is often circled.

Facing lines

The pattern cutter usually traces a separate pattern piece for a facing from the main pattern piece and then adds any necessary seam allowances and other annotations to this new pattern.

It is also helpful to draw the facing line onto the main pattern piece, too. This is helpful during the production process because the technician can check the facing against the pattern and spot any mistakes, such as a missing seam allowance, for example.

The facing line is drafted with a line of alternate dots and dashes.

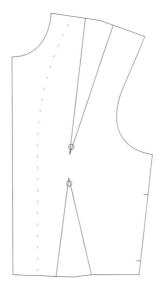

Sewing lines

Ideally, the sewing line where seams are sewn together, should be indicated on the pattern. If time is short, however, it is acceptable just to indicate the sewing lines at both ends of the seam only. The sewing line is equivalent to the line marking the seam allowance on the paper pattern.

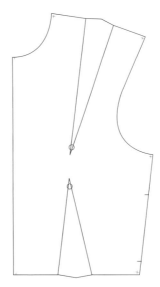

Shading

The pattern cutter can add areas of shading using light or broken diagonal lines to indicate the position of a particular detail. When adding a pocket to the front of a jacket, the manufacturer would apply a piece of interfacing along the pocket opening to provide extra strength along the cut line. The pattern cutter should mark the exact position and size of the interfacing on the main paper pattern piece with light red or broken diagonal lines.

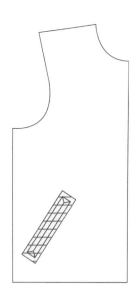

Technical writing

Handwritten annotation on paper patterns must be very clear and easy to read, as this will save time and prevent misunderstandings between the pattern cutter and technician or manufacturer and thus avoid expensive mistakes. It is, therefore, useful for the pattern cutter to learn the art of technical writing, which is usually written in upper case letters in a blocked and uniform style.

Of course, today, computers have taken over much written communication and so there is less need to write by hand. Nevertheless, the skill of technical writing is still a useful one.

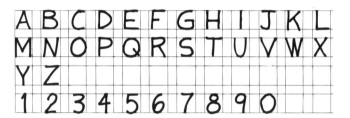

True corners

Some things only become evident at garment stage, such as the requirement to true the corners of all seams when two fabric pattern pieces are put together, such as the corners at the shoulder neck points, the shoulder points where they meet the top of the sleeve crown, underarms and hems of garment (right).

A quick and easy way to finalize a set of paper patterns is to place them together, as though they were being sewn, then redraw the meeting points to true and finalise the pattern by redrafting a smooth line (far right).

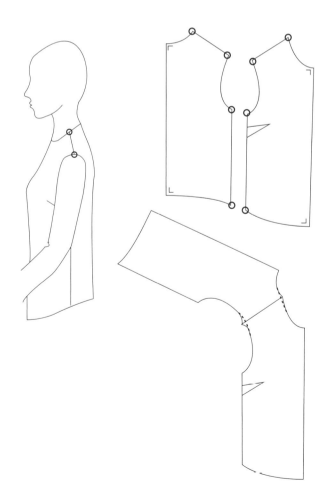

THE TOILE

The toile is an essential part of the pattern cutting process. Making a toile will help you see if your pattern cutting strategy has worked – if it meets the design brief and resembles the working drawing – and allow you to make any necessary adjustments for fit.

The first stage of making a toile is to select the correct fabric – one that will most closely resemble the characteristics of the fabric from which the final garment will be made. Once the toile is sewn, it is then usually fitted on a mannequin, this being the most convenient method of seeing the garment in three dimensions. There are, however, pitfalls in doing so as a mannequin is not an exact representation of human anatomy. To ensure that the toile is successfully altered, knowledge of the differences between the mannequin and human anatomy is vital, and we shall also explore these potential fitting pitfalls in this chapter.

Once the fitting is complete, the necessary adjustments are made to the pattern, and a second toile is usually made before the final pattern is completed.

CALICO OR NO CALICO

Most experienced pattern cutters and sample machinists in the industry will make a calico toile as a quick method of gauging proportion and checking the accuracy of the pattern. But why is the toile made from calico and does it need to be?

Calico is a 100 per cent cotton fabric that is usually reasonably priced, which is one reason why it is often used to make toiles. Made from unbleached cotton, it is usually off-white in colour and often has a slight slub in the weave. It comes in several weights from fine (muslin or cheesecloth), through light and medium to heavy. It is coated to make it crisp and flat, but it can be washed to make it hang in natural folds. Unwashed calico may shrink if pressed with steam.

When making a toile it is important to select the weight of calico nearest to the final fabric that will be used for the garment. Even then, using calico can impose limitations on the accuracy of the toile, principally because it will not always behave in exactly the same way as the final fabric. A woven wool fabric used for a tailored jacket with a two-piece sleeve, for example, would be stretched along the back seam using steam at elbow level to allow for the shape of the bent elbow and also to allow the arm to move forwards. Calico cannot be manipulated in this way, and so the toile will not be accurate. In this case it might be best to make a set of sleeves out of wool.

A pattern cutter, therefore, needs to understand and take these limitations into consideration when adjusting the pattern according to the calico toile. Knowledge of what will not work in calico but will work in the final fabric is vital. It is also advisable, when deciding whether to make a toile in calico or not, to consider how accurately it will resemble the final garment. Lace or fur, for example, cannot be imitated in calico and it would be a waste of time to try.

To overcome these problems, some pattern cutters in the industry prefer to work in the final fabric during the toiling process in order to rectify technical problems right at the beginning of the process, and manufacturers do sell sample lengths of fabric at a special (though often more expensive) rate to enable them to do so.

Practical alternatives for the student, if the final fabric is not available or calico is still too expensive, are inexpensive fabrics sourced at markets, wholesale shops and second-hand or charity shops. Cheap curtain fabrics, lining purchased in bulk, old bed sheets, tablecloths or duvet covers can also be used.

Woven wool fabric (right) would be manipulated using steam to accommodate the shape of the elbow in a two-piece sleeve. Calico (left), however, cannot be manipulated in this way and so the toile will not be accurate.

FITTING ON A MANNEQUIN

In the same way that the pattern cutter needs to be aware of the limitations of using calico for the toile, he or she also needs to be aware of the limitations of using a mannequin for fitting. Apart from the obvious difference between a stiff, lifeless dummy and a body made of flesh and bones that moves, mannequins also have several features that differ from human anatomy and which need to be borne in mind during fitting. To overcome these problems, it is usually also best to fit the toile on a live model as well as on the mannequin. Eventually, as an experienced pattern cutter, you will be able to analyze the fit and accuracy of a paper pattern when it is made into a toile and fitted on both the mannequin and the live model and will also be able to assess how a standard-sized garment might fit various body shapes. In the meantime, try assessing your own body against a mannequin in a mirror looking at some of the differences outlined here. You could also assess the way your clothes move as you walk, swing your arms and stretch.

FITTING: AIDE MEMOIRE

When a toile/test garment is ready for fitting, try to keep to these rules:
- the Centre Front and Centre Back should be clearly marked.
- the toile fabric must be pre-shrunk before cut and make.
- if there are fastenings, these should be applied in order to assess the suitability in size and quality (however, in most cases using dress pins to fasten the garment is acceptable).
- the garment should be made up using machine stitch, not with pins.
- it is acceptable to draw pockets by pen onto a toile to save time, but it's best to try out the construction method of a complicated pocket.
- other small details can also be drawn on if they are basic or classic, e.g. top stitching.
- try not to cut the toile right away unless you are absolutely sure. If there is excess fabric, always try to pin it up (or pin away).
- there should be someone to take notes.
- the toile should be tried on more than one model in order to justify a more realistic fit, unless it is made to measure.

Step-by-step guide to fitting

1. Look at the 'frame' of the garment i.e. the length and width.
2. Length: look from the front, back and side to see whether the garment needs to be lengthened or shortened. Check front is same length as back.
3. Width: check that the garment isn't too big or too small? Is there too much or too little tolerance?
4. Look at the CF and CB lines: they should hang visually vertical. If not, this may be affected by different shoulder slant on a real person. Another possibility is the actual cutting out of paper pattern or fabric is asymmetrical. Finally, this could be due the garment being cut on an 'off-grain' angle on the fabric.
5. Neckline width: check for shoulder neck points standing too close or too far from both sides of the neck. In case of gaping at CF or CB, a small amount can be taken out from CB neckline vertically down the garment to zero. The same can be done for front CF neckline. The actual outline of the neckline should be according to sketch and working drawing.
6. Shoulder line: does it go too far to front or to the back? The length could be adjusted easily but this will be related directly to crown height of sleeve.
7. Armhole: does it feel restricted when moving arms upwards and forwards? Making it deeper or shallower is fairly straightforward but check how the sleeve is affected.
8. Side seam: if this is not hanging vertically, it is very easy to move the side seam by cutting and pasting the actual side seam on the paper pattern.
9. Darts: are bust darts too big (too much suppression)? A too large bust dart would create too much excess room for the body. You could let out the dart by opening the sewn dart and letting the garment lay flatter on the body. When darts are too small (not enough suppression), the garment will appear to be taut – an extra dart would need to be placed, then this extra dart could be transferred or combined to an existing dart during the flat pattern cutting process. For the rest of the darts at the back, the process is much simpler and you can just take in or let out the darts as appropriate.
10. Other details: anything that has no direct relation to the fit of the garment should be discussed with the designer.

Movement

Human beings walk, stand, sit, climb stairs, bend and stretch their arms. Clothes, therefore, cannot be too tightly fitted and we have already discussed the need to add tolerance. The toile should, therefore, not be adjusted to fit the mannequin exactly and should be tried on a human model, if possible, in order to assess ease of movement.

Fabric

A mannequin is made from compact fibres covered by a layer of cotton or linen. This allows a garment to be pinned to the mannequin. Human beings are, of course, made covered with soft, flexible flesh that has elasticity – which cannot be pinned. Aside from the issue of the effect upon gravity of pinning a garment to the mannequin (see page 24), there is also a question of fit. A strapless dress, for example, might be made to fit the mannequin, but as soon as it is fitted on a real person, if it is too tight it might create an unattractive dent across the bust as it presses into the flesh. (In this case a boned bodice would be the best solution.)

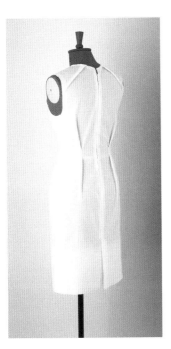

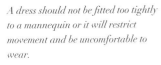

A dress should not be fitted too tightly to a mannequin or it will restrict movement and be uncomfortable to wear.

A strapless dress can easily be made to fit a mannequin, but when worn on the human body the elasticity of the flesh can cause an unattractive dent across the bust if the dress is made tight in an effort to hold it up. The solution is to add a corset inside the bodice.

Arms

Detachable arms can be purchased for mannequins and attached by means of two circular metal plates that slot together. They are, however, unwieldy and quite expensive. They also do not move in the same way as the human arm, so again trying the toile on a live model is the best solution.

With or without arms, the mannequin has a metal or plastic plate at the armhole. It should not, however, be mistaken for the shape of the actual armhole, which is much more complicated than a mere circular shape. The armhole on a garment should certainly be made lower to accommodate the movement of the arm. If the toile is made to fit the shape of the metal plate it will be too tight.

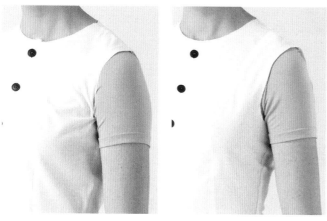

An armhole cut to fit a mannequin will be too tight when worn by a model (left). The armhole should be lowered to fit the model (right).

Legs

Full body mannequins with legs, but no feet, can be used to try on trousers, shorts, swimwear and jumpsuits. Again they have their limitations. The legs do not bend and the lack of feet means it is impossible to check if the bottom of the trouser is wide enough for the ankle to slip through. The fabric covering also means that it is difficult to pull some fabrics over the legs, especially tightly fitted jeans that might be pulled on the human body with the assistance of the skin's flexibility and a 'wiggle' of the hips.

Figure shape

When using a dress mannequin, it is also important to select the best shape. Mannequins are available in two styles – BSA and BSD (see size charts on pages 12 and 13). The BSD reflects an hourglass figure, a style more common in the years up to the 1950s. Today, changes in lifestyle mean that the BSA mannequin, with its larger waist and hip measurements, is more appropriate.

The 'ideal' figure has changed across fashion history and continues to change. In the 1950s the preferred shaped was the hourglass, while today our modern lifestyle has led to a straighter line.

Neck

The neck on a mannequin tends to lean forwards and the upper back has a slight slouch if you compare it to a human being standing up straight. The pattern cutter fitting the toile on a mannequin needs to be aware, therefore, that it is acceptable to have a slight gap between the neckline of the mannequin and the centre back of the collar. If the neckline is adjusted to fit the mannequin and the gap filled, when the garment is worn by a live model there will be an excess of fabric at the base of the collar as the neck pushes the collar back.

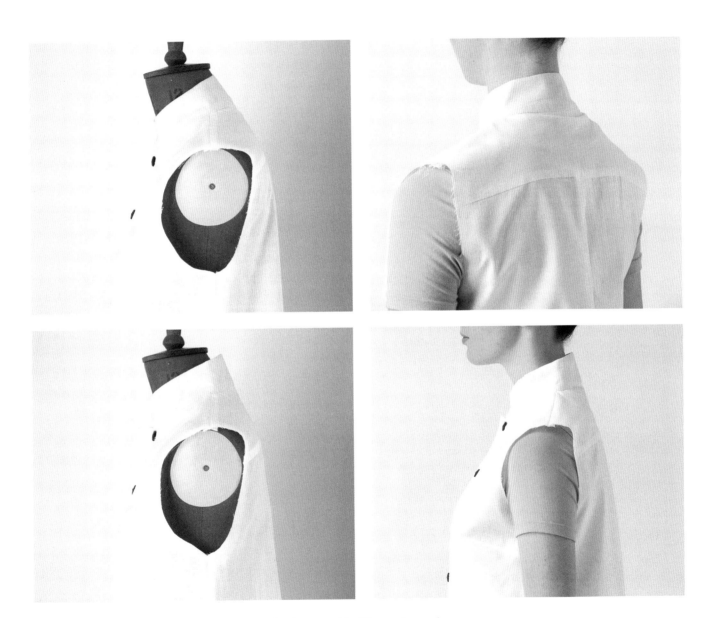

When fitting a toile on a mannequin, the pattern cutter needs to be aware of the differences between human anatomy and that of the mannequin. A collar adjusted to fit the mannequin, for example, will not sit comfortably at the neckline on the body. When fitting the toile on the mannequin, the pattern cutter needs to be aware that it is acceptable to have a gap between the collar and the neck.

Head

Most dress mannequins are made without the addition of a head. This can cause problems if you are fitting a toile with a hood where it is impossible to assess the fit. Toiles with high collars (above 8cm/3in) are also difficult to assess on the mannequin and the pattern cutter would need to consider the shape of the back of the head, the position of the ears and the jaw line.

Abdomen

The abdomen, below the waist seam, of mannequins is slightly rounded. Most women also have a slightly rounded abdomen, while for young, slim girls this area is completely flat. However, as we have seen (see page 75) it is preferable not to use darts in this area to avoid exaggerating the abdomen. The pattern cutter fitting a toile, therefore, need not try to mimic the shape of the mannequin exactly and will also be helped by the elasticity of human flesh, which will adjust itself to a certain extent to fit inside the garment.

Pelvis

On a mannequin the side of the hip is made completely smooth and nearly circular. A human body, however, has pelvic bones in this area, which are especially prominent on slimmer and younger people. In the latter case, therefore, the side of the hip should be made flatter than on the mannequin. This also affects the waistband, which could also be made slightly straighter than on the mannequin where it will stand away at the waistline.

Buttocks

The back of the hip area is always completely flat on a torso mannequin, unlike the human body shape, which is rounded. It is, therefore, important when fitting the toile in this area not to make it too tight. Full body mannequins, however, resemble the shape of the buttocks more closely.

Nape to waist

As we have seen, the nape to waist measurement is normally cut shorter than the actual body measurement (see page 79) to accommodate both shorter and longer measurements in this area and avoid having the garment 'sit' on the hips. It is, therefore, necessary to compare the measurement of the mannequin to the set of measurements you are using.

MAKING & ADJUSTING THE TOILE

Making a toile provides the pattern cutter with an opportunity to test the pattern. The best strategy, therefore, for pattern cutting is to take advantage of this stage by first understanding the garment construction, considering the pattern cutting approach and then drafting a pattern quickly, using the toile to correct any mistakes. By accepting that the first draft of the pattern is very unlikely to be completely accurate, the pattern cutter can then be allowed to speed up the process by making a quick first draft rather than labouring over a pattern that is then just as likely to contain mistakes.

Here we will look at the process of making a pattern and then adjusting a toile for a skirt from the Betty Jackson Autumn/Winter 2009 collection.

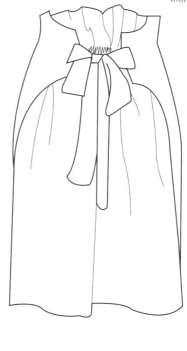
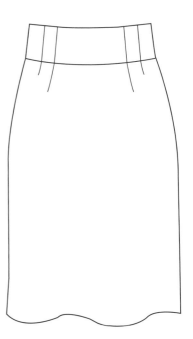

Working drawing of the Betty Jackson skirt, showing front and back

Pencil skirt featuring gathering at the centre front of the waist from the Betty Jackson Autumn/Winter 2009 collection.

Step 1
Select a block

A basic skirt block was used as the starting point for the pattern. As the design is quite relaxed in feel either a basic skirt block one size up could be selected or 8 to 10cm (3 to 4in) tolerance could be added to the block. Trace the block onto a piece of pattern cutting paper and add tolerance, if necessary.

Step 2
Adjust length

Work out the length of the skirt. In this case the hem is about 8 to 10cm (3 to 4in) above the knee, so the centre back should be 55cm (21in).

Step 3
Create front panel extensions

From the side front dart, draw a line parallel to the side seam from waist to hem. Cut the pattern open along this line. Add panel extensions to which you will add the ties. Each extension should be 10cm (4in) long. Draw a curved line at the top and bottom of each extension, according to the working drawing.

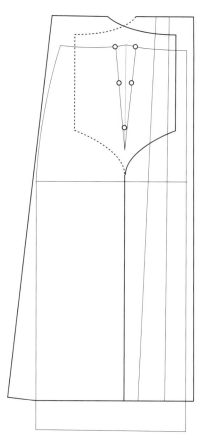
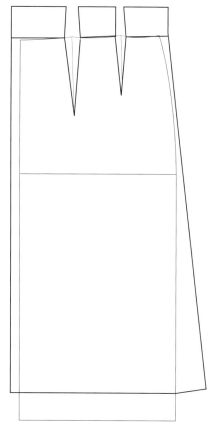

Above diagram shows steps 1 to 5

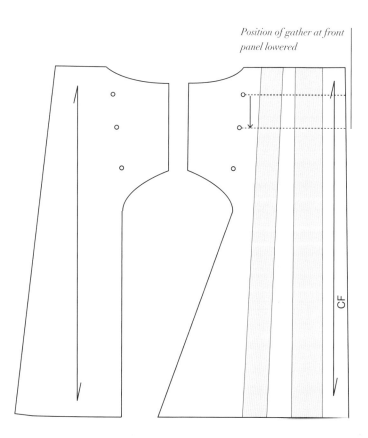

Position of gather at front panel lowered

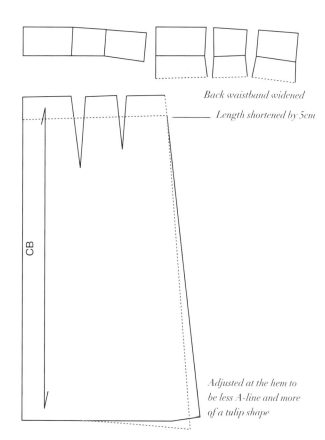

Back waistband widened

Length shortened by 5cm

Adjusted at the hem to be less A-line and more of a tulip shape

Step 4
Extend width of skirt front

Cut and split the new centre front panel vertically in two places. Add an additional allowance of fabric along both lines and at the centre front to extend the panel so that it is twice as wide as the original block, in order to gather this extra width back to the original measurements.

Step 5
Create back waistband

From the top of the back panel, measure down 6cm (2¼in) at the centre back and side seam. Draw a line across the back to create the waistband. Cut the pattern along the line. Remove the darts from the waistband sections and re-draw them as one pattern piece by tracing and combining these steps onto a new piece of paper.

Step 6
Make first toile

A toile was then made and fitted on a mannequin.

Step 7
Adjust line of skirt

Assess the toile against the working drawing. The first thing to note is that the toile is more A-line than the working drawing, which is more of a tulip shape. The pattern should, therefore, be adjusted at the hem, in this case by taking it in 10cm (4in) – i.e. 2.5cm (1in) on all side hems of front and back.

Step 8
Reduce length of frill

The frill at the front needs to be made deeper. This can be done by lowering the position at which the front panel is gathered. The back waistband also needs to be widened.

Step 9
Make back waistband wider

The waist also seems too large. In this case it can be taken by reducing the length of the elastic at the waist by approx. 2.5cm (1in).

Step 10
Make second toile

A second toile is then made and used to double-check all the details and that the pattern matches the original working drawing and specification. Allowing for the crispness of the calico in contrast to the wool from which the skirt will eventually be made, this second toile seems much better. Not quite perfect, it could be shortened by 5cm (2in) before going into production, where it can be used by the manufacturer as a construction template to ensure accuracy during the bulk production process.

The first toile, created in calico cotton.

The second toile, made in the actual fabric that the final piece will be produced from.

Stitching the toile

You can machine or hand stitch the toile. If hand stitching, always use 100 per cent cotton tacking thread as it is much stronger than sewing thread. Pinning is not recommended, especially along curved seams.

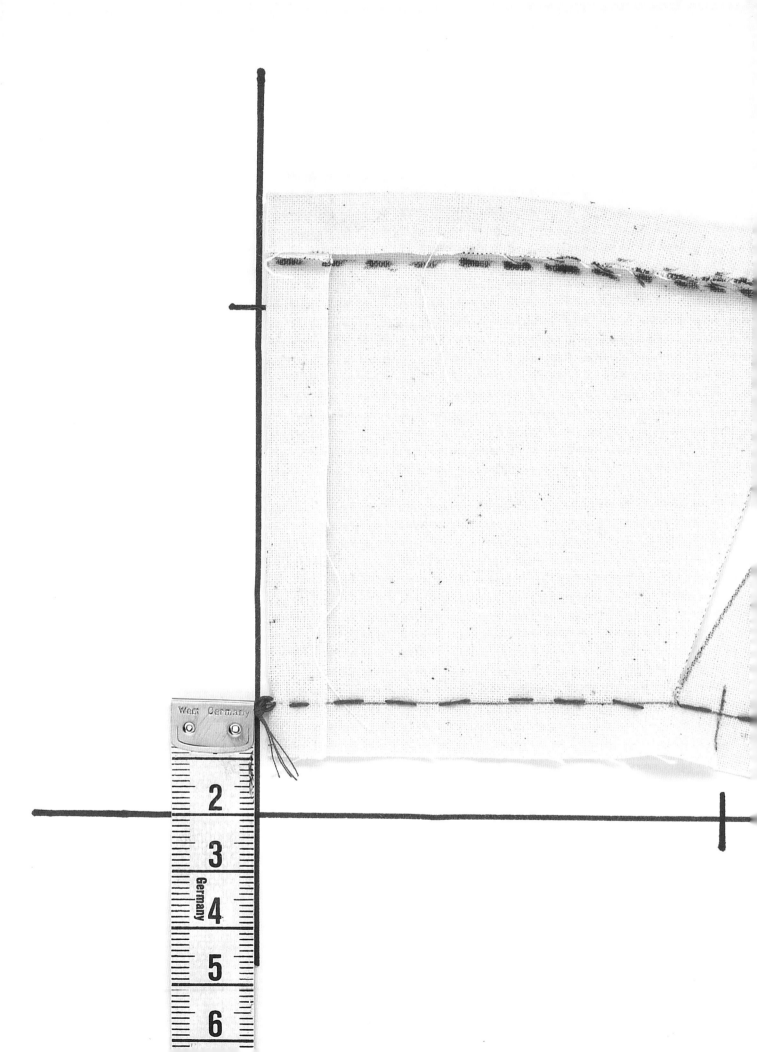

CHAPTER 5
CONVERTING THE BLOCK INTO THE DESIGN

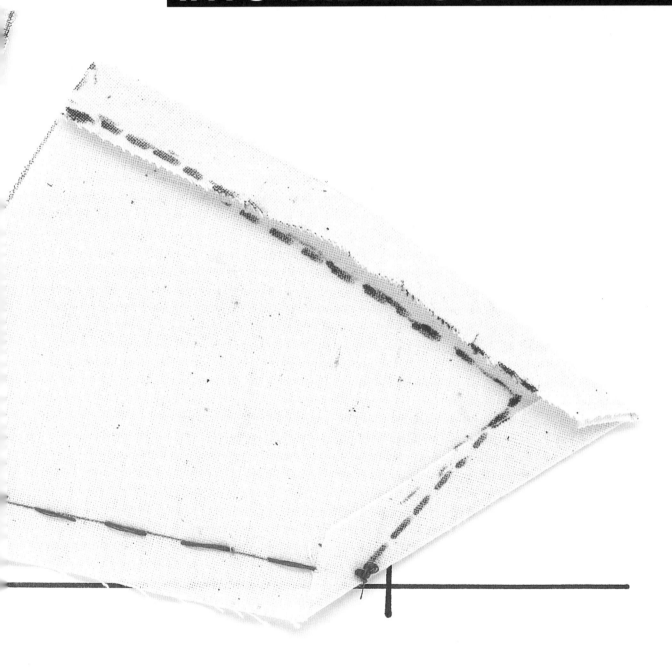

A set of basic blocks offers the pattern cutter a selection of simple garment shapes that can be modified into an endless number of different garment styles. It is very rare for a pattern cutter not to modify the block.

Most modifications entail either adding or eliminating seams, moving, manipulating or eliminating darts, or adding pleats, tucks and gathers. Once you have understood these basic principles you will be able to convert the block into a brand new paper pattern for any style of garment. Also in this chapter, we will look at adding collars, fastenings and openings to the pattern. Finally, we will discuss how to create a completely new style from a bodice block – a jacket – demonstrating how easy it is to combine the modification techniques explored in this chapter to create a new block or pattern.

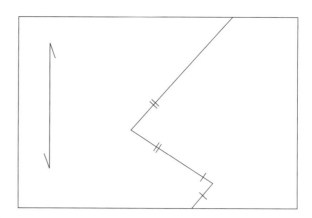

ADDING SEAMS TO PAPER PATTERNS

In theory seams can be added anywhere on a pattern. You just need to decide where to put the seam, whether it will be straight, curved or even a zigzag shape.

Step 1
Mark the seam on the pattern & add notches
Mark the line for the seam on the pattern. Then add notches to enable you to find how to line up and join the pattern together again.

Step 2
Cut the pattern open & add seam allowances
Using a fresh piece of paper, trace both sections of the pattern, transfer the notches and add relevant seam allowances and drill holes. Grainlines should be parallel to the original grainline.

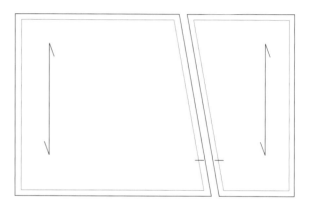

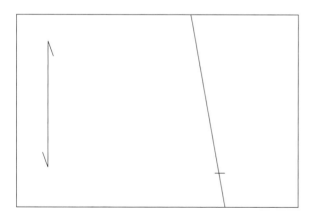

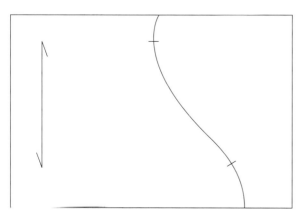

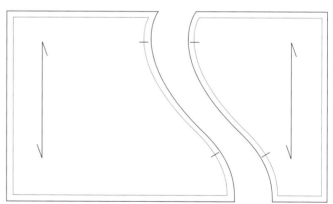

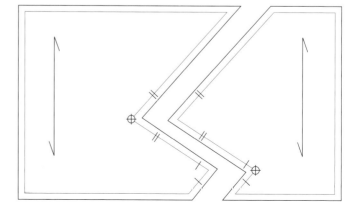

Step 3
Sew the new seam together

Make a toile from the pattern. Once the new seam is sewn together, only a line will be visible on the surface of the garment.

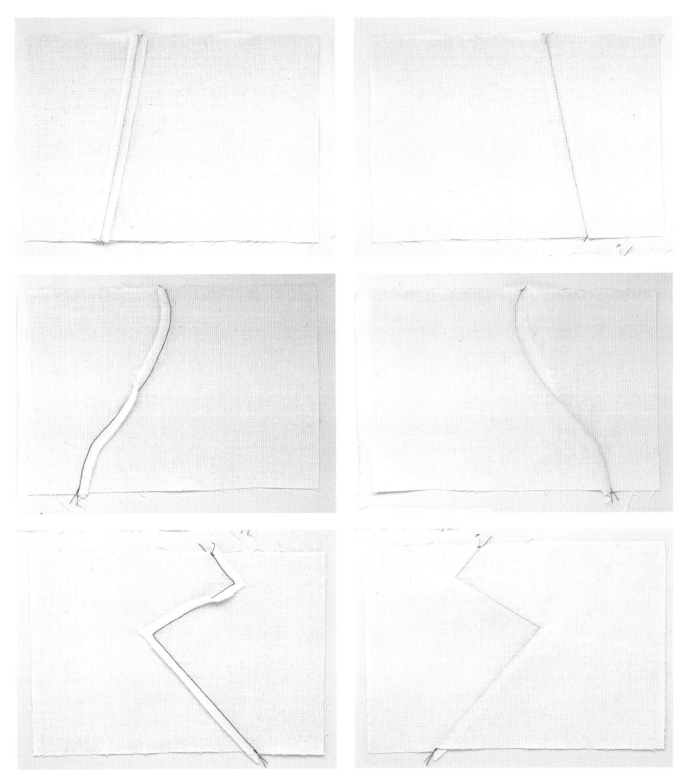

For curved and zigzag seams, we often use a technique called 'twisting' seams, shown in the above photos.

ELIMINATING SEAMS

Most garments have a combination of the following types of seam:

- Side seams
- Centre back seam
- Shoulder seam
- Armhole seam
- Centre front seam
- Yoke seam

What is and is not a seam?
A seam should join two completely separate pattern pieces together. A dart, therefore, is not a seam because it is constructed in the middle of a pattern piece.

COMBINING TWO STRAIGHT SEAMS

The simplest method of eliminating a seam is to align two straight seams on two pattern pieces that are meant to be joined together and combine them on one pattern piece.

Step 1
Lay one sewing line next to the other
Lay two straight seams next to each other. If the seam allowance has been added, overlap the allowances so that the sewing lines sit directly on top of each other.

Step 2
Draft the single pattern piece
Draw around the two pattern pieces to create one shape.

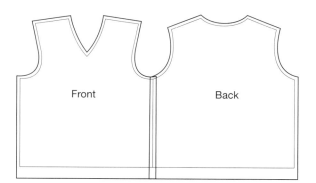

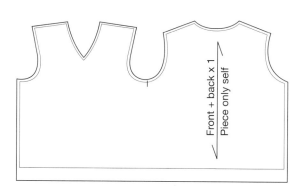

COMBINING TWO SHAPED SEAMS

Knowing how to combine two shaped seams is a matter of practise. The first step is to lay the two pattern pieces side by side to judge how it can be done.

Eliminating the side seam on a pair of slim-legged trousers

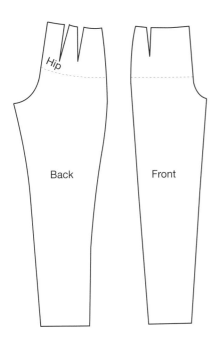

Step 1
Place the two pattern pieces side by side

Place the two pattern pieces side by side with the grainlines parallel to each other and the hip points touching. Do not overlap the pattern pieces, or the trouser leg will be too narrow. Aim to make the pattern larger rather than smaller; it can always be taken in later at the toile stage. Notice how the shape of the waist creates a dart between the two pieces.

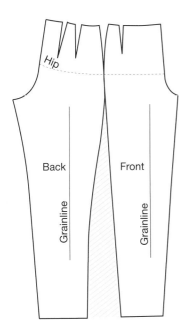

Step 2
Draft the single pattern piece

Trace around the two pattern pieces, adding a dart to accommodate the shape of the waist. The new pattern now has a much wider and straighter leg because the shaping created by the side seam has been removed.

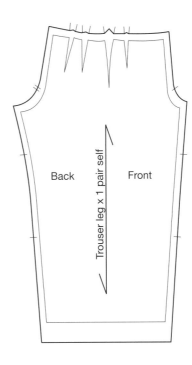

Trouser leg x 1 pair self

ELIMINATING THE SIDE SEAMS ON A JACKET

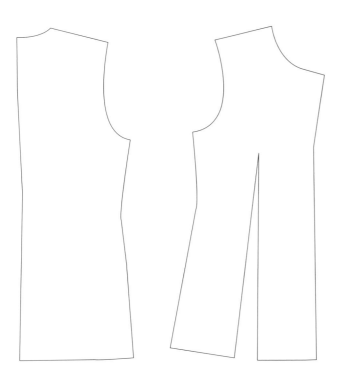

Step 2
Draft two new seams

It is now necessary to re-distribute the shaping at the waist, and this can be done be creating two new slightly curved seams, each starting part way along the armhole seam.

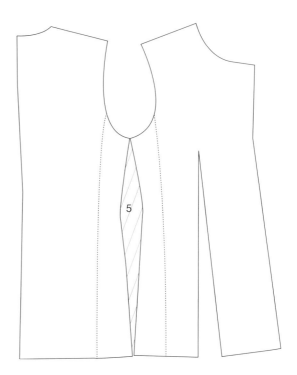

Step 1
Lay the patterns side by side

Lay the front and back bodice patterns pieces side by side. Measure the gap between the two pattern pieces at the waist (in this case 5cm/2in).

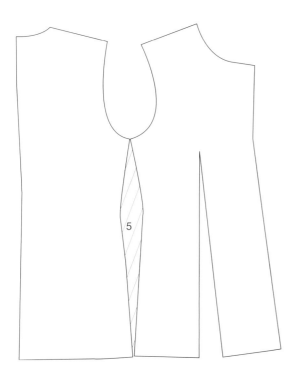

Step 3
Create two new darts

Re-distribute the 5cm (2in) shaping from the side seam dart into a 3cm (1¼in) dart at the side back seam and a 2cm (¾in) dart at the side front seam at waist level. An additional adjustment might also be necessary on the centre back seam to accommodate the female shape.

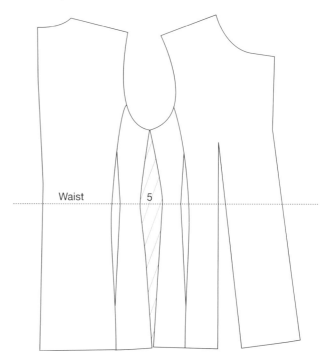

Trace the new pattern

Trace off the three new pattern pieces, adding seam allowances, notches and annotation.

The consequence of creating large pattern pieces can be to jeopardize the economy of the layout plan. Larger pattern pieces take up more space on the width of the fabric and it can be difficult to fit smaller pieces in next to them. Pattern cutters should, therefore, take into account the width of the fabric, which usually measures 90, 144 or 160cm (36, 54 or 66in) wide, and the likely outcome of the layout plan when creating larger pieces.

Centre back x 1 pair self

Side panel x 1 pair self

Front x 1 pair self

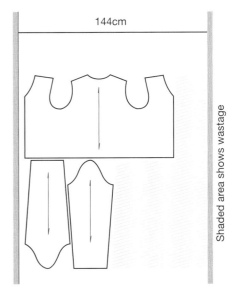

144cm

Shaded area shows wastage

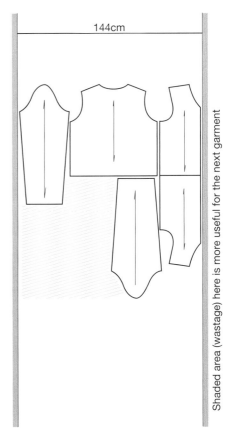

144cm

Shaded area (wastage) here is more useful for the next garment

A large pattern piece creates wasted space, whereas smaller pieces leave enough room to include additional pattern pieces from another garment on the same width of fabric.

RE-POSITIONING THE GRAINLINE

Joining two pattern pieces together can affect the grainline. The pattern cutter, therefore, needs to consider the probable consequences of eliminating seams.

When the front and back bodice of a simple shirt are joined together at the shoulder, three issues immediately become apparent. There is no right or wrong to these issues, but it is important that the pattern cutter takes everything into consideration.

1. The centre front is now on the bias, and so the button stand will not be on the straight grain.

2. The back side seam is sitting on the straight grain, whereas the front side seam is now on the bias. Joining two such seams will tend to create a wavy seam, and the shirt might also not hang properly, depending on the stability of the fabric.

3. If the fabric is striped or checked, the pattern will look different on the front and back of the shirt.

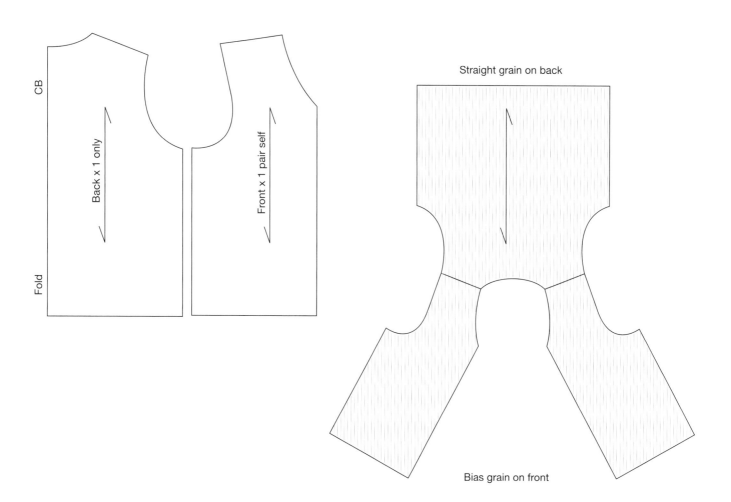

Straight grain on back

Bias grain on front

MOVING DARTS ON THE PAPER PATTERN (PIVOTING)

Darts, as we have seen, are used to manipulate the fabric of the garment so that it fits around the three-dimensional shape of the body. It is easy to locate darts on a pattern that is designed to fit closely to the body because it is clear where darts are needed.

RE-POSITIONING DARTS

If the basic block is adapted and made larger, then darts can be re-positioned according to the new proportions of the garment. The darts can also be reduced in size if the garment is not intended to be as fitted as the original block. A winter coat, for example, might not need the same bust shaping as the bodice block from which it is adapted.

On a tightly fitted garment made from a woven fabric, darts are used to create the three-dimensional shape.

On a loose-fitting winter coat darts are not required to mould the garment to the shape of the body and so are either reduced inside or removed altogether. Instead, subtle shaping could be introduced in the vertical side and centre back seams.

For woven pattern cutting, darts are usually positioned in the following locations:

- Bust
- Front waist (in direct relation to the bust)
- Back shoulder blade
- Back waist (in direct relation to the back shoulder blade)
- Front waist (in direct relation to the front hip)
- Back waist (in direct relation to the back hip)
- Back hip/buttocks
- Side seam at the hip (usually disguised by a shaped side seam)

Moving darts when the garment is made wider

If the garment is made wider at the underarm point by 2cm (¾in), the bust dart should also be moved in proportion. In this case it will be necessary to move the dart by 1cm (⅜in) towards the side seam, and at the same time lower the end of the dart by 1cm (⅜in).

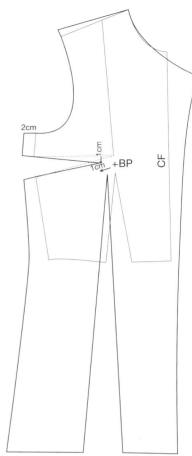

Moving darts when the garment is made longer

If a pattern is lengthened from a bodice block to create a jacket, then the bust dart could also be lowered in proportion by 1cm (⅜in). If the jacket is then lengthened to a coat, the point of the dart could be lowered by 2.5 to 4cm (1 to 1½in). In this case the block could be also made wider at the side seam by 4.5cm (1¾in) at the underarm point. The armhole could also be lowered by 3cm (1¼in) and the dart moved towards the side seam and reduced by 2.5cm (1in) if the fit of the coat is looser than that of the jacket.

Dart direction

When moving darts, the direction of the dart should still point towards the area of the body to which it relates — the bust point, the back of the hip and so on.

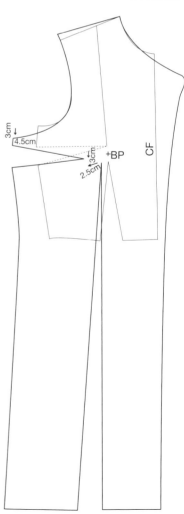

IS IT POSSIBLE TO REMOVE DARTS COMPLETELY?

A pattern cutter might remove darts on a loosely fitted or oversized garment if they are no longer needed to perform the function of creating a three-dimensional shape, retaining them only if they are used as a design feature. It is easier, however, to design such a garment using a dart-less block, and many pattern cutters will feature such blocks – shirt, top, dress and jacket – in their studios.

DART MANIPULATION

The highest point on the front bodice is the bust point and, therefore, darts on the bodice front should point towards this area. As long as the darts point towards the BP, it does not matter whether they start at the shoulder, side seam, waistline or from the centre front – or even how many darts are used. The key is that each should start from a seam and be positioned to create the desired visual effect on the garment.

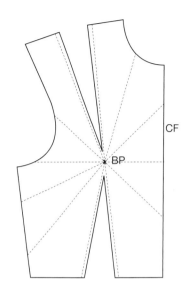

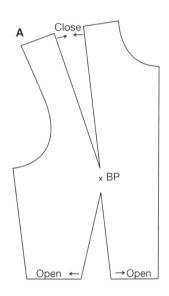

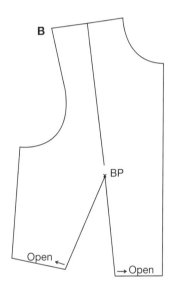

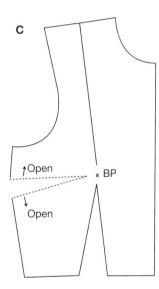

In diagram A the shoulder and waist darts are shown open. Diagram B shows the effect of closing the shoulder dart, which opens the waist dart further. A large dart at the waistline could be avoided by opening a second dart at the side seam, diagram C.

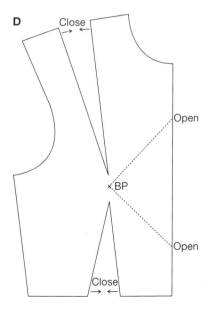

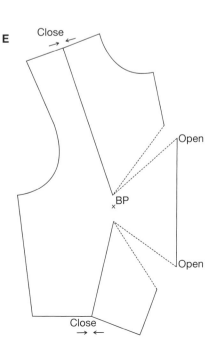

Diagrams D and E show the effect of closing both shoulder and waist darts and opening up two darts at the centre front.

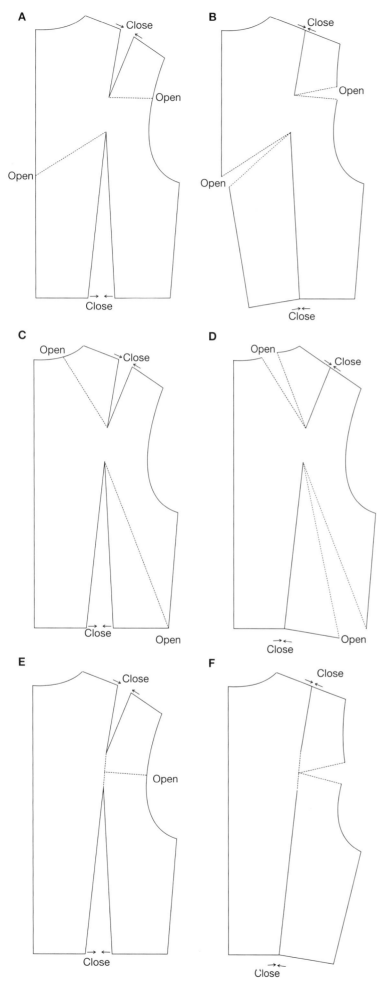

On the back of the bodice, in order to provide a good distribution of fabric and avoid interfering with the grainline, darts are generally placed at the shoulder and waistlines. However, as long as the darts point towards the shoulder blade, again it does not matter if they start at the shoulder, side seam, waistline, armhole or from the centre back.

Diagrams A and B show the effect of closing the shoulder and waist darts and opening darts at the centre back and armholes.

Diagrams C and D show the effect of closing the shoulder and waist darts and opening up corresponding darts at the neckline and bottom of the side seam.

Diagrams E and F show the side seams at the shoulder and waist closed and a single dart opened at the armhole seam pointing towards the centre of the shoulder blade.

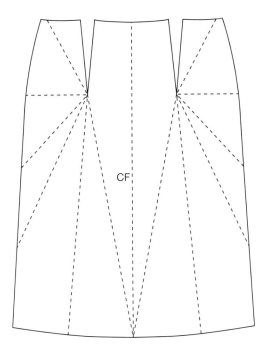

Darts can also be similarly manipulated on any pattern piece, including skirts and trousers.

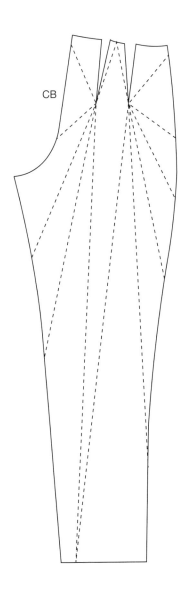

ADDING SEAMS TO ELIMINATE DARTS

Darts are a necessary construction feature of woven pattern cutting, but they can look intrusive and spoil the look of a garment. An alternative is to design the seams of the garment so that they include and thus eliminate the darts. To do this, the darts may have to be moved to different positions.

BACK YOKE OF A SHIRT

The back yoke of a shirt is a classic design that in fact serves to eliminate a dart. By moving the shoulder dart to the armhole seam and incorporating it in a new horizontal seam across the back of the shirt, a new pattern piece and design feature of the garment can be created to accommodate the position of the shoulder blade.

The shoulder dart can be moved to a horizontal position on the back armhole. Then a seam, incorporating the dart, can be created to add a yoke.

Step 1
Transfer the shoulder dart to the armhole

Take the back of a basic shirt pattern, and close up the shoulder dart, opening up a horizontal dart at the back armhole.

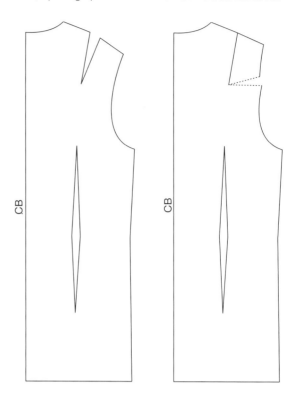

Step 2
Create the yoke seam

Draw a horizontal line from the end of the dart at 90° to the centre back line.

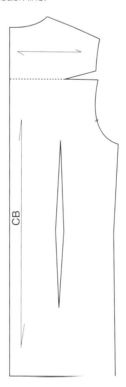

Create the two pieces of the pattern

Trace off both pieces of the paper pattern, add seam allowances, notches and annotation.

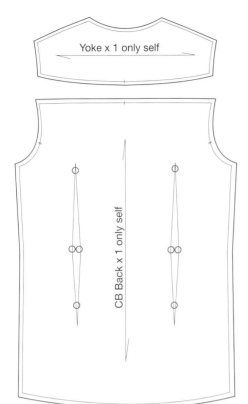

BACK YOKE SEAM OF A PAIR OF JEANS

Alternatively, the designer could design the garment to include graphic seam lines and then investigate whether the seams could be used to incorporate darts. The back yoke of a pair of jeans is one such example. The concept is the same as for the back yoke of a shirt, but the methodology derives from a designed line, rather than from the need to move a dart.

The classic back yoke of a pair of denim jeans eliminates the need for darts at the back waistline.

Sewing lines

Ideally, the sewing line where seams are sewn together, should be indicated on the pattern. If time is short, however, it is acceptable just to indicate the sewing lines at both ends of the seam only. The sewing line is equivalent to the line marking the seam allowance on the paper pattern.

Step 1
Draw the yoke

On a trouser pattern, draw a yoke shape on the back trouser.

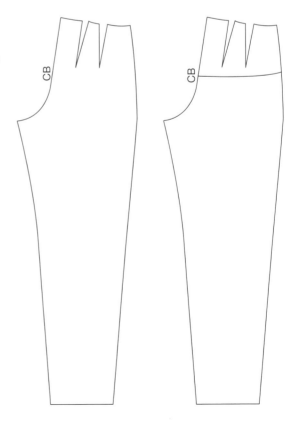

Step 2
Eliminate the darts

Trace the new yoke shape, then fold and eliminate the darts.

Step 3
Create the paper pattern

Trace off both pieces of the back trouser leg, adding seam allowances, notches and annotation.

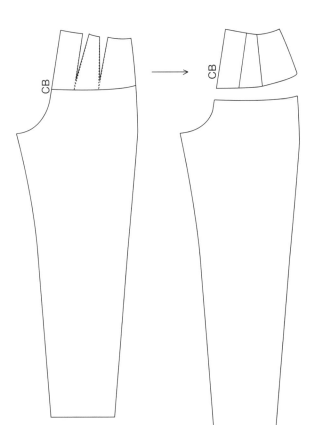

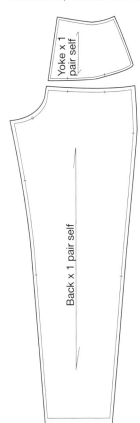

INCLUDE TWO DARTS ON ONE SEAM

Step 1

If the ends of two darts are close together, aesthetically it can be advantageous to cut and include both in one seam.

Step 2
Create a single seam

Draw a line through both darts.

Step 3
Create the paper pattern

Trace off both pattern pieces, adding seam allowances, notches and annotation.

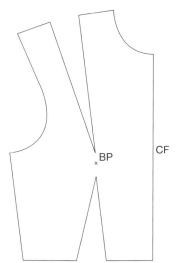

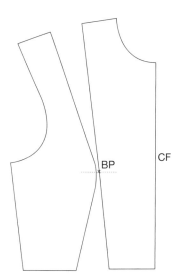

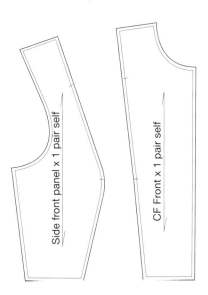

THE PRINCESS LINE

There is a practical problem when sewing the end of a dart; the machine has to back tack in order to secure the sewing thread, but at the point of the dart there is no seam allowance to carry the tension. On heavier fabrics, especially on tailored garments, a bespoke tailoring technique would be needed to finish the end of the dart and balance the tension and thickness of the fabric. On lighter fabrics the triple line of stitching can cause the fabric at the end of the dart to become slightly puckered, or the sewing thread may detach itself from the fabric after the garment has been worn a few times. A practical solution to the problem from a pattern cutting point of view is to introduce the princess line. The princess line seams curve from the armhole over the bust and then down the garment, to either side of the centre front.

Step 1
Mark the beginning of the princess line

On a bodice pattern with darts at the shoulder and waist, draft the curve at the beginning of the princess line from the armhole seam to the end of the shoulder dart.

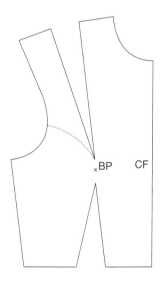

Step 2
Extend both existing darts

Extend the shoulder and waist darts so that they meet at the bust point.

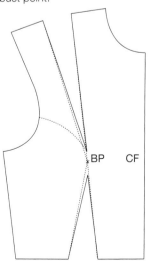

Step 3
Close the shoulder dart

Close the shoulder dart and move it to the armhole, opening a dart where you marked the beginning of the princess line in Step 1.

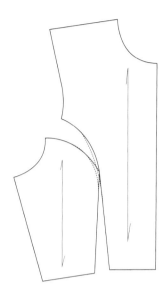

Step 4
Create the paper pattern

Trace off both pattern pieces, adding seam allowances, notches and annotation.

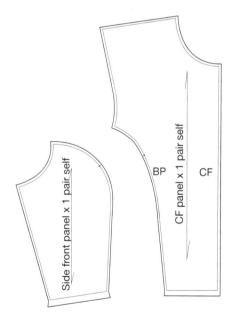

ADDING PLEATS & TUCKS

The concept behind both pleats and tucks is the same – the folding of fabrics at regular or irregular intervals, the folds then being secured to a seam or sewing line. Pleats and tucks can be used to:

• create and enhance design details
• add extra room to certain parts of a garment when worn
• offer flexibility of fit

Pleats are constructed with a directional fold line from one point to another. They are then either pressed along the pleat line with a steam iron, sewn along their length parallel to the fold, or are permanently pleated by industrial pleaters.

A pleated skirt with engineered pleats constructed by the machinist, who hand presses the pleats before securing them with a machine stitch at the waistline.

Tucks are drafted in the same way as pleats on the paper pattern, but once they are secured in the seam they do not have a definite directional line, being left open to move naturally and provide flexibility and volume to the garment. Pleats and tucks can be constructed either by using existing darts or by cutting open the pattern.

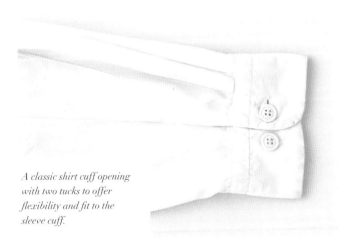

A classic shirt cuff opening with two tucks to offer flexibility and fit to the sleeve cuff.

CONSTRUCTION USING EXISTING DARTS

Pleats and tucks can be added to garments to provide softer, three-dimensional shaping in the garment in place of the 'cone shape' provided by a dart.

Step 1
Extend the darts on the bodice

On a bodice pattern, extend the shoulder and waist darts so that they meet at the bust point.

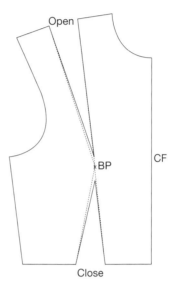

Step 2
Close the waist dart

Close the waist dart, leaving approximately 1.5cm (½in) as tolerance, and open the shoulder dart. Measure the width of the newly constructed dart (Y).

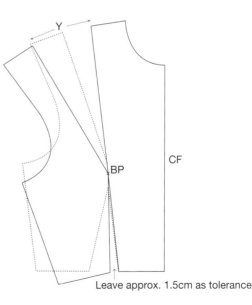

Leave approx. 1.5cm as tolerance

Step 3
Divide the tucked area into three

Re-draw the shoulder seam and divide Y into three tucks. These are not the same width – the middle tuck should be the largest and the one next to the armhole the smallest to provide more shaping across the middle of the bust and avoid excess fabric bunched up under the arm.

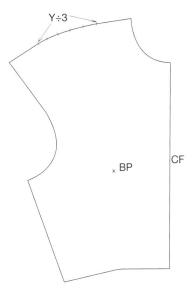

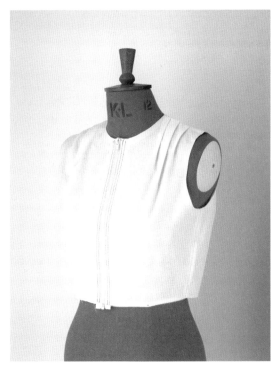

Toile of the top with tucks at the shoulder seams replacing the shoulder and waist darts of the bodice.

Step 4
Create the paper pattern

Trace the newly drafted pattern, adding the seam allowances, notches and annotations, including those to indicate the position of the tucks and the direction in which they should be folded.

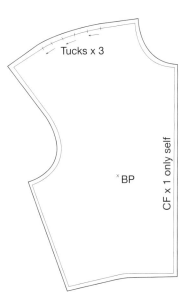

CONSTRUCTION ACHIEVED BY CUTTING THE PATTERN

In this method pleats or tucks are added to the garment by first locating their position on the working drawing or on the paper pattern. The depth of the pleat should also be worked out according to the width of material that is to be added into the garment.

The additional fabric added to the garment for each pleat or tuck is equivalent to its depth multiplied by two. In the example given here, each pleat added to the skirt has a depth of 2.5cm (1in), so the paper pattern will be opened 5cm (2in) for each pleat (2.5cm/1in x 2).

The front side seam should remain exactly the same length so that the front of the garment, which will be pleated, can be joined accurately to the back. The hem of this tulip skirt should also be kept the same width and straight, not curved.

Step 1
Locate the position of the tucks
The working drawing shows that the design has three tucks on either side of the skirt, which are attached to a yoke at hip level.

Step 2
Draft the yoke & position of the tucks
Trace a basic skirt block, draft the design lines showing the position of the yoke and the position of the three tucks.

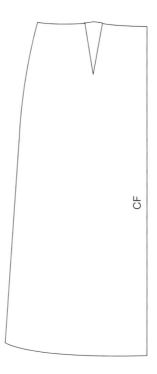
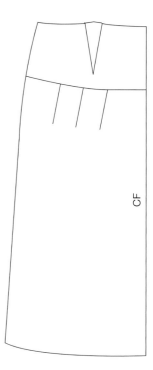

Step 3
Create the yoke
Close up the waist dart and trace the paper pattern to create a separate pattern piece for the yoke. Mark three design lines to show the position of the three tucks, indicating the measurement of the opening required for each.

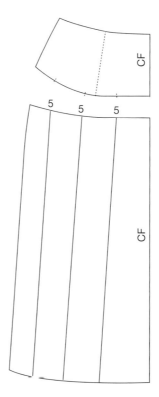

Step 4
Open up the tucks

Cut and open up the pattern 5cm (2in) on each design line.

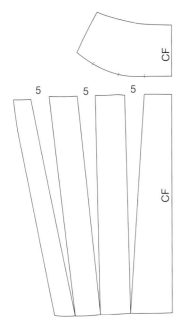

Step 5
Complete the tucks

Trace the pattern onto a new piece of paper and close up the tucks with sticky tape. Use a tracing wheel, draw along the waistline. Carefully cut through the sticky tape, open out the darts and re-draw the shape of the waistline along the line of holes created by the wheel.

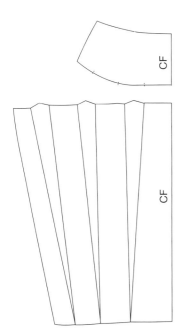

Step 6
Complete the paper pattern

Trace off both pattern pieces, adding seam allowances, notches and annotation, including annotation for tucks.

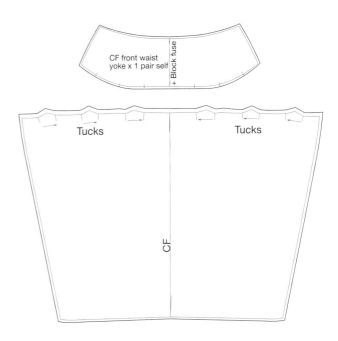

Toile of pleated skirt with yoke.

CONSTRUCTION USING MEASUREMENTS

Tucks can be used to reduce the width of fabric when joining a wider pattern piece to a narrower one, such as at the hem of a sleeve where it is joined to the cuff. The width of the cuff is controlled by the measurement of the wrist. The hem of the sleeve where it joins the cuff, however, is controlled by the width of the sleeve. The width of the sleeve cannot be reduced from the underarm point to the exact width of the cuff because the underarm seam would then be on the bias and would be difficult to sew. This directly affects the fit and accuracy of the elbow. Tucks are, therefore, used to manipulate the sleeve hem into the exact measurement of the cuff.

Step 1
Draft a sleeve using measurements
Draft a sleeve with a crown height of 12cm (4¾in), a sleeve length of 52cm (20½in) and a sleeve width of 34.5cm (13½in). Square off the hem of the sleeve. Draft a separate pattern for the cuff 20cm (8in) wide.

Step 2
Reduce the underarm seam
Reduce the width of the sleeve hem by 4cm (1½in) on either side. Re-join the underarm seam. Re-measure the width of the sleeve hem, in this case 34.5cm (13½in) – 8cm (3in) = 26.5cm (10½in).

Step 3
Calculate the tucks
The difference in measurement between the sleeve hem and width of the cuff is 6.5cm (2½in) [34.5cm (13½in) – 28cm (11in) = 6.5cm (2½in)]. This is the allowance for tucks. Each tuck, therefore, measures 3.25cm (1¼in).

Step 4
Draft the tucks
Locate two tucks of 3.25cm (1¼in) each on the sleeve hem, positioned towards the back of the sleeve.

Step 5
Create the paper pattern
Trace the sleeve pattern, adding seam allowances, notches and annotation, including annotation to mark the position of the tucks.

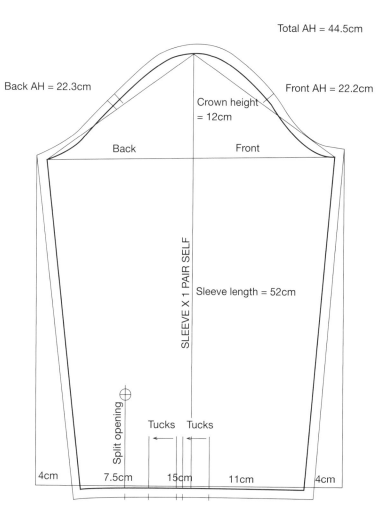

Total AH = 44.5cm

Back AH = 22.3cm

Front AH = 22.2cm

Crown height = 12cm

Back

Front

SLEEVE X 1 PAIR SELF

Sleeve length = 52cm

Split opening

Tucks   Tucks

4cm   7.5cm   15cm   11cm   4cm

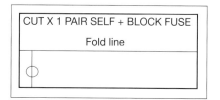

CUT X 1 PAIR SELF + BLOCK FUSE

Fold line

ADDING VOLUME

Adding volume to a garment is synonymous with letting a garment out, or making it less fitted. In doing so, the pattern cutter still needs to consider how to fit some parts of the garment to the shape of the body, but can usually be less precise. Adding volume can be achieved by combining one or all of the previous three sections of this chapter:

- moving darts
- adding seams to eliminate darts
- adding pleats, tucks or gathers

Here, we will look at how all three methods can be combined to create a semi-fitted dress, the only area of which is fitted is across the bust.

Front and back views of a dress with an inset pleated panel on its front bodice, gathers, narrow shoulder straps and an elasticated section at the centre back.

Working drawing of the dress.

17cm

Waist

77cm

90cm

The measurements for the dress are worked out by the designer
and pattern cutter according to those supplied for the original
block and from the working drawing.

Length	77cm (30¼in)	The total CB length i.e. 60cm (23½in) below waist level
Bust	95cm (37½in)	This is taken from the basic block i.e. 90cm (35½in) + 5cm (2in) tolerance
Waist	104cm (41in)	To provide a loose-fitting dress
Hip	N/A	This measurement is not needed because the dress is loose fitting
Hem circumference	180cm (71in)	The whole circumference of the hem
Front neck drop	11cm (4¼in)	Taken from CF from base of neck point to edge of garment
Armhole depth	17cm (6¾in)	This is 2.5cm (1in) less than the basic block measurement to ensure modesty on this sleeveless garment
CB length	17cm (6¾in)	This measurement is needed to work out the CB length of the bodice. It is measured up from the waistline.

Step 1
Create the basic shape of the dress

The starting point for this dress is not a dress block but a bodice block, because the only area where the dress needs to fit the body accurately is above the waist.

- Trace the bodice block.
- Extend the centre back and centre front lines to measure 60cm (23½in) below the waist.
- Divide the waist measurement and the measurement of the circumference of the hem into four, since you are working on patterns for half the back and front [26cm (10¼in) and 45cm (17¾in) respectively]. Extend the waistline to 26cm (10¼in) and draft the hem at 45cm (17¾in).
- Raise the armhole by 2.5cm (1in).
- Mark the position on the centre front of the new neck drop from the centre front neck point.
- Mark the position of the new centre back length, measured up from the waistline.

Step 2
Add design lines to the pattern

Following the working drawing, add the design lines to the pattern:

- On the front, draft the new neck edge from the centre front to the position of the strap. Then draft a curve from the strap to the new raised underarm point.
- Mark the position of the tucked panel by drafting a line from the end of the original shoulder dart to the centre front.
- On the back, draft a slightly curved line from the top of the new centre back measurement to the new raised underarm point.
- Then draft the side seams from the new underarm point, through the new waistline point to the hem.
- Mark the position of the straps on the inside of the now eliminated shoulder dart. Measure the length of the strap a + b (43cm/17in).

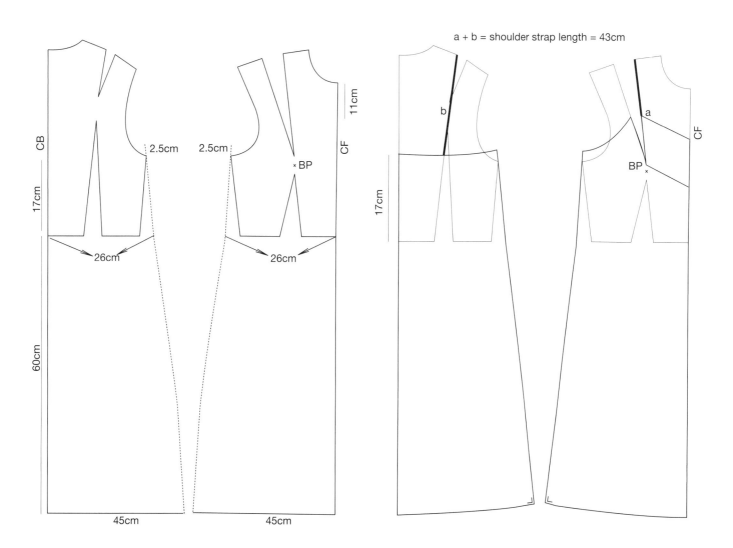

a + b = shoulder strap length = 43cm

Step 3
Complete the pattern

- Trace the new front panel off the pattern.
- Trace the remaining front and back half patterns onto a new sheet of paper, mirroring them to create complete pattern pieces. Add the position of the centre front and back lines and notches, seam allowances and annotation.
- Draw the pattern for the 43cm (17in) strap.

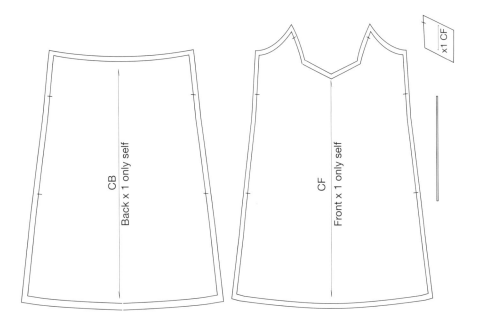

Step 4
Create the tucked front panel

- Trace the front panel shape onto a piece of paper or card. Add the seam allowances. Draw lines to indicate 11 pleats onto the card as a guideline. Measure the depth of each pleat (in this case 1.2cm/½in).

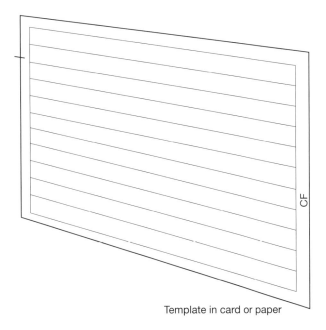

Template in card or paper

- Cut out a piece of fabric, larger than the paper or card template. The grainline should run along the width of the pleats to make it easy to fold the fabric and provide stability to the edge of the pleats. Make the pleats by folding one of 2.4cm (1in), leaving a 1.2cm (½in) gap, then folding another of 2.4cm (1in), and so on.

- Lay the paper or card template on top of the pleated fabric, and mark the shape of the panel, including the seam allowances, with tailor's chalk. Top stitch the edge of the pleats before cutting out.

2.4cm
1.2cm

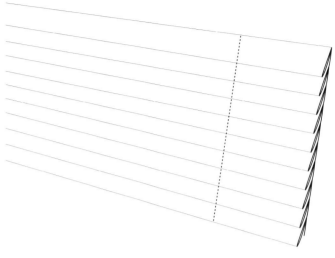

- Create a second pleated panel, mirroring the first, and join at the centre front.

- Stitch the inside edges of each pleat and secure the outside edges with edge stitching as you fold and pleat the fabric.

Step 5
Adding volume

Draw lines onto the front pattern, parallel to the centre front, wherever you want to add volume beneath the front panel. To add volume to this summer dress, double the length of the seam at the bottom of the front panel (in this case 10cm/4in as you are working on half of the dress pattern). Cut along the lines and open each up 4cm (1½in); add 2cm (¾in) at the centre front. Do not, however, alter the width of the hem.

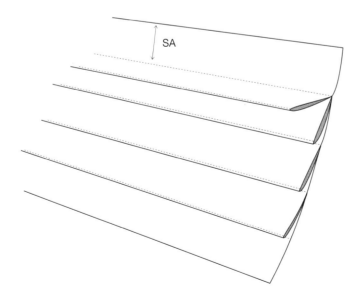

SA

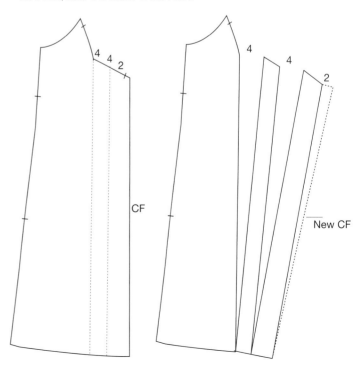

Adding volume to different weights of fabric

The amount of volume you can successfully add to a garment depends upon the quality and weight of fabric.

• For a medium-weight fabric, such as cotton and dress fabrics, you should aim to add fabric equivalent to double the measurement of the seam you cut open.

• For a heavy fabric, such as thick wool or heavy jersey, aim to add half the measurement of the seam.

• For delicate fabrics, such as silk chiffon, you can add up to 3 to 4 times the measurement of the cut seam.

Step 6

Complete the paper pattern

Trace both the front and back of the dress, mirror each along the centre front and centre back lines. Trace half the front panel pattern only, as this is made in two sections, and create the pattern for the shoulder straps. Add seam allowances, notches and annotation.

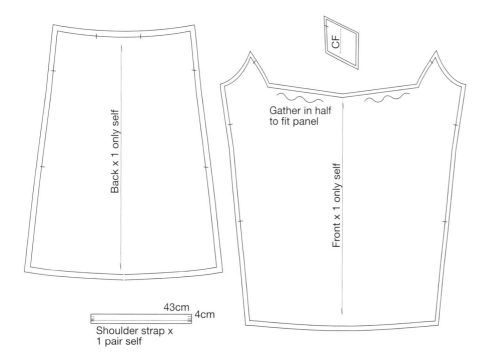

Adjusting gape at the centre back

The centre back pattern of the bodice block will include a small amount of tolerance across the back because of the original tolerance of the basic block. This may cause the dress to gape, in which case a small piece of elastic could be added at the top edge of the dress at the centre back. See the back of the dress and the working drawing on page 151. This will allow flexibility to fit different people with slightly difference bust measurements.

COLLARS

At its most basic, a collar is a strip of fabric that is wrapped around the neck and attached to the bodice at the neckline. The neck is similar in shape to a tube that narrows towards the top. The basic collar shape can, therefore, be likened to a trapeze-shaped tube. The neckline itself, as we have seen, is higher at the shoulder neck point, sloping down towards the centre front (see page 47).

This most basic of collars is called a standing collar. It is also equivalent to a collar stand, which forms one part of a two-piece shirt collar. A collar can also have a relationship with the shoulder line. A shirt collar, for example, with or without a collar stand, rises up the neckline and is then folded down towards the shoulder. It is, therefore, wider at its lower edge than the width of the neckline so that it can sit comfortably on the shoulders.

The leaf edge of a two piece collar is wider than the width of the neckline so that it can sit comfortably on the shoulders.

Parts of the collar

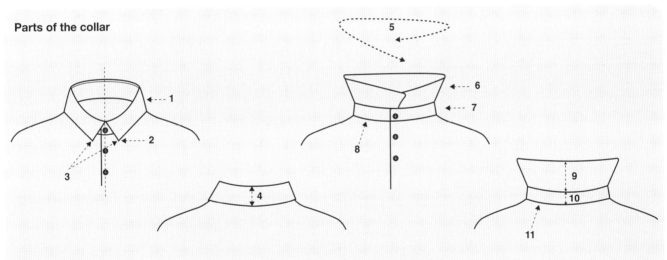

1. top collar layer
2. collar point
3. spread
4. fall
5. leaf edge
6. under collar layer
7. collar stand (band)
8. front neckline
9. depth/height of collar at CB
10. depth/height of collar stand (band) at CB
11. back neckline

DRAFT A SIMPLE STANDING COLLAR OR COLLAR STAND ON THE MODEL

A collar can be drafted from a rectangular strip of fabric or from a set of measurements.

To fit around the neck, the collar is wider at its base than at the top and, when laid flat, the necessary curved shape of the pattern can be seen.

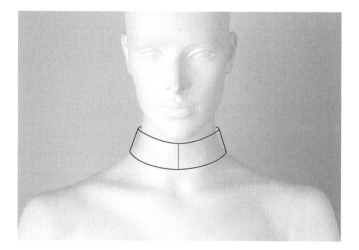

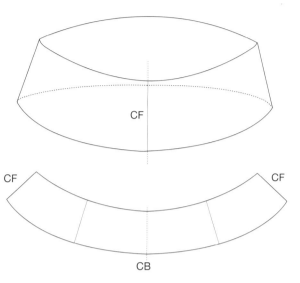

Step 1
Measure the collar & create a frame

Create the collar by first drafting a frame, in the same way that we drafted each block. First measure the front and back necklines of the bodice. This is the width of the rectangle. Then work out the height of the collar (the average collar is usually 6 to 7cm/2¼ to 2¾in high). Add the seam allowances, notches and annotation to the pattern.

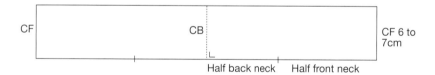

Step 2
Cut the rectangle from fabric & stitch to the bodice

It is easiest to understand the concept of the collar if you take the measurements and cut the rectangle out of fabric, and then machine or hand stitch it to the neckline of a bodice toile. As you can see, the rectangular collar is too wide and is standing away from the neck.

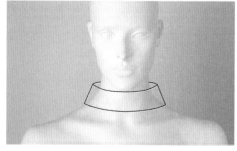

Step 3
Adjust to fit the neck

To adjust the collar, take small tucks (using pins, sticky tape or masking tape) to fit it more closely to the shape of the neck. The tucks could be taken on the shoulder neck point, and halfway between the shoulder neck point and the centre front on both sides. Minimal amounts could also be taken in tucks from the centre back and also halfway between the shoulder neck point and centre back on both sides. It is better, however, to remove as little fabric as possible from the back of the collar because to do so will restrict movement of the head and neck when lifting the chin to look up (see page 123).

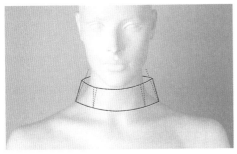
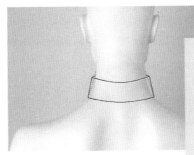

Step 4
Remove & re-draft

Unstitch the collar from the bodice and lay it out flat. A new pattern, which will be curved inwards to reduce the length of the top edge, can then be drafted.

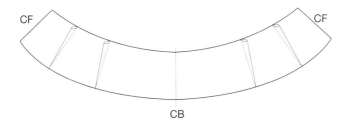

When to measure the collar
Since the length of the collar is equal to the length of the front and back necklines, the collar pattern cannot be cut until the front and back bodices have been completed and the length of the neckline finalized.

DRAFT A SIMPLE STANDING COLLAR OR COLLAR STAND FROM A SET OF MEASUREMENTS

Step 1
Draw two lines at 90° to create a frame

Draft the collar in half by first drawing two lines at 90° to each other. The vertical line is the centre back and should be the height of the collar (again, we will use the average collar height of 6cm/2¼in). The horizontal line should be equal to half the width of back and front necklines.

Step 2
Adjust the neckline edge

Raise the end of the horizontal line by 2.5 to 3cm (1 to 1¼in). This is to allow the centre front of the collar to rise as the top edge of the collar decreases in width. This measurement of 2.5 to 3cm (1 to 1¼in) is the average by which the neck point will rise; if it is much larger the top edge of the collar will become too narrow and the collar will be uncomfortable to wear.

Step 3
Adjust the top edge

Measure in 3mm (⅛in) from end of the raised line and draft a line, 5cm (2in) long, at 90°. This 3mm (⅛in) is removed from the end of the line to compensate for the lengthening of the line when this lower edge is curved (as seen already, a curved line is longer than a straight line), or simply re-measure the half neck to readjust the length. This new centre front line is only 5cm (2in) compared to the 6cm (2¼in) line at the centre back so the front of the collar is not too high under the chin.

Step 4
Draft the curved lines at the neckline & top edges

Draft a curved line at the neckline edge. Check that the measurement of this new neckline edge matches the measurement of the front and back necklines of the bodice. If not, adjust and re-draw the line. Then, from an angle of 90° at the centre front, draft a curved line along the top edge.

Step 5
Finish the collar

Mirror the final pattern, then add seam allowance, annotation and notches.

DRAFT A ONE- OR TWO-PIECE COLLAR WITH STAND, ON THE MODEL

Step 1
Measure the collar & create a frame

The length of a one-piece collar (with no collar stand) is equivalent to the length of the finished neckline on the bodice. The length of the collar stand of a two-piece collar is also equivalent to the length of the finished neckline, while the length of the top collar is equivalent to the length of the top edge of the collar stand from one centre front point to the other.

To find the height of a one-piece collar at the centre back, measure how high you want the collar to stand at the back of the neck, then double that measurement and add 1cm (⅜in) so that when the collar is turned down (fall) the outside edge (leaf) hides the seam at the neckline. So if the collar is 3cm (1¼in) in height, add an extra 4cm (1½in).

The top collar of a two-piece collar should also be wider than the collar stand so the stand is hidden when the collar is turned down.

Start by drafting a pattern for half the collar. Since a collar usually ends in two points at the centre front, add a triangular shape to each end of the collar to imitate the required shape. (Alternatively, this shape can be created and added on later.)

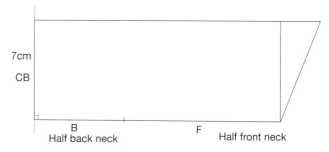

One-piece collar

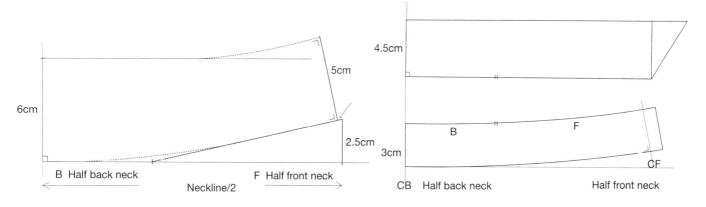

Two-piece collar with stand

Step 2
Cut the rectangle from fabric & stitch to the bodice

Machine or hand stitch the one-piece collar to the bodice toile at the neckline. Machine or hand stitch the top collar to the collar stand of the two-piece collar and then sew the collar stand to the bodice.

In both the case of the one-piece and two-piece collars you will see that back of the collar is rising up above the neckline.

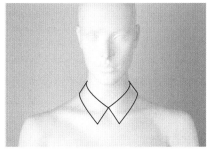
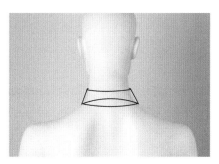
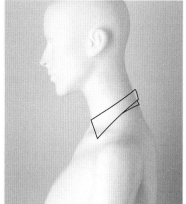

One-piece collar

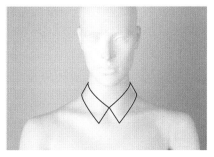
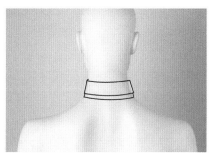
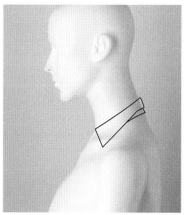

Two-piece collar with stand

Step 3
Adjust to fit the neck

In the case of both the one-piece collar and the top collar of the two-piece collar, cut the collar open to relax its shape around the neckline and to allow it to sit on the shoulders more comfortably. This could be done at the shoulder neck point and either side of the centre front. A small area either side of the centre back could also be released in this way. Measure the space introduced at each opening along the collar leaf edge.

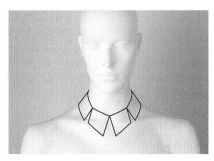
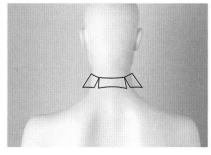
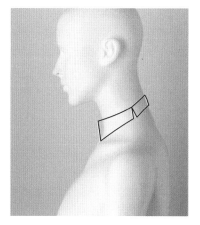

Two-piece collar with stand

Step 4
Remove & re-draft

Unstitch the collar from the bodice and lay it out flat, incorporating the measurements you noted in Step 3. A new pattern can then be drafted.

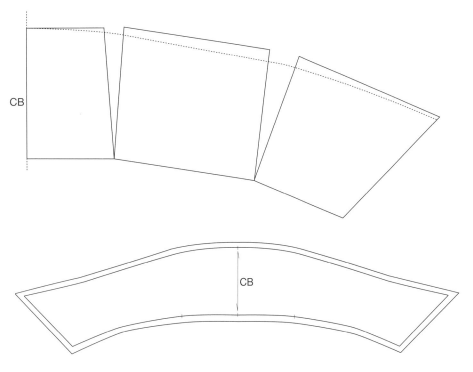

One-piece collar

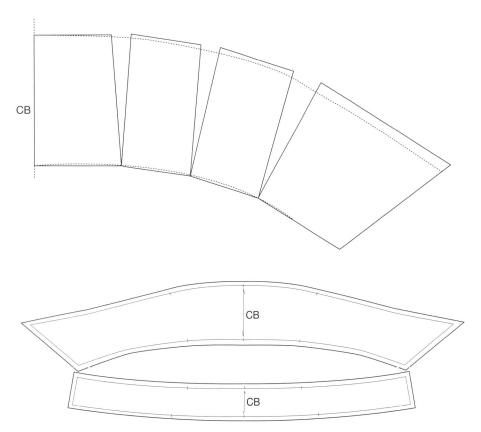

Two-piece collar with stand

DRAFT A TWO-PIECE COLLAR FROM A SET OF MEASUREMENTS

Step 1
Draft the collar stand

Draft the collar stand in exactly the same way as for the standing collar (page 160).

Step 2
Extend the centre back line vertically & draft the top collar

Extend the centre back line. From a point 5cm (2in) above the top edge of the collar stand, draw a curve down to meet the centre front of the collar stand. This distance of 5cm (2in) between the collar stand and top collar is not fixed, because the depth of the curve will depend on the extent to which you want to collar leaf edge to curve to enable it to sit on the shoulders. The larger the number, the longer the leaf edge, so it would sit more outwards from the neckline towards the shoulder.

Step 3
Draft the centre back measurement & the collar leaf edge

The centre back of the top collar fall should always be wider than the collar stand so the stand is hidden when the collar is turned down. In this case it is 4.5cm (1¾in). Draw the centre front slightly wider, in this case 6cm (2¼in). Draw a curved line to form the collar leaf edge.

Step 4
Draft the point at the front edge of the collar

Draft the point of the collar according to the design.

Step 5
Add a button stand

Add a button stand to the front of the collar stand large enough to fasten the collar. The addition of this button stand means that the top collar need only be drafted from centre front to centre front; there is no need to add an additional allowance because the top collar is not overlapped at the centre front.

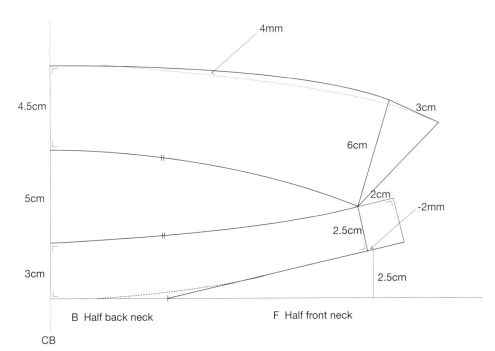

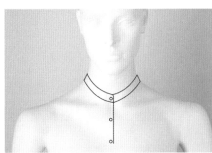

The button stand is overlapped at the front to fasten the collar, while the top collar is drafted from centre front to centre front so that it does not overlap.

PETER PAN & SAILOR'S COLLARS

The basic principles for constructing a collar – creating a shape that fits around the tapered cone shape of the neck for a standing collar and collar stand and to allow the top collar to sit comfortably on the shoulders – can also be applied to draft patterns for other types of collar.

A Peter Pan and sailor's collar look different in design, but are constructed in the same way.

Step 1
Draft the collar shape

After the bodice pattern has been finalized, align the front and back bodice patterns at the shoulder as if they are sewn together. You might want to move the shoulder darts away first. Trace the shape of the front and back bodices onto a fresh sheet of paper. To avoid confusion and ensure an accurate pattern, do not include the seam allowances.

Next draw the collar shape directly onto the front and back bodices according to the working drawing.

Draft the collar from the pattern

The collar construction, as we have seen, should not be undertaken until the bodice pattern has been finalized. It is also important to remember not to try to make a collar from a basic block, but always to use the actual pattern constructed from that block, otherwise you risk drafting a collar that will not fit if changes are made from the block to meet the final design.

Seam allowances and developing the pattern

When developing any section of the pattern, do not include seam allowances until the pattern piece is complete. This is to avoid confusion and the accidental inclusion of the seam allowance in the overall shape of the pattern piece, rendering it too large or the wrong shape so that it will not fit or work with the other pieces of the pattern.

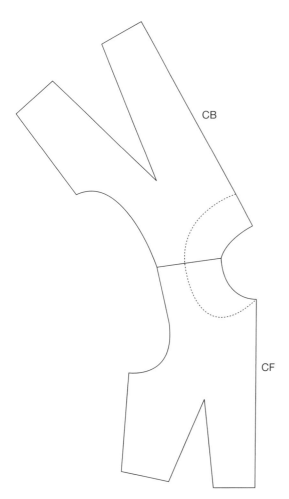

Step 2
Trace the collar pattern

Trace the collar pattern and add seam allowances, grainline notches and annotation.

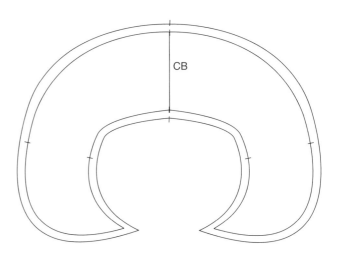

This pattern creates a collar that will lie flat on the shoulders because it is cut to mirror the shoulder line of the garment exactly.

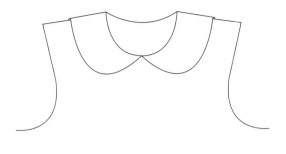

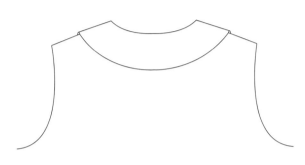

Sometimes the pattern cutter needs to cut a collar that does not lie flat on the shoulders. This can be done by making the collar leaf edge narrower so that the collar leaf edge is forced to sit straighter because it cannot lie flat, creating a small collar stand and a more three-dimensional effect.

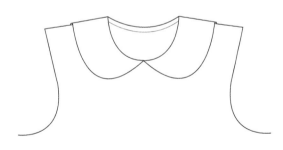

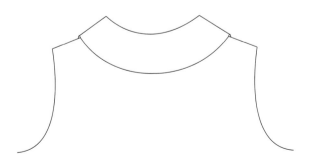

There are two methods of reducing the collar leaf edge.

Method 1
Reduce the leaf edge of the collar by overlapping the shoulder seam

Again, after the bodice pattern has been finalized, align the front and back bodice patterns at the shoulder as if they are sewn together and trace the shape of the front and back bodices onto a fresh sheet of paper (not including seam allowances). Now overlap the shoulder line by up to 4cm (1½in), but do not reduce the neckline or the collar will be too small. Then draw the shape of the collar onto the front and back bodices and proceed as in Step 2. The effect is to reduce the measurement of the outer edge of the collar leaf edge.

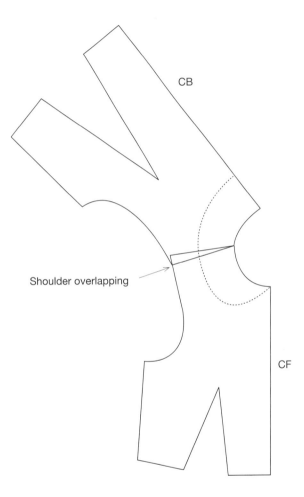

Method 2
Reduce the leaf edge of the collar by adjusting the collar pattern itself

Alternatively, draft the collar pattern as in Steps 1 and 2, but do not add the seam allowance. Then fold away sections from the front, shoulder, back and centre back to reduce the leaf edge of the collar. Re-trace the pattern and add the seam allowances, notches, grainline and annotation.

Two-dimensional vs three-dimensional collars

The basic principle is that the longer the collar leaf edge, the flatter the collar. The shorter the leaf edge, the more three-dimensional the collar is, with a tendency to stand up.

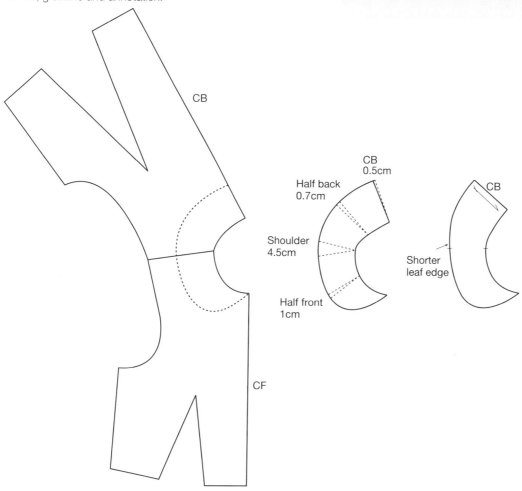

CONVERTIBLE COLLAR

A convertible collar has a more casual look than a buttoned-up one or two-piece shirt collar. The centre front placket, or button stand, forms the lower section collar, which looks similar to a notched collar with a lapel, but when it is buttoned up it looks like a one-piece shirt collar.

A convertible collar uses the front placket or part of the button stand to form the lower part of the collar.

Step 1
Amend the neckline

First, complete the pattern for the front and back bodices. Then straighten the neckline at the centre front so that the seam is 'straight' when it is converted into the lower part of the collar. The button stand could also be extended by a further 0.5cm (¼in) to achieve a more obvious shape to the lower section of the collar.

Step 3
Work out the position of the notch point

Using sticky tape or pins, attach a rectangular shape to the front neckline to work out the position of the notch point (the place at which the upper and lower collar meet). It should be positioned on the front neckline, but not on the centre front line, to ensure that the collar could still be buttoned up to the top without it overlapping at the front.

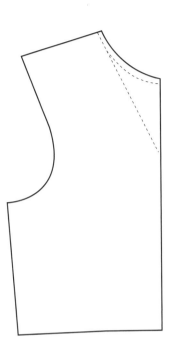

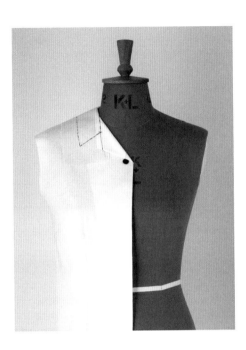

Step 2
Make up a toile & find the position of the first button

You can check the length of this lower section of the collar by making up a toile using this new pattern for the front bodice and folding the bodice back towards the shoulder neck point from the level of the first button. You can also do this by folding the paper pattern in the same way. This will help you gauge the shape of the lower collar and check the position of the first button.

Step 4
Measure the front & back necklines and the height of the collar

Measure and record the length of the back neckline (in this case 9.8cm/3¾in).

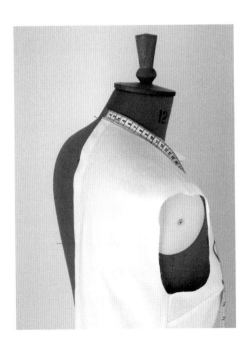

Measure the front neckline up to the notch point (in this case 10.8cm/4¼in).

Measure the height of the collar at the centre back by using a tape measure to measure up the neck to the desired height and then draw the tape measure back down to the desired depth of the collar fall so that it covers the seam at the neckline (in this case 9cm/3½in, which we will round up to 10cm/4in to allow for any necessary adjustments). It is easier to start with a pattern that is slightly too large than one that is too small as it is impossible to add in fabric, but easy to remove).

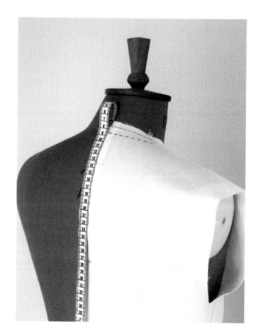

Step 5
Draft the first paper pattern

Start by creating half of the top collar pattern. Draw two lines at 90° to each other. The vertical axis is the centre back and the horizontal the back and front necklines. Measure 10cm (4in) up the vertical line and the length of the back and front necklines along the horizontal line [9.8cm (3¾in) + 10.8cm (4¼in) = 20.6cm (8in) in total].

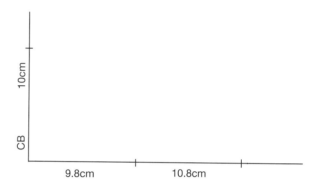

The height of the collar at the centre front could be re-drawn from the scrap paper or fabric you used to mark the notch point.

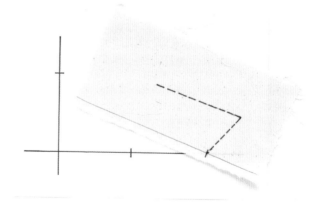

Step 6
Complete the first paper pattern

Complete the first paper pattern by adding the seam allowance and the position of the shoulder neck point (between the front and back necklines).

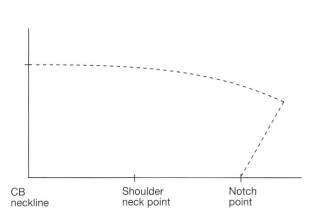

CB
neckline

Shoulder
neck point

Notch
point

Step 7
Cut a first toile

Cut a toile and fold in the seam allowance at the leaf edge of the collar and iron flat (do not use steam as steam might stretch or shrink the fabric).

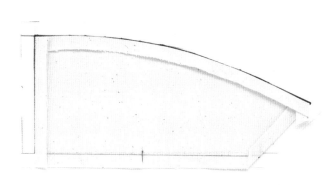

Step 8
Attach the first toile to the bodice

Hand stitch the toile to the neckline of the bodice from the centre back to the notch point. Do not pin as it is not easy to pin a curved seam accurately.

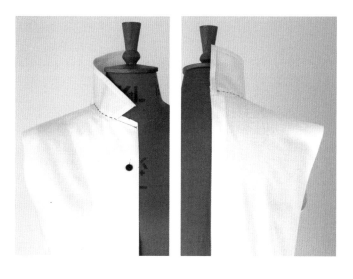

Step 9
Line up the centre back

Pin the toile to the centre back of the mannequin to ensure that the half toile will behave in exactly the same way as the full size collar when the centre back is lined up vertically straight with the centre of the neck at the back.

Step 10
Evaluate the collar leaf shape

Check if the collar is too wide or too narrow and mark any adjustments with red pen.

Step 11
Evaluate the way the collar sits

Check if the collar is sitting comfortably on the shoulders – is it too loose or too tight? If it is too tight, slash the collar open, usually near the shoulder line. Measure the new opening at the level of the collar leaf edge. In case it is too loose just pinch in the excess leaf edge as desired with a pin.

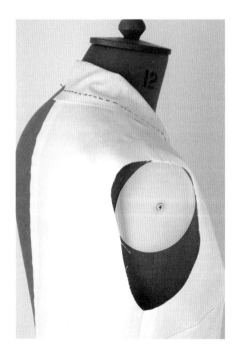
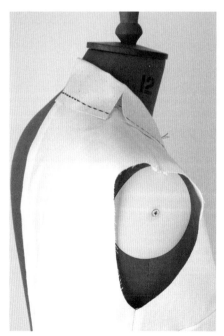
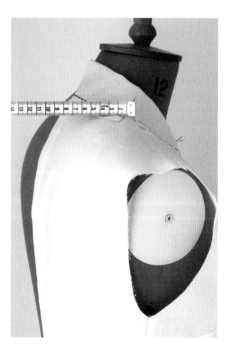

Amend & make the paper pattern

Unpick the hand stitching and lay the toile flat on a fresh piece
of paper incorporating the measurements you noted in Step 11.
Trace around the amended toile.

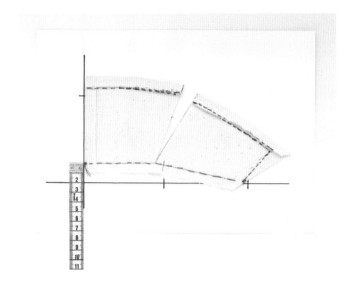

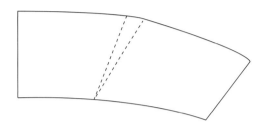

Create the final pattern by adding the seam allowances, folding
the paper in half and tracing off the second half of the pattern to
create the whole collar pattern.

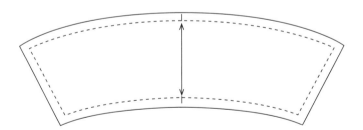

Cut out a final toile using one half of the adjusted paper pattern. To create an accurate final toile of a collar the fabric should be stabilized in some way, just as it would be on the final garment when it would be block fused. For a quick toile, fusible stay tape could be ironed on around the edges of the collar. This should be done with the paper pattern underneath to ensure that the fabric has not been stretched in the process. Turn under the seam allowances along the outer leaf edge and centre back.

Finally, hand stitch the toile to the neckline, lining up and pinning the collar at the centre back.

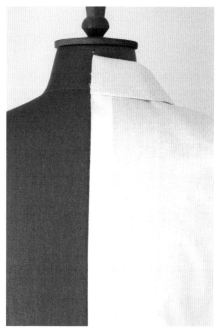

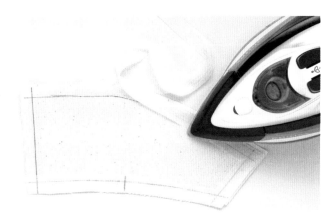

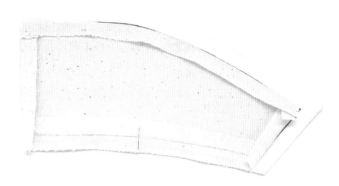

ALTERNATIVE METHOD FOR DRAFTING A PATTERN FOR A CONVERTIBLE COLLAR USING MEASUREMENTS

Instead of working with a toile, a convertible collar pattern can also be drafted using a set of measurements.

1. Draft a vertical line (centre back line) approximately 15 to 20cm (6 to 8in) long (point A being the lowest point and point B the highest).

3. Mark a point 2cm (¾in) from A up the vertical line (point C). This is to lengthen the leaf edge.

2. Using a set square, from point A draft a horizontal line at 90° approximately 25cm (10in) in length. This is the baseline (temporary neckline).

4. Mark a second point a further 8cm (3in) along the vertical line (point D). This is the actual centre back of the collar with collar stand and fall.

5. At 90° from point C draft a horizontal line of 9.8cm (3¾in) (point E). This is the actual half back neckline.

7. Smooth out the line from point E to point F with a curved ruler. Also mark a notch at point E. This is the notch for the shoulder neck point, matching the collar to the bodice of the garment.

6. From point E, draft a straight line 10.8cm (4¼in) in length to touch the base line (point F). This is the actual front neckline.

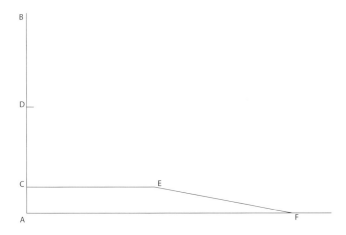

8. At point F, draft a vertical line at 90°, 5.5cm (2¼in) in length (point G). This is the length of the top collar meeting collar notch.

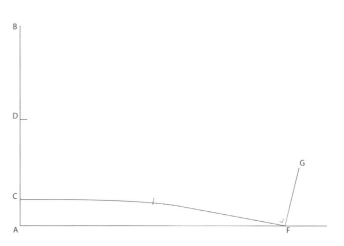

9. At point G, draft a vertical line at 90°, 1.5cm (½in) in length (point H). This is to create a prominent collar spread.

Using this method of drafting a collar is easy, but it does not provide the understanding of how a collar works that is demonstrated by drafting a collar using a toile. In the latter method, the derivation of the 2cm (¾in) gap between point C and the baseline is more easily understood.

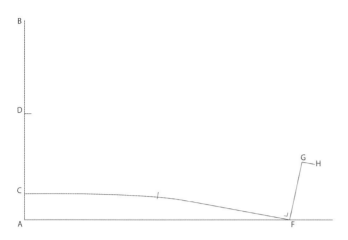

10. Finally, join points D and H using a curved ruler. This is to finalize the leaf edge.

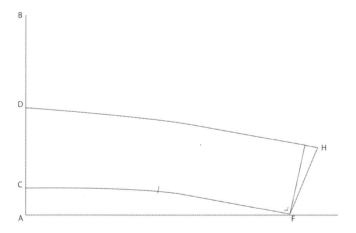

OPENINGS & FASTENINGS

When a garment does not have an opening or fastening, it is usually because it is made from a stretch fabric or is oversized and can just be pulled on. Most garments made from woven fabrics do, however, need some form of opening and fastening, the most obvious being an opening at the neckline, which is usually necessary to enable the head, with its larger circumference compared to the neck, to pass through.

There is no particular rule about where the opening should be, but it is usually at the centre front – the fly on a pair of jeans, a white shirt, denim or tailored jacket. The opening on an asymmetrically designed garment may, however, be at centre front or positioned anywhere else that seems most appropriate.

Buttons, buttonholes & the button stand

When a garment has a centre front opening, the buttons and the outer end of the buttonhole must be positioned on the centre front. The width positioning vertically where the button sits is called the button stand.

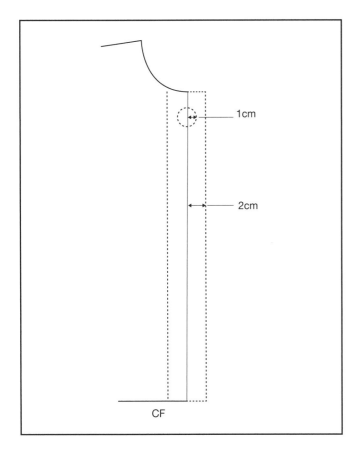

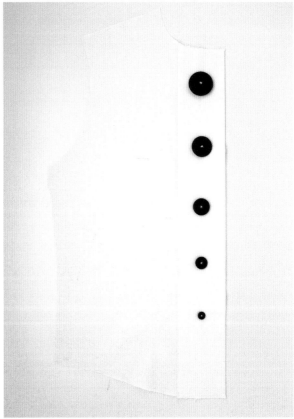

The centre of the button should always be sewn on the centre front line.

Button sizes

The size of the buttons chosen for a garment is usually specified so that they meet the practical requirements of fastening the garment – too large or too small and they will be of no practical use. Buttons are, therefore, usually in proportion to the size of the garment, or to the area of the garment where they are used.

The actual size of a button is specified according to the internationally recognized standard of ligne (L).

Ligne = circumference of the button measured in millimetres ÷ 2

To calculate the ligne of a button you therefore need to measure the diameter of the button (which is twice the radius) and then use the following equation:

Ligne = diameter of button x π (3.142) ÷ 2

Button size chart (mm)

Ligne	16	18	20	22	24	26	28	30	32	34	36	38	40	42
Diameter	10	11.4	12.8	14	15	16.5	18	19	20.3	21.6	22.9	24	25.4	27

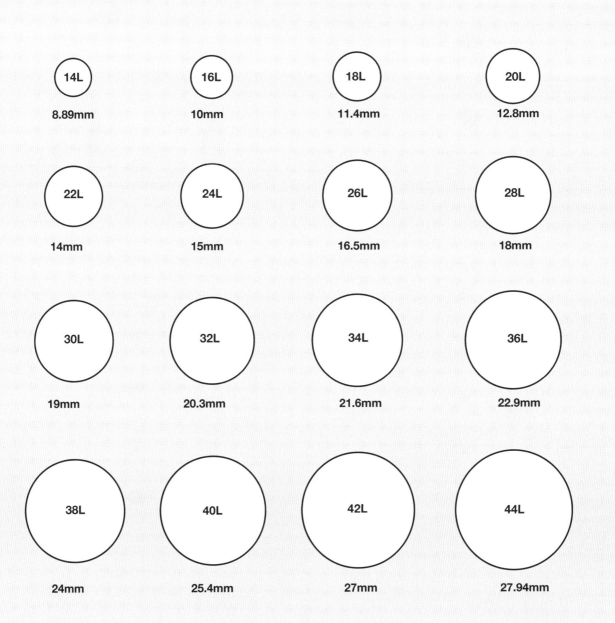

14L — 8.89mm 16L — 10mm 18L — 11.4mm 20L — 12.8mm

22L — 14mm 24L — 15mm 26L — 16.5mm 28L — 18mm

30L — 19mm 32L — 20.3mm 34L — 21.6mm 36L — 22.9mm

38L — 24mm 40L — 25.4mm 42L — 27mm 44L — 27.94mm

Button stand

The width of the button stand depends on the size of the button. As the button is placed on the centre front, half of the button sits on bodice and half will require an extension on which to sit. Usually, for aesthetic reasons, this extension is wider than half the width of the button, but there is no rule about how much wider it should be.

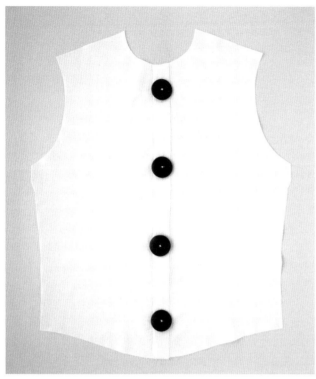

A large button seems to overwhelm width size of the narrow extension.

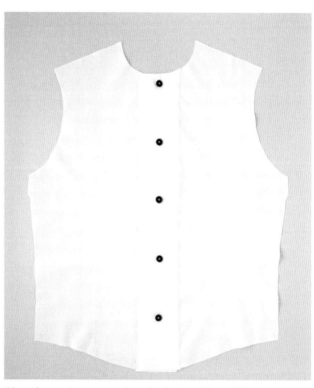

The wide extension seems too large for the size of the small button.

The size of the button here seems to be compatible with the width of the extension, which is the same as the width of the button itself.

A button that is wider than the extension seems aesthetically less acceptable. The edge of the button sits too far outside the garment's button stand

Generally, however, the button and button stand work best when the extension is the same width as the button itself. The button stand is, therefore, twice the width of the extension. The larger the width of the button, the wider the button stand, and vice versa.

Alternatively, the button stand extension can simply be measured as half the diameter of the button plus 1cm (⅜in), so that there is always a 1cm (⅜in) gap between the edge of the button and the edge of the garment. This system is widely used within the industry, such a standardized system saving time and confusion.

Vertical button stand

This is the most commonly seen and used fastening on many modern garments, including shirts. The buttons are sewn on the centre front.

A button stand extension of half the width of the button plus 1cm (⅜in) also looks acceptable aesthetically and provides a standardized system for specifying the width of the button stand within industry.

A shirt has a vertical button stand with the buttons positioned on the centre front.

Double-breasted fastening

A double-breasted fastening is usually used on outerwear, such as trenchcoats. Although the fastening looks asymmetrical, both left and front extensions are in fact symmetrical. Instead of being sewn on the centre front line, the buttons are equidistant from it on the right- and left-hand sides.

The buttons on a double-breasted jacket are positioned equidistant from the centre front line.

The left and right extensions of the jacket are the same width, with the centre front line positioned halfway between the buttons and buttonholes.

Centre front

Centre front

ZIPS

Zips are used on many types of garments. Like buttons, they are usually located on the centre front line, and the question is whether to adjust the width of the garment at the centre front to allow for an exposed zip where the teeth are visible or leave it for a concealed edge-to-edge zip where the teeth are visible or leave it for a to be adjusted so that the zipper tape may be attached to it.

Concealed edge-to-edge zip

For a concealed edge-to-edge zip the seam allowance needs to be made wide enough to accommodate the width of the zipper tape and the top-stitching.

Exposed zip

If the teeth of the zip are to be exposed the width of the teeth needs to be subtracted from the width of the garment. So, if the teeth are positioned on the centre front and are 1.6cm (½in) wide, then 0.8cm (¼in) needs to be subtracted from each side of the centre front line before the seam allowance is added.

An allowance must be made to the width of the garment to take into account the introduction of the additional width of the zipper teeth.

A concealed edge-to-edge zip sitting on the centre front line of a garment needs only an adjustment to the seam allowance to accommodate the width of the zipper tape so that zip can be top-stitched to the garment.

Like the concealed edge-to-edge zip, an invisible zip needs no adjustment to the centre front line, but the width of the seam allowance must be adjusted to accommodate the width of the zipper tape. The seam allowance could also be made even wider to create a self-binding for the zipper tape.

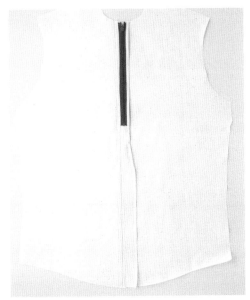

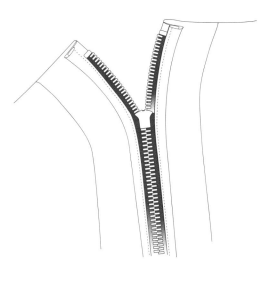

The seam allowance can be extended to self-bind the zipper tape of an invisible zip.

CONCEALED PLACKET

A concealed placket is a self-grown placket that is extended from the centre front without any seams. It must, therefore, be made on the straight grain, otherwise the fabric will not fold well. Its purpose is to hide all the buttons, or fastenings, using an extra layer of fabric.

A concealed placket hides both the buttons and the buttonholes.

Work out the size of the button stand

If the size of the button is 38L, the width of the extension would be 2.4cm ÷ 2 + 1cm = 2.2cm (1in ÷ 2 + ⅜in = ⅞in). The whole button stand is, therefore, 4.4cm (1¾in).

Draft the concealed placket

From the centre front line, extend the front of the garment out by 4.4cm (1¾in) x 3. Add the seam allowance.

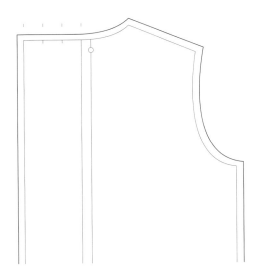

Step 3
Construct the placket

The placket can be folded to the right or wrong side of the garment.

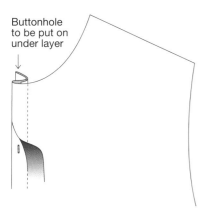

Buttonhole
to be put on
under layer

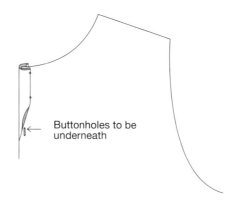

Buttonholes to be
underneath

Concealed placket folded to the wrong side of the garment.

Concealed placket folded to the right side of the garment. Then additional stitches would be needed to secure the concealed placket on the right side of the garment.

FLY FRONT

A fly front is a standard method of fastening trousers. The zip extends exactly from the top of the trousers underneath the waistband to at least hip level, to allow the trousers to be pulled on over the hips.

The zip guard, or zip bearer, is a rectangular-shaped piece of self fabric stitched behind the zipper tape. Its purpose is to prevent the skin from being rubbed by the zip's teeth.

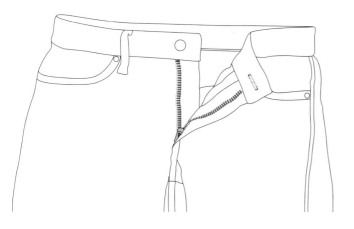

The zip extends from the lower edge of the waistband to hip level.

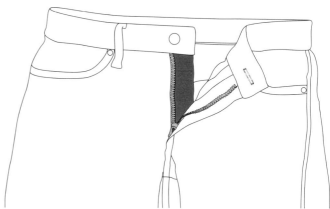

Zip guard

The front zip facing lies on the top of the zip, along the centre front seam. The shape of this facing acts as a guide for the top stitching on the front of the trouser.

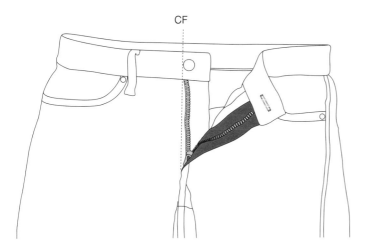

CF

Front zip facing

The seam sandwiching the zip between the left trouser front and the zip guard should be extended at least 0.5cm (¼in) outside the centre front line to allow the zip to be hidden underneath the zip facing.

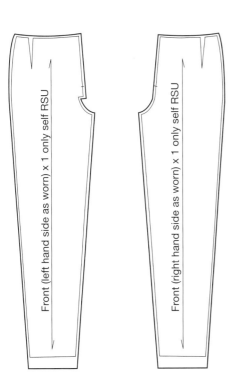

Front (left hand side as worn) x 1 only self RSU

Front (right hand side as worn) x 1 only self RSU

Extended min 0.5cm

The right trouser (as worn) has an extension at the centre front that allows the zip to be concealed by the zip facing. This means that the left and right front trousers cannot be cut as a pair.

CONVERTING A BODICE BLOCK INTO A JACKET BLOCK

Blocks are the most efficient starting point for all pattern cutting. In the earlier part of this chapter, we have seen how they can be converted into different styles by moving darts, eliminating seams or adding volume. In this final section we look at how to use a block and convert it into a different type of garment – from a bodice block to a jacket block. Once you understand the principles, then you can convert the same block into a shirt block or even a coat block.

The starting point is to compare a toile made from a bodice block to a jacket. How much longer is the jacket than the bodice? How much lower or higher is the armhole of the jacket, etc? This can be done by taking a photo of the bodice block toile then drawing the jacket over the top.

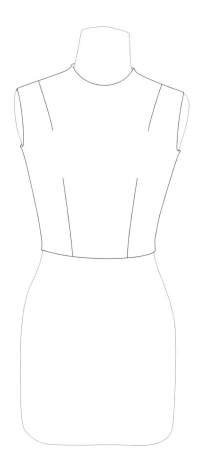
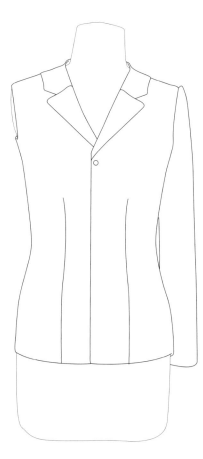
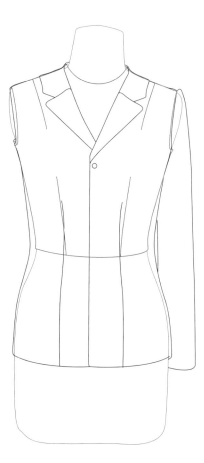

Compare the similarities and differences between the bodice and the jacket. Look at the position of the darts, the shape of the waist, the length of the garment and the position and shape of the armhole.

From an evaluation of the two garments, it should be possible to make a list of measurements for a jacket block.

NOTES		**MEASUREMENTS**
Length of jacket	The sketch of the jacket suggests that the finished length of the garment extends below the hip line to about the level of body rise (crotch).	Bodice block + 30cm (12in)
Bust	The bodice block has approximately 4 to 5cm (1½ to 2in) tolerance. Since this is a jacket, and therefore outerwear, add a further 4cm (1½in) tolerance.	Bodice block + 4cm (1½in)
Waist	The bodice block has 5cm (2in) tolerance. It is easier, however, to work out the bust and hip measurements first, then to draw a smooth curve on the pattern itself from the underarm to the hip to create the side seam. This is because the side seam should not have a curve inward of more than 2.5cm (1in) at the waist, otherwise the fabric will 'pull' and create a tension mark at the waist, especially on woven fabrics. The pattern should not, therefore, be forced to fit the waist.	To gauge after hip and bust are worked out, curving the side seam inwards by 2 to 2.5cm (¾ to 1in)
Hip	Again, as this is a piece of outerwear, additional tolerance should be added at the hip. In this case the total hip measurement should be 100cm (39¼in) [92cm/36¼in (hip measurement on the size chart) + 8cm/3in].	Divide 100cm (39¼in) on hip evenly
Shoulder length	Modern womenswear jackets tend to have narrow shoulder lines. In this case as the measurement on the size chart is approximately 11.5cm (4¾in), then finished jacket shoulder length should be more or less the same.	Bodice block + 0.5cm (¼in)
Shoulder slant	Unless specified, a jacket should include a pair of moderate shoulder pads in order to achieve a 'smart' look. The shoulder slant, therefore, should include the actual thickness of the shoulder pad.	Bodice block + 1.5cm (½in)
Armhole depth	The basic bodice block includes excess depth of 1 to 1.5cm (⅜ to ½in), and with the raised shoulder slant of the jacket, there should now be enough room for movement of the arm (sleeve). The depth of the armhole of the jacket block can, therefore, stay the same, or be increased by 0.5 to 1cm (¼ to ⅜in) further; jacket armholes are usually tidy with little excess fabric.	Same as bodice block or + 1cm (⅜in) max
Neckline	The neckline of the basic bodice block hugs the base of the neck with no excess tolerance. The neckline of the jacket, as a piece of formalwear, acts in the same way.	No change
First button position	The first button should be levelled to the intersection of break line to the front edge of the garment.	On CF level near bust level
Button size	Although there is no specific rule for the size of buttons, for most outerwear the button size should start from 44L.	50L

Adapting the darts on the bodice block for the jacket

The darts on the bodice block can, as we have
seen (see pages 139–40), be moved to any
position on the bodice as long as the point
of the dart remains in the same place.

Back shoulder dart

Most modern garments do not have a back
shoulder dart, and this dart can be eliminated
by moving it to the armhole seam when attaching
sleeves, but this can create a gap on the back
armhole. This excess fabric could be eased
into the seam, which is a standard procedure
with wool fabrics. The pattern cutter can,
therefore, move half the dart to the armhole
seam and ease half into the shoulder seam.

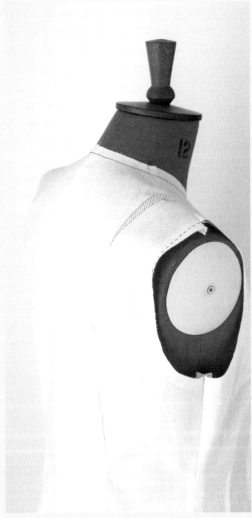

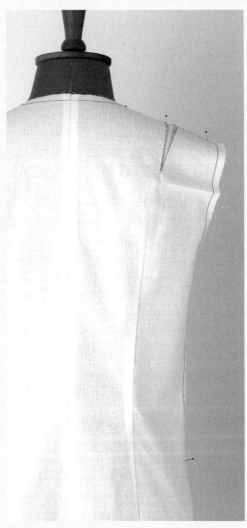

Transferring a shoulder dart to the armhole seam creates a gap at the back armhole.

To eliminate the gap at the back armhole, transfer half the shoulder dart to the armhole seam and ease half into the shoulder seam.

Front shoulder dart

The front shoulder dart is the upper half of the bust dart, but it is too large and looks intrusive on jackets. To eliminate it by closing it up and opening up the lower half of the dart from the bust point to the waist, however, creates an excessively large dart and disturbs the side seam, which would move to the bias grain. Instead, the shoulder dart can be removed in one of two ways:

- Opening up the shoulder dart moving the excess fabric to the armhole seam. Rather than creating a dart at the armhole, the pattern could just be re-shaped along the shoulder line and armhole and the excess fabric left to create additional room for the movement of the arm.

- Closing up the shoulder dart and moving half to the side seam and half to the armhole seam. You will need to fill in the gap under the arm at the side seam, which is created when you fold the dart when redrafting the pattern.

Opening up the front shoulder dart creates excess fabric at the armhole, but this excess could be used as additional tolerance for movement of the arm.

Once the sleeve is attached, the excess fabric at the armhole disappears.

Moving half the dart to the armhole seam and half to the side seam is unobtrusive because the sleeve will hide the dart. You will need to fill in the gaps under the arm.

Step 1
Trace the bodice block & move the darts

Trace the bodice block, aligning the front and back pieces next to each other along the bust line. Alter the darts according to the working drawing. Here half the back shoulder dart has been moved to the armhole seam and the other half will be eased away into the shoulder seam. The front shoulder dart has been closed and a dart opened up on the armhole seam.

Step 3
Adjust the bust

To increase the bust by 4cm (1½in), it would be usual to add 1cm (⅜in) at both underarm points (since we are working on half the pattern). For a jacket, we'd create a larger back than the front to allow the arms ease of movement. In this case, increase the bust by 1.5cm (½in) at the back and 0.5cm (¼in) at the front.

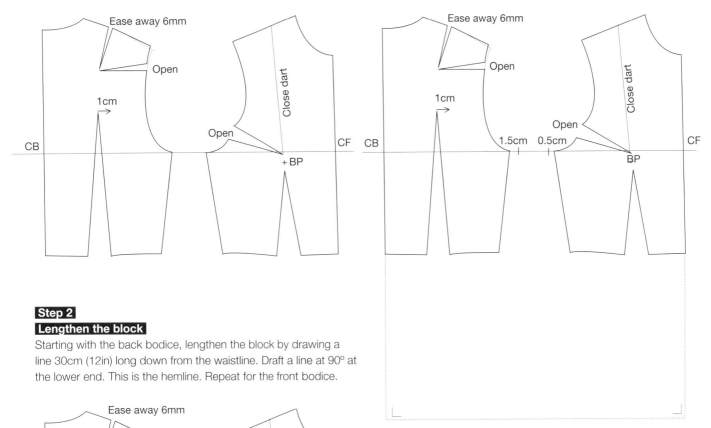

Step 2
Lengthen the block

Starting with the back bodice, lengthen the block by drawing a line 30cm (12in) long down from the waistline. Draft a line at 90° at the lower end. This is the hemline. Repeat for the front bodice.

Step 4
Draft the back side seam

- Increase the hip measurement by first locating the hip line 19cm (7½in) below the waistline on the centre back. Draw a dotted line measuring 25cm (9¾in), at 90° to the centre back (one quarter of the finished hip measurement of 100cm/39¼in).
- Draw a straight line from the new underarm point to the hemline. At the waistline mark a point 2cm (¾in) from this straight line, measuring towards the centre back (to achieve a reasonable curve at the waist). Draw a line from the underarm point, and use a hip curve at this new waist point to achieve the smooth curve.
- Then extend this new side seam back out towards the end of the straight line at the hem. This section of the line should curve outwards slightly to accommodate the hip.
- Since the side seam is now curved, re-measure the line and mark a point 30cm (12in) from the waistline. Draft a new hemline at 90° to the side seam and curve it back towards the centre back (true corners).

Step 5
Adjust the shoulder, neckline & armhole

- Raise the back shoulder point by 1.5cm (½in) to accommodate the thickness of the shoulder pad. Draft a new shoulder line from the shoulder neck point to new shoulder point. This line should be 12.6cm (5in) long (12cm/5in + 0.6cm/¼in ease, replacing part of the shoulder dart).
- Draft a new back armhole, starting the line at 90° to the new shoulder point. This will now include the new armhole dart.
- Raise the front shoulder point by 1.5cm (½in) and draft a new shoulder line measuring 12cm (5in).
- Draw the front armhole curve using an armhole ruler. (see illustration on next page.)

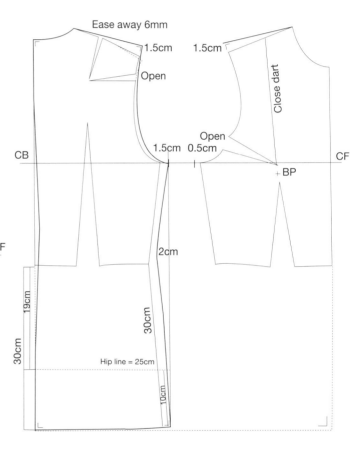

Step 6
Create a dart at the centre back

The centre back could be kept straight, but usually a dart is added to create a closer fit at the waistline. Mark a point 0.6cm (¼in) from the centre back along the waistline (to create a dart of 1.2cm/½in). Using a hip curve, re-draw the centre back line.

Step 7
Move the side back darts

The side back dart could be created as an extension of the dart on the bodice. As the jacket has been made larger, however, it would be better, aesthetically, to increase its size and position proportionally.

• Move the top point of the dart approximately 1cm (³⁄₈in) towards the side seam. At the same time lower the top of the dart by 1cm. Draft a vertical line from this new point to finish approximately 4 to 5cm (1½ to 2in) above the hip line. Reduce the width of the dart from 4cm (1½in) to 3cm (1¼in) by measuring 1.5cm (½in) either side of the vertical line. Draw the dart. This is to give additional tolerance to the waistline of the jacket, as outerwear.

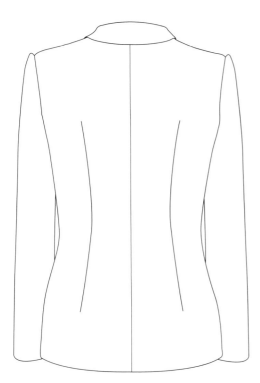

Side back darts left according to the bodice block (bust darts remain at the basic block position).

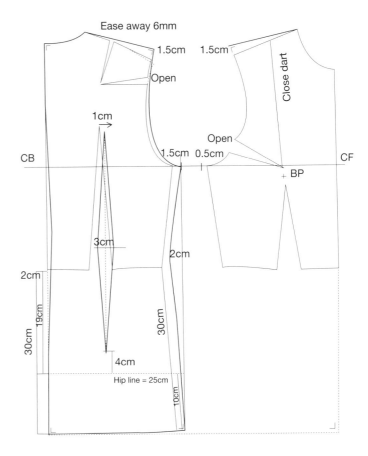

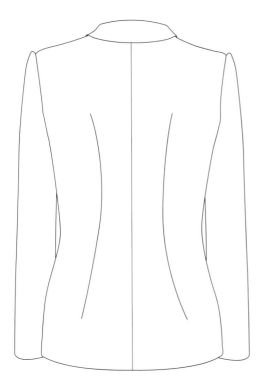

Side back darts moved and re-sized (graded dart positions).

190 CHAPTER 5: CONVERTING THE BLOCK INTO THE DESIGN

Step 8
Move the side front darts & draw the armhole

In a similar way to the side back darts, the front side darts would also benefit aesthetically from being moved.

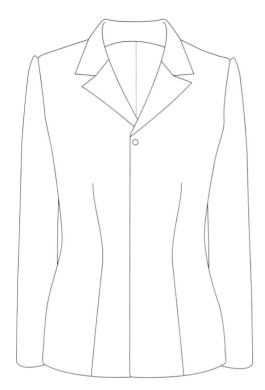

Side front darts left according to the bodice block (bust darts remain at basic block position).

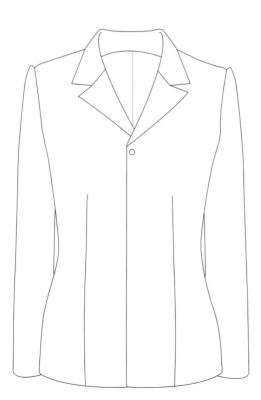

Side front darts moved and re-sized (bust darts graded to new position and straightened).

(Please see enlarged diagrams over the page)

- Move the top of the side front dart 1cm (⅜in) towards the side seam. At the same time, lower the top of the dart by 1cm (⅜in). Again, draw a vertical line from the top of the dart, this time extending it to the hemline. Reduce the width of the dart from 4.5cm (1¾in) to 2cm (¾in) at waist level.

- Extend the dart to the hemline by drawing two lines of exactly the same measurement. Re-draft the hemline by drawing lines at 90° to both sides of the dart. The dart is not reduced back to a point on the front, as it was on the back, because the front of the jacket is flatter than the back.

- Having removed fabric from the hips in this dart, it is important to check, and if necessary, adjust the hip measurement at the side seam. Locate the hip line at the same level as on the back (in this case 10.5cm/4in from the hem). Measure the width of the front, excluding the dart, which in this case should be 25cm (9¾in).

- Draw a straight line from hip line on the side seam to the new underarm point. Measure 2cm (¾in) towards the centre front from this straight line, and draw the side seam from the underarm point to the hemline, creating the curve at the waist using a hip curve. Re-measure the front side seam, which should be exactly the same length as the back side seam. Any discrepancy between the two can be taken up by the making the front armhole shorter than the back by raising the underarm point, or dividing the discrepancy between the length of the armhole and the hem.

- Draw the front armhole using an armhole curve.

- Finally, add a 2.5cm (1in) dart towards the side seam to provide extra fit. Extra side or front darts can also be added throughout the fitting stage.

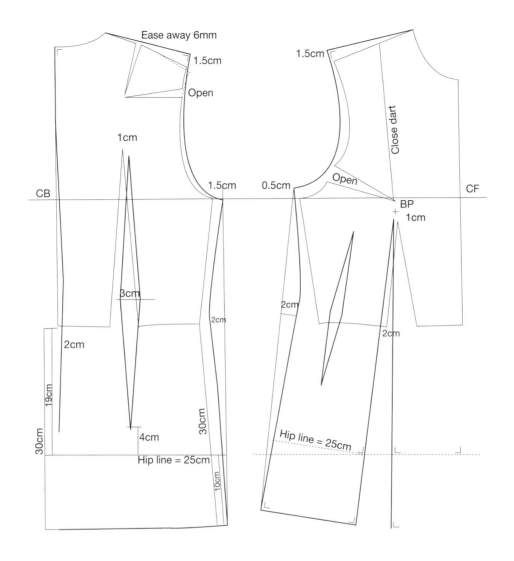

Position of the collar

The longer the extension from the shoulder neck point, the closer the collar will sit on the neck. A convertible collar, therefore, has very little or no extension so that it sits flat on the shoulders. A jacket, however, has an extension of 1.5 to 3cm (½ to 1¼in) from the shoulder neck point so that it sits further up the neck.

The break line of a jacket collar (above left and centre) sits closer to the neck than that for a convertible collar (above right), which can consequently lie flat on the shoulders.

Adjust the front neckline/break line lapel

- Create the button stand extension by adding 2.6cm (1in) to the centre front (half the diameter of a 50L button plus 1cm).

- Work out the break point of the collar. To do this, locate the position of the first button level with the bust point (the standard position for a three-button jacket – for a single button jacket the button would be at waist level). This is the position of the break point. Mark the position with a horizontal dotted line.

- Continuing from the line outward from the shoulder, mark a point 1.5cm (½in) from the shoulder neck point. Draw a dotted line from this point to the break point. This is the break line, where the lapel will roll over extended from front of garment.

- Front the position of the break line, draft the shape of the lapel and top collar using dotted lines. Mirror the shape of the lapel along the break line to complete the front neckline and the front edge of the jacket.

- The top collar construction will be same as for the convertible collar (see page 161).

- Mark the position of the first button (draw the size of the actual button on the button stand), mark the position of the centre front line and the break line.

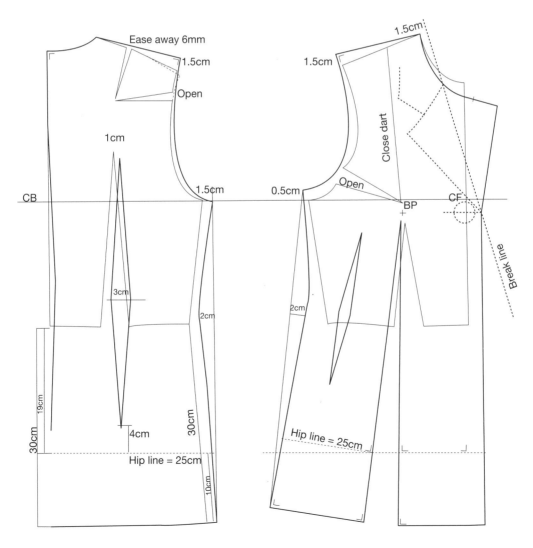

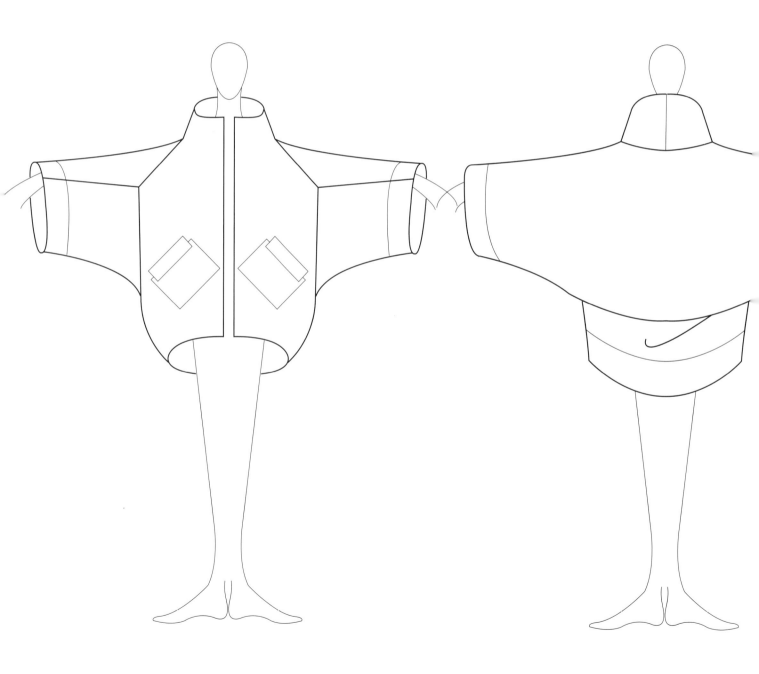

CHAPTER 6
INSPIRATIONAL
PATTERN CUTTING

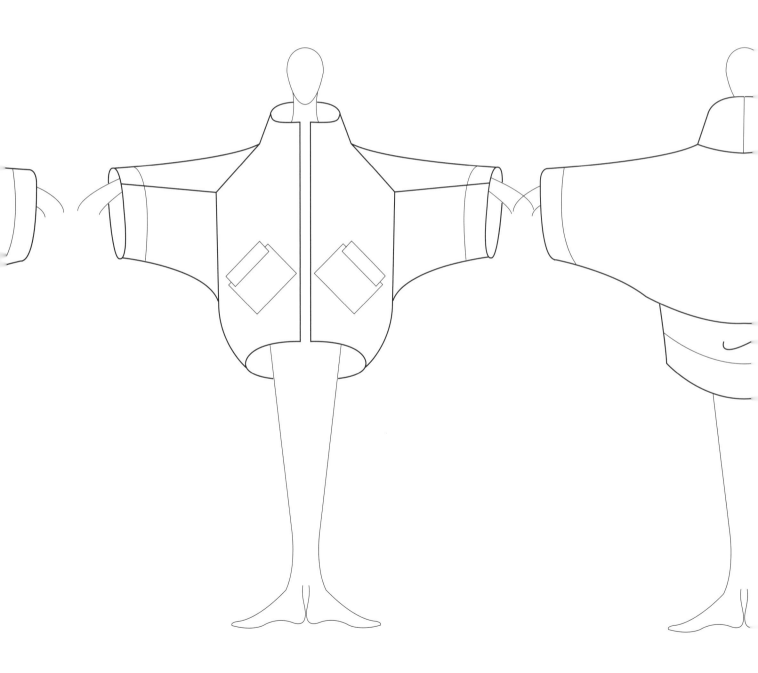

It is a fashion designer's job to take initial ideas and concepts and transform them in new and interesting ways into desirable garments. The sources of inspiration available to a fashion designer and the directions in which they can be taken are almost limitless. They include exploring silhouettes, contrasting colours, reinventing historic references, introducing new lengths, combining unusual textures, introducing prints, distorting proportions, enlarging or reducing details – the list of possibilities is endless.

It is the job of the pattern cutter to translate the designer's ideas into wearable garments, and they can do so using almost exactly the same approach as the designer, taking the basic block and, with an understanding of how it is made, adapting it in an almost equally limitless number of ways.

In this chapter we will look at some basic but equally interesting pattern cutting skills that use a combination of geometry, extension, mirror imaging and repetition and are based on the basic blocks. We will see that pattern cutting need not be complicated or intricate and that sometimes the approach you take to pattern cutting can inspire a creative outcome in the simplest way.

The garments we will explore were designed by Lo and Cabon, a design partnership between the author of this book and Darren Cabon, exploring new shapes through pattern cutting as well as drawing, with pattern cutting as their key inspiration. The approach is minimalist, but also shows an intellectual approach to clothing architecture taken through pattern cutting. The garments discussed, rather than demonstrating a particular 'trick' or 'skill' to cut a paper pattern, show the essence of all pattern cutting – the thought process.

A PIECE OF STRING

A Piece of String is a garment from the 1995 collection, Wearing the Cloud, a collection of evening and wedding outfits for both men and women. The collection was made in shades of blue from navy to light blue and in white, taking inspiration from the colours of the sky. To imitate the ethereal quality of the sky the collection was made from silks and mixed silk fabrics.

The concept behind A Piece of String was to use woven fabrics to imitate knitwear. The result is a unique lace that is used to mask the body in a similar way to a wedding veil.

A Piece of String aimed to combine the qualities of woven and knit fabrics by taking a continuous piece of woven fabric, made to resemble a length of yarn, folding and twisting it in a random pattern, and securing each intersection in the pattern with a hand or machine stitch. When it is stretched, the areas between the intersections distort, much like a knitted fabric.

The lace veil of A Piece of String is in fact a high front collar piece that is hooked onto the ears. The garment itself has an asymmetric hemline and is fastened at the back with two strings – each being one end of the continuous piece of string.

The base garment is a simple white dress with a mandarin collar made from a double layer of silk habotai designed to enhance the comfort of the wearer and at the same time give a sense of luxury to the garment.

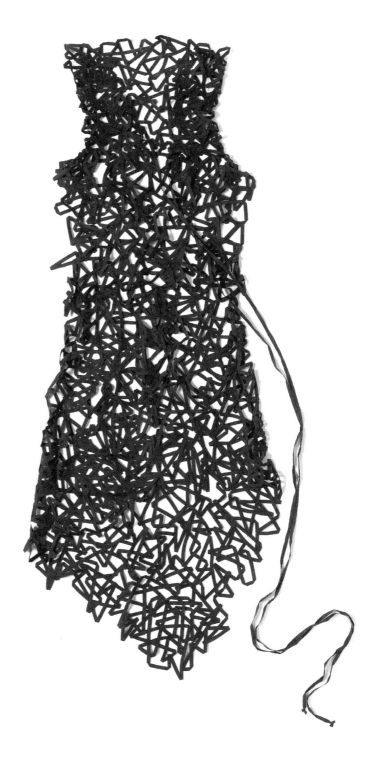

THE MATERIAL

The fabric used was silk habotai, a crisp, delicate but tough fabric that is naturally flat and can, therefore, be easily cut, stitched and ironed.

To create the continuous yarn, the silk was cut and the folded into bias strips, which were then joined together to create one continuous strip approximately 30m (100ft) in length. Bias strips are cut at a 45° angle to the straight grain of the fabric.

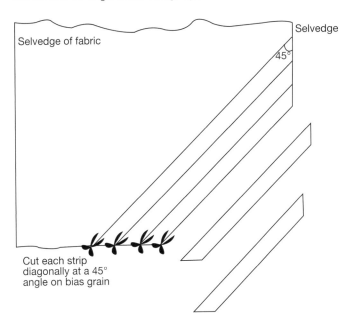

Cut each strip diagonally at a 45° angle to the straight grain.

Each strip of fabric should then be joined with a 45° diagonal seam to maintain the slight stretch of the bias strip.

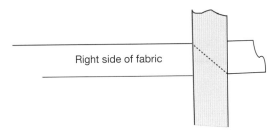

With the right sides together, sew a 45° diagonal seam.

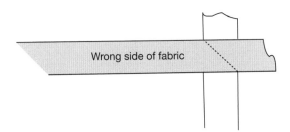

Bias strips can either be made by hand, by using an industrial binder working in conjunction with a flat-lock machine foot, or by using a simple hand-held binder.

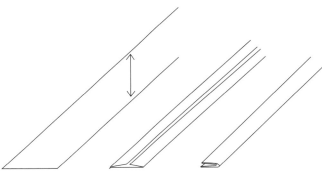

The sides of each strip can be folded in by hand. The strip is then folded in half and stitched together along its entire length.

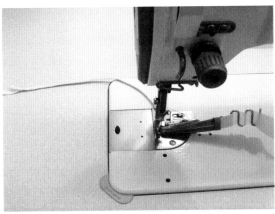

Manufacturers often install a binder next to a flat-lock sewing machine. As the bias strip is fed through the binder it is pulled under the machine foot and folded and stitched at the same time.

A hand-held binder can also be used.

Step 1
Draft a dress block

Using a size chart or a set of personal measurements, draft a one-piece dress block.

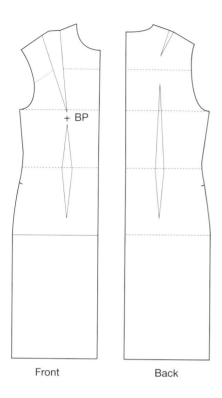

Front   Back

Step 2
Move the darts on the front

Close the shoulder dart and re-distribute part of the allowance to create a small side bust dart and part of the allowance to create a dart extending to the hem. This creates an A-line shape.

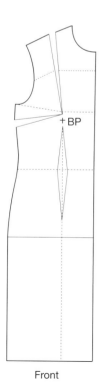 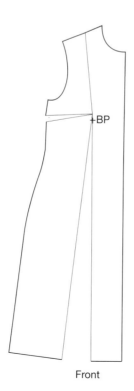

Front   Front

Step 3
Create the complete front pattern

Because the front of the garment has an asymmetrical hem, you need to work with one pattern piece, rather than half. At this stage, therefore, you need to draw around the pattern and create a mirror image along the centre front line.

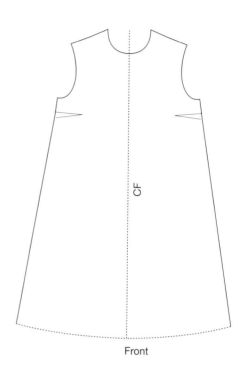

Front

Step 4
Create the front collar

To create the veil, widen the shoulder neck point so that the width of the veil will coincide with the width of the face measured from ear to ear. Then raise the shoulder neck point so that it will be level with the top of the ears.

Step 5
Lower the armhole & create the asymmetric hem

As this is an outer garment, it should not be too tight. It is also open at the back when worn. Lower the armhole by 3cm (1¼in) and increase the bust by 4cm (1½in) [2cm (¾in) on each side].

Work out the length of the garment at its lowest point on the asymmetric hem. From the side seams, which should come just above the knee, draw the asymmetric hem, remembering that the lowest point of the hem is on the right-hand side when the garment is worn.

Step 6
Create the back pattern

As you did for the front, raise the shoulder neck point to the level of the top of the ears. Mark a split point 3cm (1¼in) down from the shoulder neck point along the seam; this creates the opening for the ears from which the veil is hung. Lower the armhole by 3cm (1¼in) to coincide with the new front armhole measurement. Adjust the side seam so that it is the same length as the front side seam. From the point at the top of the collar, work out the line of the back opening, curving it towards the side seam, which flares out to match the front. Make sure that the two sides meet at the centre back at a point level with the armhole for the fastening.

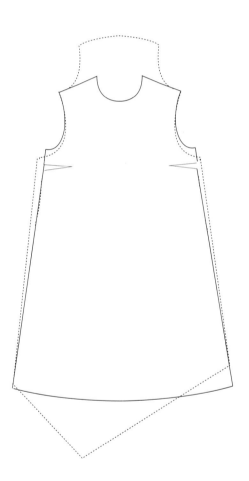

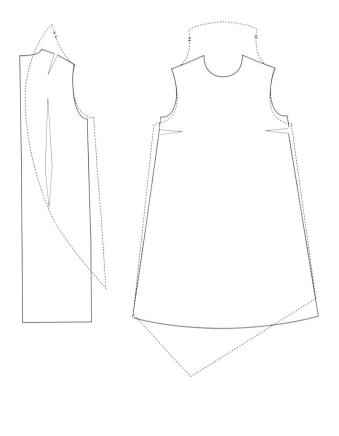

Step 7
Make a test garment

Make a toile to test the overall shape and fit. As this is a lightweight garment, made from silk, the most suitable fabric for the toile would be a light silk organza or a calico muslin.

Step 8
The paper pattern

Once the fitting is finalized, make the paper pattern.

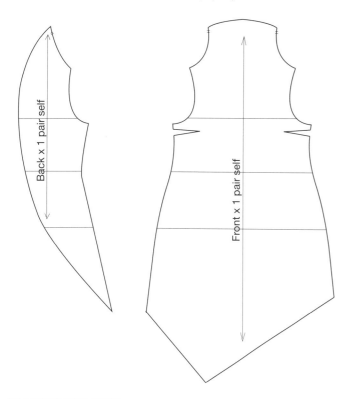

CONSTRUCTION

The final paper pattern is used as a template to construct the 'lace' garment.

Using the 30m (100ft) long stitched bias strip, work on the front and two back pattern pieces separately (the strip is, therefore, not strictly continuous).

Create a network of zigzag lines, crossing and re-crossing each other. Place a hand stitch at each junction where the strips cross. You will need to bear the following in mind:

• The density of the pattern is random, however if the network is too large the silk may not be able to hold its shape; if it is too close, then the bias will begin to stiffen and lose its stretch quality.

• The network should, however, be particularly dense along the side and shoulder seams and along the darts to create sufficient strength and allow the seams to be hand sewn.

• A long piece of the bias strip should be left on each side of the centre back to tie the garment.

Finally, tack the darts, side seams and shoulder seams with a contrasting coloured thread before sewing the seams by hand.

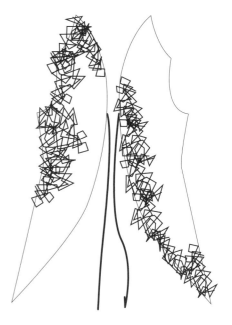

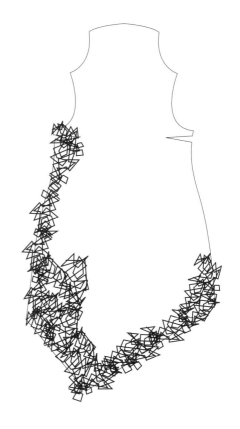

THE 'T' COAT

THE MATERIAL

The concept for this project was the alphabet, and the letter 'T' was literally pulled out of a hat. Allowing fate to take a hand like this, and exploring the resulting avenues it opens up, can lead to interesting shapes and new and innovative pattern cutting techniques.

The 'T' formed an obvious silhouette for the garment, with the horizontal bar of the letter forming the sleeves and the vertical bar the body. The neckline was placed in the middle where the two bars crossed. Unbalancing the front and back of the garment like this broke all the rules of pattern cutting, but produced an interesting shape.

The coat was made from different fabrics for the Spring/Summer and Autumn/Winter collections. Each fabric altered the character of the garment in a different way, demonstrating that the choice of fabric is as important as the skill used to cut the pattern. For the Spring/Summer collection the 'T' coat was presented as an opera coat made from a crisp silk satin organza with a slight sheen; in a laminated chiffon it became an oversized raincoat. For the European Autumn/Winter market the collection included versions in simulated fur and embroidered, quilted silk habotai imparting warm, cosy characteristics with the glamour of a 1930s silhouette.

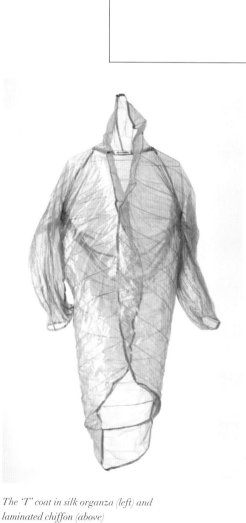

The 'T' coat in silk organza (left) and laminated chiffon (above)

The sleeves of the 'T' coat consist of a simple tube of fabric, open at both ends. They can be cut as wide or as narrow as desired. Similarly, the body of the coat can be straight, or can be shaped with darts.

With the neckline in the middle, the balance of the garment is altered and when the coat is worn it is automatically pulled towards the back with the excess fabric hanging from the mid-shoulder blade to the hip level, creating an almost alien-like shape. To compensate for the raising of hemline at the front, the centre front of the garment could be drafted up to 5cm (2in) longer.

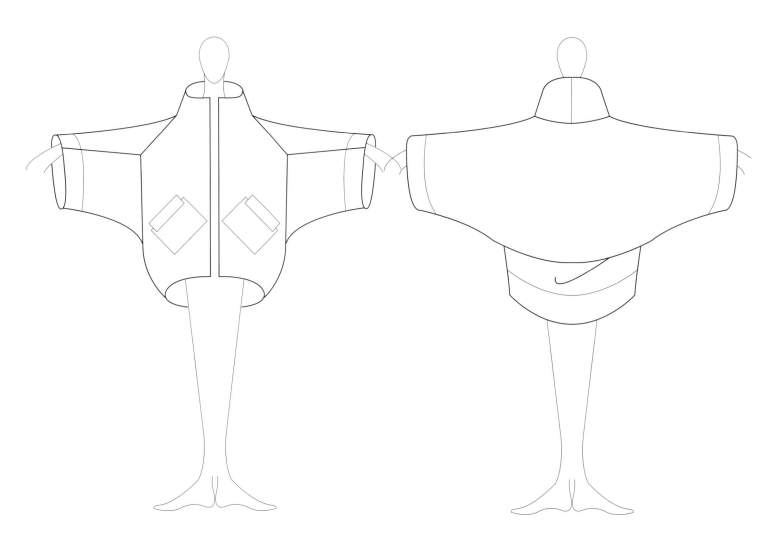

The front and back of the 'T' coat, showing the raising of the front hemline, caused by the unconventional position of the neckline, and the corresponding excess of fabric at the back.

Step 1
Draft the sleeves

First work out the length and width of the sleeves. The length is the measurement from wrist to wrist with arms outstretched. The width is the width of the tube shape and should not be too narrow as the essence of this garment comes from its oversized shape. Draw a rectangle using these measurements.

To identify the position of the sleeves, shoulder and necklines, notches are marked along the length of the rectangle. First measure and mark the length of the sleeves from the wrist to the shoulder/underarm point. Then mark the position of the back neckline in the centre of one long side. It should be approximately 16 to 18cm (6¼ to 7in) in width and 1.5 to 2cm (½ to ¾in) deep. Using these measurements draw a curve so that the collar can sit comfortably at the centre back.

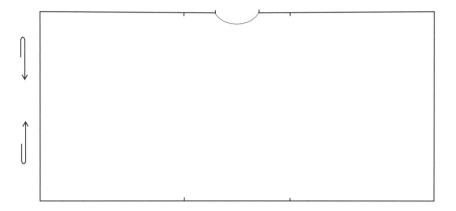

Step 2
Make the sleeves

Cut the sleeves from cloth and fold the tube in half and join the sides of the tube from the wrist to the notches representing the shoulder/underarm points.

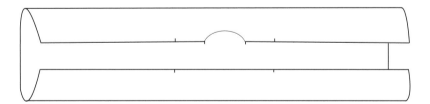

The open edge along the top of the tube will be joined to the main body of the coat from the shoulder to the neckline. The open edge at the bottom will be sewn from the shoulder/underarm points and along the back of the bodice near the waistline.

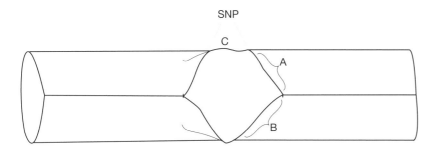

Step 3
Draft the front & back bodice

As this is an oversized garment, the bodice is also drafted using geometric shapes, rather than from a block.

Again, we start by drawing a rectangle, taking the measurements from the tube created for the sleeves, and this time drawing half the pattern only from centre front to centre back.

The length of the rectangle is calculated by adding the shoulder length measurement from the shoulder neck point to the notch on the sleeve tube (A) to the half of the measurement taken between the two notches along the back of the coat (B). The notch where A and B meet is effectively the side seam of the garment. The measurement from A to the centre front is dependent on the final design, since this is an oversized garment.

To create the collar, measure half of the back neck length (C). Draw a line of that measurement at a 45° angle to the top of the rectangle at the shoulder neck point. Then draft an oversize collar shape.

The pattern, though unconventional in cut, now has a centre front, centre back, side seam, sleeve, collar and shoulder seam.

Step 4
Cut the fabric

Cut a pair from cloth and then sew the centre back seam and also the centre back collar seam. This creates an almost circular seam to which you will now attach the sleeve tube.

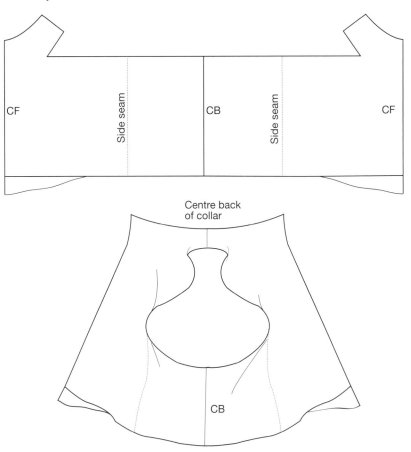

Step 5
Join the sleeves to the bodice

Attach the sleeves to the bodice, matching the notches on the sleeves to the side seams, and sew around the circular seam.

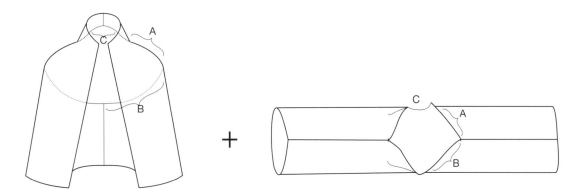

THE BIAS TUBE

Most clothes we wear today have vertical seams, the majority of which are cut on the straight grain. Garments cut on the bias also tend to have vertical seams, but because the fabric gives and then bounces back under the tension of the machine foot when the seams are sewn, these seams tend to be wavy.

The concept of the Bias Tube is to engineer a garment on the bias, without wavy seams. To do this, the seams of the garment are diagonal, or spiral, but are sewn on the straight grain. The garment itself works on the bias grain and therefore has a slight stretch and tendency to cling to the body.

Transferring straight seams into a spiral seam

To transfer straight seams into a spiral seam, there are a few rules and limitations with which the pattern cutter must comply:

- The original side seams of the garment should be completely straight with no shaping.
- The garment should be cut with very little shape.
- The pattern should not have darts.
- When the garment is cut, it will hang on the bias.
- Usually, garments cut with a spiral seam will work best if they are made from light fabrics, such as chiffon or silk crêpe, as these will hang closely to the body. Heavier fabrics such as calico or denim will not hang as well.
- Once the spiral seam has been created, further fitting using fastenings and suppression can be made on the first toile.

Because it is cut on the bias, the dress is flexible and able to expand and contract to fit the curves of the body when worn.

The top of this chiffon outfit from the Lo and Cabon Autumn/Winter 2003 collection is cut on the bias and sewn with vertical seams, which consequently are wavy. The skirt, however, is also cut on the bias but sewn with a single spiral seam, which because it is sewn on the straight grain of the fabric, is perfectly flat.

THE PATTERN

Step 1
Create the basic, straight pattern shape

Taking a basic front and back pattern for a sleeveless dress, lay them side by side and remove any shape on the side seams.

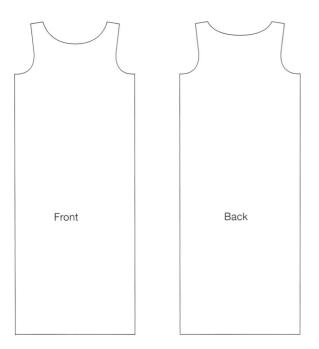

Step 2
Join the back & front at the side seam

Then either join them together along one side seam using sticky tape or retrace the paper pattern, eliminating one of the side seams. Mark the position where the spiral seam will start, in this case three-quarters of the way down the armhole at the back.

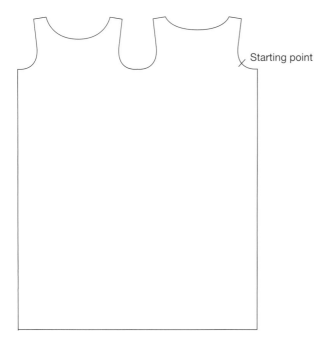

Step 3
Draw the position of the spiral seam

From the starting point, draw a dotted line at 45° until it reaches the opposite side of the pattern. Add two notches along this line.

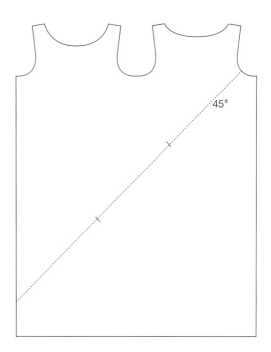

Step 4
Cut the pattern in two

Cut the pattern along the dotted line.

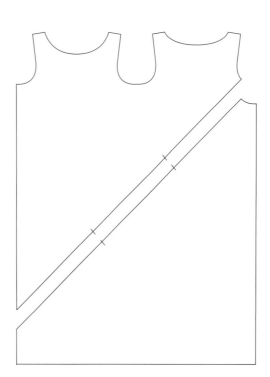

Join the vertical side seams

Move the pattern and reposition it so that the original vertical side
seams are lined up.

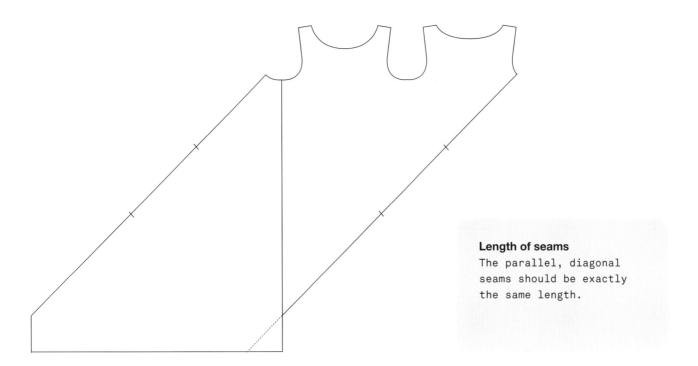

Length of seams
The parallel, diagonal
seams should be exactly
the same length.

Step 7
Lengthen the new spiral seam as necessary

If the original side seams are matched perfectly, then the pattern is
complete. However, if the garment is long it is likely that sections
are either overlapping or missing at the hemline. In this case
remove the overlapping section and reposition it to extend the
side seam that is falling short.

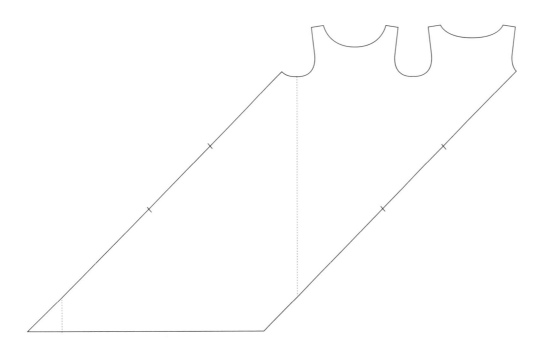

Step 8
Add grain lines

Add the grain line to the pattern, which runs parallel to the new spiral seam.

Step 9
Cut the pattern from the fabric

Position the pattern along the straight grain of the fabric and cut out.

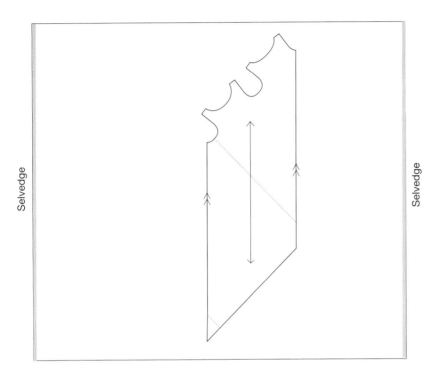

CONSTRUCTION

Sew the garment together along the single spiral seam.

The garment now has no straight side seams and, as it is entirely cut on the bias, it will give both horizontally and vertically, so that it is flexible at the bust, waist and hip, fitting and clinging to the wearer's body.

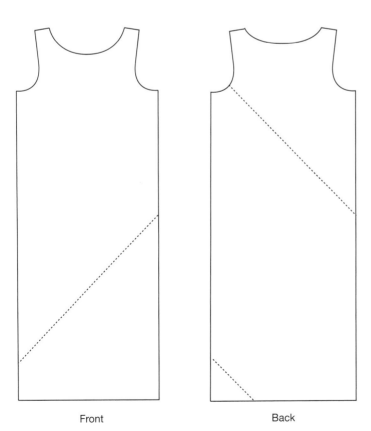

Front   Back

THE PARACHUTE DRESS

The Parachute Dress was created for the maid of honour at a summer safari wedding. The concept was that it should be elegant and 'simple and modern with a twist'.

THE MATERIAL

Recreating or re-designing the fabric is one way to create a unique garment. For this dress, two off-white inexpensive silks – silk habotai and silk chiffon – were used to create a light 'parachute-like' fabric for the outer shell of the dress. The lining was made from flesh-coloured silk crêpe de chine.

The lengths of off-white silk habotai and silk chiffon were cut into strips of increasing width along the warp.

The toile of the finished Parachute Dress showing the twisted, draped hem.

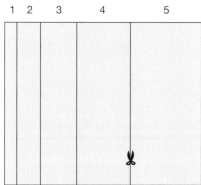

Silk habotai

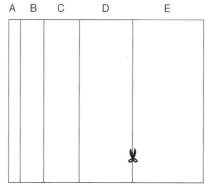

Silk chiffon

These were then joined together with French seams (see page 222) in an alternating pattern. The fabric was then washed with warm water in a washing machine.

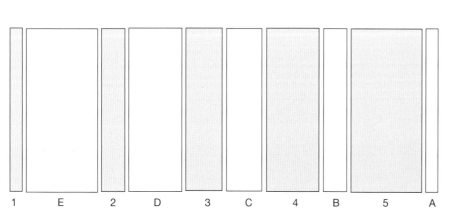

The effect of the washing was to create a slight ripple effect along the seams as the silk chiffon, with its more open weave structure, shrank substantially in contrast to the more dense weave of the silk habotai.

THE PATTERN

The Parachute Dress consists of a simple dress with shoulder straps that is based on the basic dress block. The lining is cut on the bias from flesh-coloured silk crêpe de chine. The shell, which is made from the striped fabric, is cut in a trapeze shape that is also based on the same basic block. It is cut longer than the final length of the dress, turned up and then twisted before it is attached to the lining on the inside.

Step 1
Draft the basic dress pattern

First draft a dress block with a side bodice dart using an appropriate set of measurements.

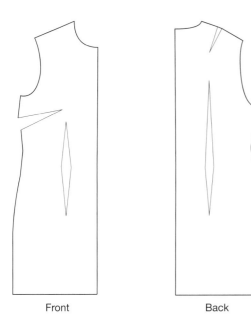

Front   Back

Step 2
Adjust the block to create a dress with shoulder straps

Raise the side seams and remove the top of the bodice. Create a gentle curve at the centre back.

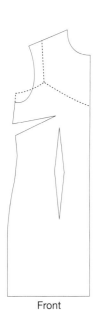

Front   Back

Step 3
Trace the pattern to create the lining

Trace the shoulder strap dress pattern to create a pattern for the lining of the dress. Create a mirror image of the front pattern along the centre front. Draw a grain line at 45° to the centre front and back as the lining is cut on the bias.

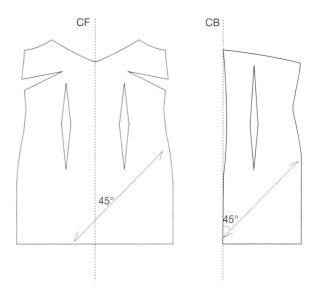

Step 4
Cut out the lining

Cut one front piece and two back pieces out of the flesh-coloured crêpe de chine on the bias grain. When cutting two sides of a symmetrical garment, the bias grain should be considered 'a pair'.

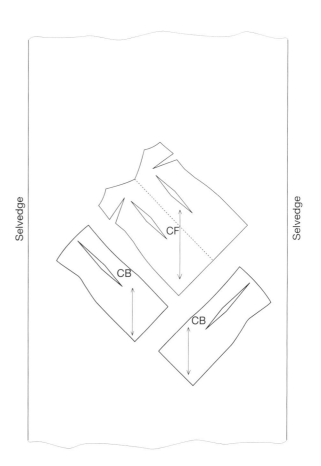

Step 5
Draft the trapeze-shaped shell

Trace the upper edge of the front bodice from the paper pattern you used for the lining. Then draft the trapeze shape, by drawing straight lines to create new side seams from the underarm points on both sides.

The length of the side seams should be equivalent to the length of the finished dress (in this case 120cm/47in from the waist) plus the measurement from the ankle to the knee level, to allow enough fabric to turn up and attach to the lining on the inside of the dress.

The width of the hem should be approximately four times the width of the lining's hem. This will vary depending on the thickness of the fabric. The lighter the fabric, the wider the hem because the fabric can be more easily gathered to fit inside the hem of the dress.

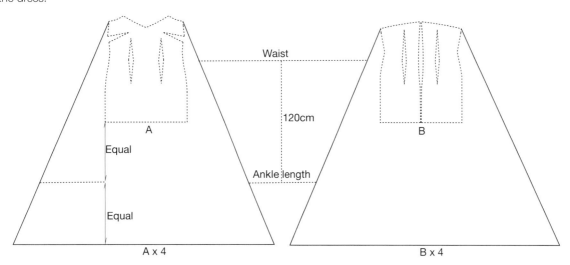

Step 6
Cut out the shell of the dress

Using your new paper pattern, cut out a front and back piece from the striped fabric you constructed earlier with the centre back and centre front along the straight grain of the fabric.

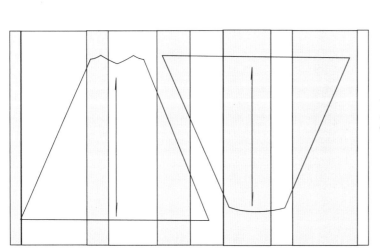

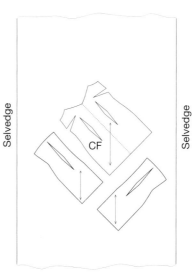

Crêpe de chine lining

CONSTRUCTION

Step 1
Make the lining of the dress

Sew the bust darts and front and back waist darts of the lining. Then, using French seams, join the centre back and side seams. The seams may be wavy, since the lining is cut on the bias, but this is acceptable for a lining. The bias cut also means that the lining will drape and cling to the body with substantial 'give'.

Step 2
Sew the shell of the dress

Sew the bust darts and side seams together using French seams. Gather the hem so that it is the same circumference as the hem of the lining.

Step 3
Sew on the shoulder straps

Make fine rouleaux straps from crêpe de chine cut on the bias. Sew the lining to the shell at the top of the dress, sandwiching the straps between the two when bagging the garment out.

Step 4
Join the shell to the lining at the hem

Divide both the lining and shell hems into four and mentally label them A, B, C and D. As you join the shell to the lining, twist the shell so that the sections line up as follows:

Shell		Lining
Section A	join to	Section C
Section B	join to	Section D
Section C	join to	Section A
Section D	join to	Section B

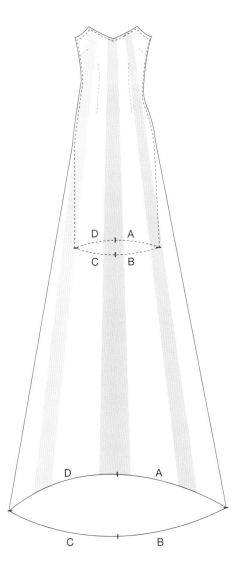

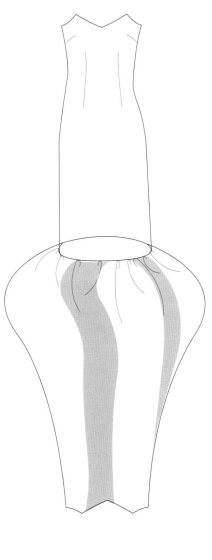

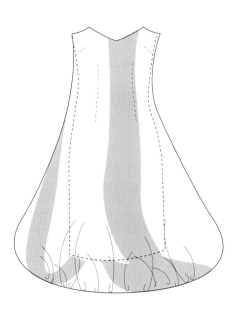

A PIECE OF CLOTH: THE BLANK CANVAS

Fashion and pattern cutting concepts come from a variety of sources. In an article in *The New York Times* in 1984, Japanese designer, Rei Kawakubo, declared that fashion designers everywhere were fooling around with folklore themes and reworkings of designs from each decade of the twentieth century. She decided that she would rid herself of these influences and start 'from nothing, from zero'. This statement is the inspiration behind A Piece of Cloth – the Blank Canvas.

'Starting from zero' may be a somewhat abstract starting point from which to design anything; if there is nothing, how or where does anything start? Lo and Cabon's interpretation of this abstract concept is 'a blank canvas'. For a painter the blank canvas is the starting point before a stroke of the brush applied; for a fashion designer, the blank canvas could as simple as a piece of cloth before it is cut and manipulated.

A Piece of Cloth featured in Lo and Cabon's Spring/Summer 2000 'Stardust' collection.

THE MATERIAL

A Piece of Cloth is made from off-white crisp silk satin organza. This should not be steam ironed during the construction process because the 'gum' that is applied to the fabric to create its bounce, shine and crispy qualities is softened by steam, destroying its flatness and making it difficult to handle. Instead it should be cleaned by a professional dry cleaner after it is made, when the garment can be softened in its entirety, rather than in random sections under the iron.

The base dress is made from a flesh-coloured washed silk habotai, which can be washed before it is used to enhance the softness of the fabric, contributing to the drape of the bias garment.

Width of the garment

The garment width is entirely dependent upon the fabric available. Raw silk satin organza is available up to 110cm (45in) wide. However, finer, coloured silk satin organza is available in widths up to 150cm (60in).

THE PATTERN & CONSTRUCTION

Step 1
Construction of the base dress

Using a basic dress block, make a strapless, knee-length (in this case 61cm/24in below the waistline) dress cut on the bias from the flesh-coloured silk habotai with vertical side and back seams. This is similar to the base dress cut for the parachute dress (see page 211).

Step 2
Basic construction of the Blank Canvas

Cut a piece of cloth 290cm (114in) long with an additional allowance of 8cm (3in) for hems at either end. Then turn the hems by folding under 1cm (3/8in) at either end and then a further 3cm (1¼in).

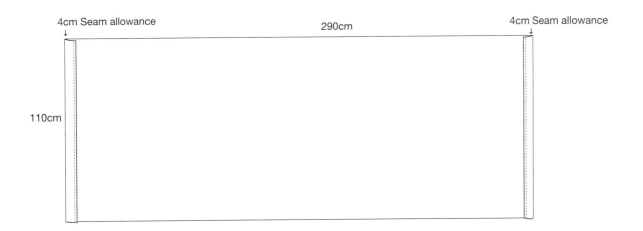

4cm Seam allowance   290cm   4cm Seam allowance

110cm

Variations on A Piece of Cloth

There are various possible ways to
construct A Piece of Cloth. One is to
make holes for the arms and neck in
random positions on the fabric. Another
is to apply buttons and sew buttonholes
across its surface so that it can be
wrapped around the body and buttoned and
worn at whim. In keeping with the idea
of going back to nothing, to the basics,
the eventual choice made was a simple
construction using A Piece of Cloth as
the back of the garment, requiring just
the front of a top and skirt to be made
and sewn directly on top of the cloth.

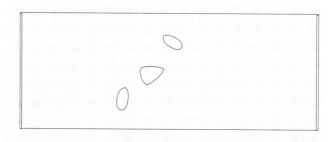

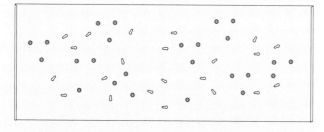

*Variations of A Piece of Cloth with randomly placed holes for the arms
and neck and buttons and buttonholes to be fastened to make a garment
according to the wearer's whim.*

Constructing the top

Take a un-darted bodice block and lengthen it so that it sits near
the hip level, in this case the centre back would be 55cm (21½in)
– 41cm (16in) nape to waist + 14cm (5½in) waist to hip level.

Widen the neckline so that it measures half the circumference of
the head, in this case 29cm (11½in) [58cm (23in) ÷ 2]. This means
that there is no need for any additional openings at the neckline to
allow the head to pass through.

Ensure that the front bust measurement is at least half the width
of the entire bust measurement, in this case 45cm (17½in) [90cm
(35in) ÷ 2].

Add seam allowances of 1.5cm (½in) to the shoulder and side
seams and a 3cm (1¼in) allowance for the hem.

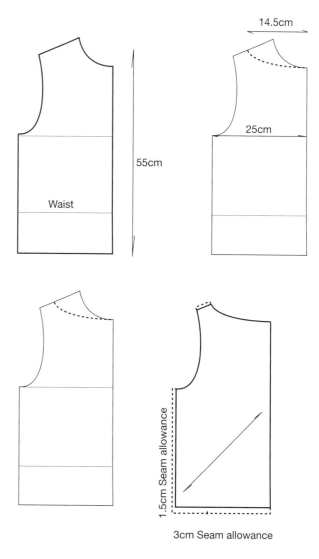

From the silk organza, cut one piece from this pattern on the
bias. Bind the armholes and neckline with bias strips of the silk
organza. Turn in seam allowances of 1.5cm (½in) on the shoulder
and side seams and top stitch. Turn under a 3cm (1¼in) hem
and finish.

Step 4
Constructing the skirt

Cut a rectangular piece of silk organza. In length this should be slightly longer than the knee-length base dress, in this case 72cm (28½in). The width should be 52cm (20½in) so that the overall circumference of the skirt is 104cm (41in). The additional width is to accommodate the lack of darts, which would otherwise provide shape.

The hips also pass easily through the skirt, which is anchored by two buttons set 34cm (13½in) apart. Since the overall circumference of the waist in this case is 68cm (27in), the skirt will sit just below waist level.

Add seam allowances of 1.5cm (½in) to the side seams, 3cm (1¼in) to the top edge (to allow for the fabric to be turned over twice) and a hem allowance of 4cm (1½in).

The skirt pattern
There is no need to use a block for the skirt pattern. Instead it is constructed from a rectangular piece of fabric which is buttoned to A Piece of Cloth, the distance between the buttons dictating whether the skirt sits at the waist or mid-hip line.

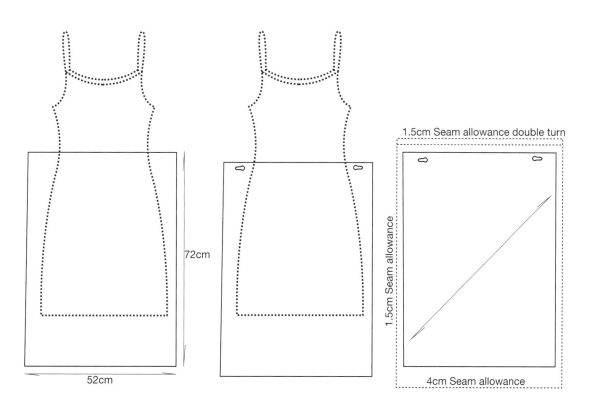

1.5cm Seam allowance double turn

1.5cm Seam allowance

72cm

52cm

4cm Seam allowance

From the silk organza, cut one piece from this pattern on the bias grain. Turn in the seam allowances at the top and side seams and turn up the hem. Make buttonholes on the top edge of the skirt, 34cm (13½in) apart.

Attaching the top & skirt to the Blank Canvas

Top stitch front of the skirt and front of the top to A Piece of Cloth.
Apply buttons to A Piece of Cloth to match the buttonholes on the
skirt. The top and skirt can be attached in any number of ways
to A Piece of Cloth, each of which will create a totally different
garment according to the resulting way in which the cloth drapes.
Variations can also be made according to the chosen length and
width of the fabric.

*Variations in the positioning of the
skirt and top on A Piece of Cloth.*

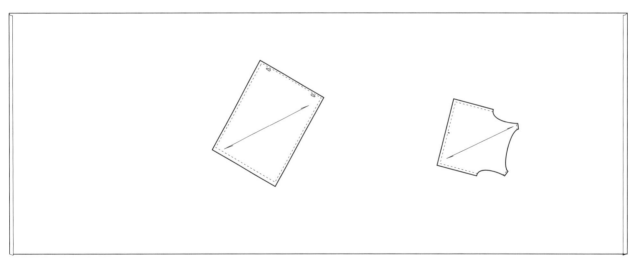

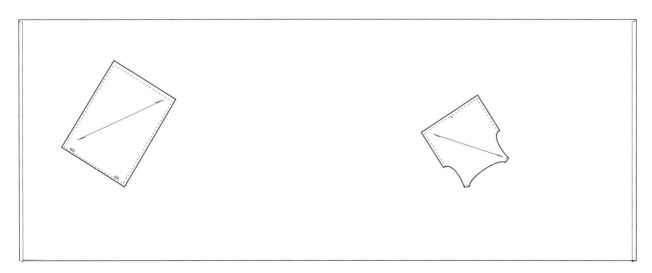

To put on A Piece of Cloth:

• Step into the skirt and fasten the buttons at the waist.

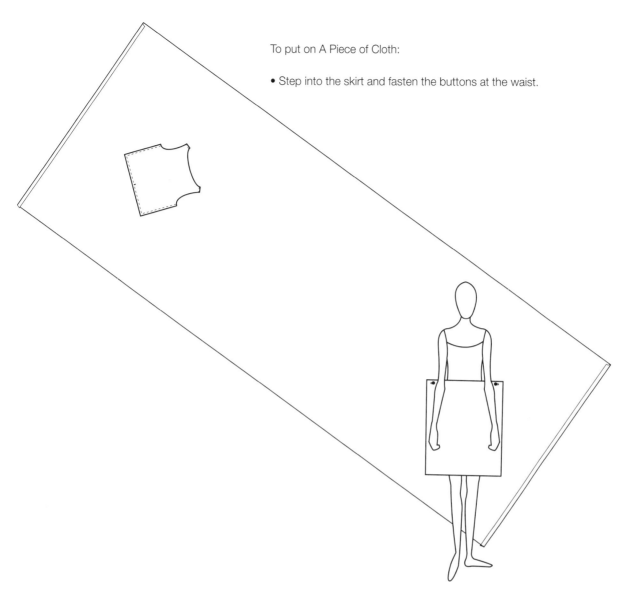

• Pull the top part over the head, like pulling on a sweater.

• Drape and twist the back depending on the positioning of the top and skirt on A Piece of Cloth.

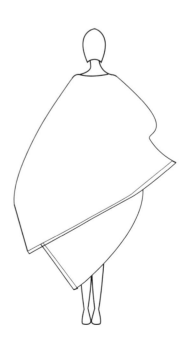

IAIDO TUXEDO

National and ethnic costumes have been a constant source of inspiration to fashion designers for the simple reason that they answer two requirements of fashion – form and function.

The inspiration behind Iaido Tuxedo is Japanese Zen Buddhism, represented through the martial art of Iaido. The trousers of the Iaido costume have an excess amount of fabric that is tucked or tied in regimented folds into the waistline, which is exaggerated by the player's bent, wide-leg stance. The pattern is cut open, extended with this additional width of fabric incorporated as a flap into the seam. Since this technique creates a simple, smart silhouette, like a Tuxedo, the outfit was named Iaido Tuxedo.

The trousers worn by practitioners of the Japanese martial art of Iaido traditionally are wide-legged, incorporating a fold of fabric into the side seam.

Front and back of the Iaido Tuxedo jacket constructed from nylon organza and lined in silk habotai.

THE MATERIAL

The incorporation of additional fabric into the seams of this outfit means that it is best suited to a light, transparent (or semi-transparent) fabric that is crisp, the ideal fabric being a silk organza. Silk organza, however, is usually associated with eveningwear. It is feminine and delicate, easy to crease and appeals to a more mature market. An alternative is nylon organza which has a similar weight and feel but is tough, easy to iron, withstands high temperatures and has a high level of shine, appealing to a younger clientele.

Both these fabrics are transparent, so a silk habotai lining is added in a contrasting colour. This also has the effect of highlighting the French seams and folds of the organza.

THE PATTERN

The outfit consists of a jacket and trousers. The jacket is a basic womenswear single-button, single-breasted jacket with a collar and lapel. It has a centre back seam and two-piece sleeves.

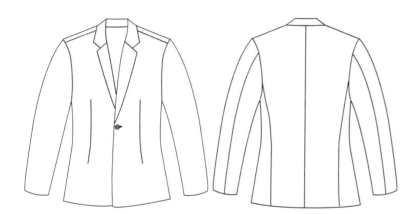

The trousers are cut slightly lower than the waist and have wide legs. They are fastened with an invisible zip in the left-hand seam.

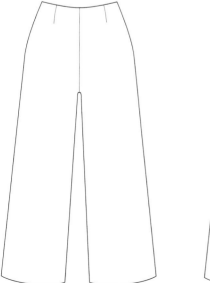 

Both are cut using a basic jacket and trouser block. The lining is cut from the same pattern, excluding the facings and turn ups.

The Iaido-inspired element is the addition of flaps of fabric, cut and incorporated into the side seams of trousers, the back sleeve seam, the centre back and into the left-hand pocket of the jacket.

Step 1
The jacket lapel

First, create a rectangular rather than a traditional Western, pointed lapel. Trace a basic jacket block. Extend and square off the base of the lapel in line with the position of the first button.

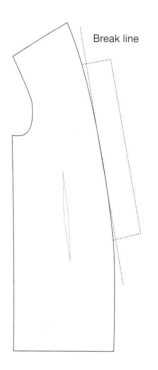

Break line

Step 2
The patch pockets

Each pocket is 14cm (5½in) in width and 17cm (6¾in) in depth. Add 5cm (2in) to the top edge to allow for a double fold of 2.5cm (1in).

The left-hand pocket incorporates an additional flap. Cut the paper pattern vertically 2.5cm (1in) from the left side seam, open it out and insert a panel 9.5cm (3¾in) long and 2cm (¾in) wide positioned 7.5cm (3in) from the upper edge. The cut lines are now the sewing lines.

To construct the pocket, fold the extended panel in half so that it sits on the right side of the fabric, stitch along the stitching lines using a French seam (see box below). Then fold in the hem allowance at the top pocket in a double fold and stitch, then top stitch both pockets to the jacket. The top of each pocket should be positioned 13cm (5in) below the first button and 10cm (4in) from the centre front.

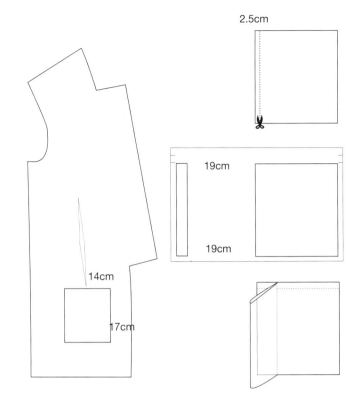

Step 3
Create the flap in the centre back of the jacket

Cut the centre back seam open. Again the cut lines now form the stitching lines. At 4.5cm (1¾in) below the neck point, insert a panel 20cm (8in) wide widening to 22cm (8½in) wide at the hem. This accommodates the natural curves of the female body and is more flattering than a strict rectangular shape.

To construct the jacket, fold the panel in half so that it extends to the right side of the fabric, stitch down the sewing lines, finishing 44cm (17¼in) from the centre back neck point (or 5cm/2in below waist level). Add a horizontal line of top stitching across the flap at this point. This leaves the rest of the centre back and flap open, acting as a vent to allow movement, especially when sitting down.

Sewing the seams

All seams on the jacket should be sewn as French seams, with the first row of stitching made inside the garment and the second stitched to the outside so that the seams also act as narrow flaps.

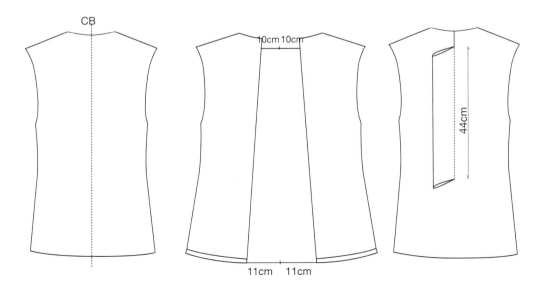

Step 4
Create the flaps in the back sleeve seams

Using a two-piece sleeve pattern, for the right sleeve as worn make a mark 2cm (¾in) from the top of the back sleeve seam. Add in a panel 20cm (8in) wide at the top and 23cm (9in) wide at the sleeve hem.

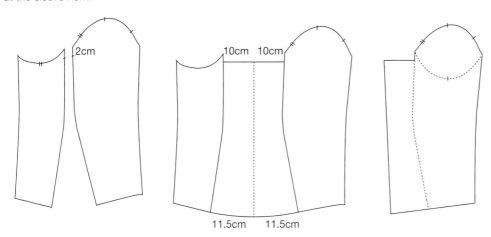

For the left-hand sleeve as worn, make a mark 23cm (9in) down the back sleeve seam and insert a panel 19cm (7½in) wide at the top and 24cm (9½in) wide at the sleeve hem.

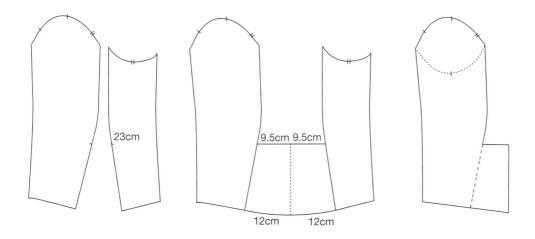

To construct both sleeves fold the extended panels in half to the right side of the sleeve and stitch down the sewing lines.

The flaps
The placing and measurement of the flaps can be adjusted according to the designer's own specification. The main criteria is that the flaps should be folded symmetrically so that they can be stitched and folded flat to the garment.

Step 5
The trousers

The front of the trousers remain unchanged.

Using a pattern taken from the back of the basic trouser block, cut open the pattern vertically from the middle of the dart nearest the centre back seam. Again the cut lines are the stitching lines. Insert a panel 22cm (8½in) wide at the top and 20cm (8in) wide at the bottom, the top being wider to accommodate the effect of the overlap at the waist.

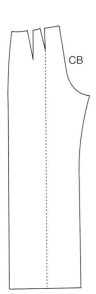
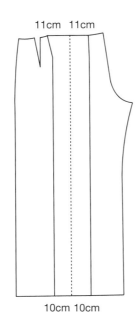
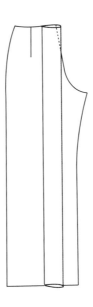

11cm 11cm

CB

10cm 10cm

To construct the trousers, fold the flap in half to the right side and stitch along the stitching lines. When the trousers are constructed the flaps, which should overlap at the centre back, should be stitched in at the waistline.

The flaps at the back of the trousers overlap at the centre back and are sewn into the waistline.

The complete Iaido Tuxedo
outfit from the Lo and
Cabon Spring/Summer
'Sugardust' show, 2000.

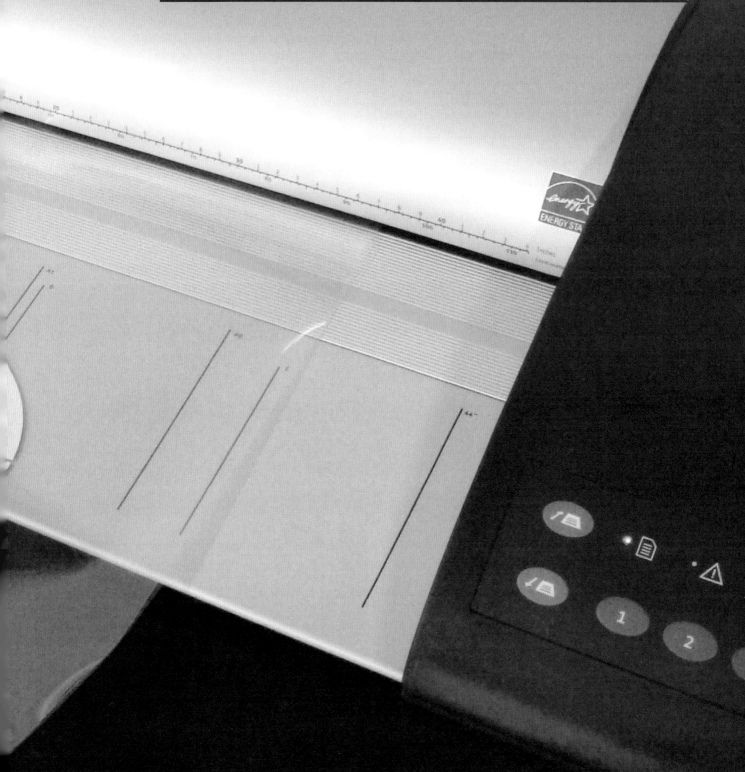

CHAPTER 7
PATTERN CUTTING
& TECHNOLOGY

It is important to realize that technology exists only as an aid to the pattern cutting process. The user of the technology must be aware of all the same theories, principles and limitations of pattern cutting and have the same knowledge and practicality as the manual pattern cutter.

The application of technology within the fashion and pattern cutting world is often referred to as CAD/CAM (Computer Aided Design/Computer Aided Manufacture). This may include a computer or laptop with pattern cutting, grading and lay planning software, a digitizer, pattern scanner, plotter and cutter. This chapter provides an overview of all of this software and hardware.

CHOOSING PATTERN CUTTING SOFTWARE

Some of the companies that supply the pattern cutting industry with CAD/CAM systems and software include Gerber (USA), Lectra (France), Optitex (Israel), Pad System (Canada), Assyst (Germany), Grafis (Germany), Vetigraph (France) and Gemini (Romania). These are just a handful of providers of professional CAD/CAM systems to the apparel industry, and you will find that there is pattern cutting software to suit all budgets and needs. Some software providers that appeal to the student, amateur, or small business on a limited budget include Telestia (Greece), Wild Ginger (USA), and Fashion Cad (Australia).

When choosing pattern cutting software, the pattern cutter must take into consideration the following:
- The operating system (for example, some software does not run on an Apple Macintosh).
- The hardware requirements.
- File formats and compatibility.
- Features and functions of the software.
- Training and support.
- Costs (including the cost of future upgrades).

Benefits of computer pattern cutting technology

All of the flat pattern cutting techniques shown in this book can be done using most of the available pattern cutting software. The computer should be thought of as a tool, like pencil, paper and scissors. Some benefits of computer-generated patterns include:
- Increased speed: reducing time to market. Digital patterns can also be emailed to factories abroad within a matter of seconds.
- Increased accuracy: for example, you are able to measure up to three decimal points within Pattern Design in Gerber Accumark.
- Storage of patterns: space is saved by eliminating the need for physical storage in pattern cutting studios. Pattern cutters are able to keep a vast archive of patterns, limited only by hard drive space.
- Multiple copies: patterns can be reproduced when needed.
- Templates: pattern cutters are able to build up a library of templates.
- Environmentally friendly: reduces paper wastage.
- Reduced costs: due to all of the above, depending on the price of the CAD/CAM package in relation to the scale of the business.

A CAD studio in college. The computer's hard drive can store and archive many thousands of patterns.

A rail of manual paper patterns: the space-saving benefits of storing patterns on computer are obvious.

WORKING FROM THE BLOCK

The most accurate way to begin pattern cutting on the computer from a block is to draft the block directly on screen using pattern-cutting software (right). The same drafting method as outlined in Chapter three can be used.

Existing manual block patterns can also be photographed, digitized or scanned into the system, and then checked over and measured for accuracy.

PHOTOGRAPHING & UPLOADING

With some pattern cutting software it is possible to photograph existing paper patterns with a digital camera, then upload them into the computer and digitize them on screen. This method of pattern input is considered more economical than the others as you do not need an expensive digitizing table or pattern scanner. However, this is not a widely used method in the fashion industry as it is not considered as accurate and a lot of time can be spent checking and adjusting the pattern.

DIGITIZING

The digitizer consists of a table with a menu and cursor. To digitize a pattern piece on the Gerber Accumark system, the pattern is first secured onto the digitizing table with masking tape. The cursor is then used to enter information about the piece on the menu, such as the piece name, piece category, piece description and sizing. This is done by placing the crosshairs of the cursor over the instruction or letter on the menu pad and pressing the 'A' button on the cursor.

The beginning of the grain line is then determined by placing the crosshairs of the cursor and pressing the 'A' button over the first and last point of the grain line on the pattern piece. The outline of the pattern piece is traced in a clockwise direction by placing the crosshairs of the cursor over points to be entered and pressing the 'A' button. Other buttons can be pressed to add graded points and notches, as well as internal markings and labels to the pattern.

Pattern input via digitizing is considered to be very accurate. Many pattern cutters prefer this method as they have complete control over every point that is added. Digitizing, however, can be very time consuming and labour intensive, and is only as accurate as the person that is doing it.

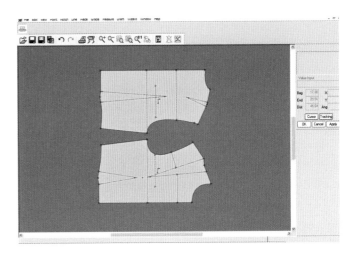

Here is a block that is being drafted on the computer using Gerber Accumark software

Digitizing a pattern piece the using a digitizer.

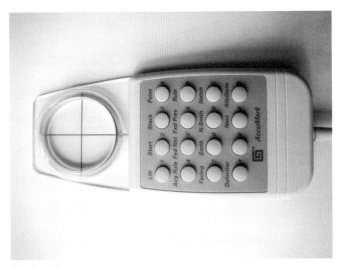

The digitizing cursor.

SCANNING

Some of the benefits of using a pattern scanner to input patterns include increased speed and ease of use. The pattern pieces are fed through the scanner between plastic sheets. The scanning software automatically digitizes the pattern. The pattern cutter then just needs to check over each pattern piece to ensure that the scanning software has picked up the correct grain line, notches, internal labels, etc., before saving in the format for the software they wish to open it in.

Once the block is stored in the system it should be saved and backed up. The block may then be retrieved an unlimited amount of times to be used for modification into styles, but should be re-saved with a new pattern name first to avoid over-writing the block pattern, like with a Microsoft Word document. The managing and storing of digital patterns is critical, and is much the same as managing other digital documents.

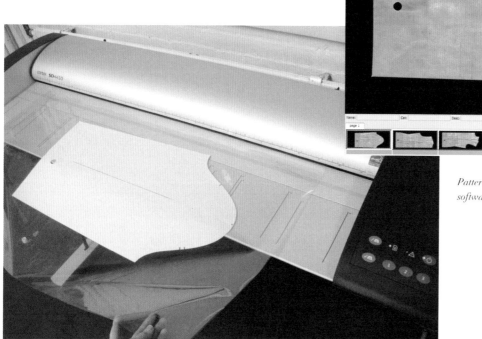

Pattern piece within Nhega scanning software, on screen.

Pattern piece being fed through a scanner.

Pattern piece converted in Gerber Accumark, ready to manipulate on screen.

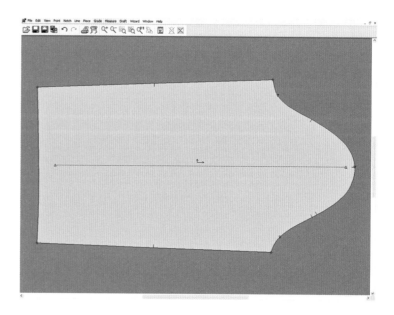

DIGITAL TECHNIQUES

Almost all of the flat pattern cutting techniques discussed in this book can be done using a computer. Here is an overview of some of the tools that can be utilized.

Folding the paper pattern

On the computer it is easy to work on the half pattern. The pattern piece can then be mirrored easily and with complete accuracy to create symmetrical patterns.

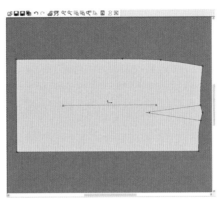 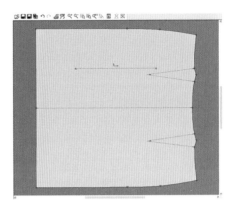

Here are the half and full-mirrored pattern pieces. Piece is mirrored in Gerber Accumark using the function Piece>Mirror Piece.

Seams

These can be easily added, removed, changed and increased without having to retrace the pattern or stick extra backing paper on to the edges. Seams can be stripped off or hidden for pattern cutting and alterations so that the true line, or the sew line of the pattern is being worked on.

There are also many functions that help to ensure the seam corners are cut correctly and most easily for the sewing of the garment. Seams can be turned back (e.g. on a tapered hem), squared off, or matched.

The pattern cutter needs to know how the garment may be sewn together to be able to choose which special seam corner they need to apply.

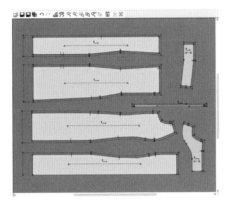

Pattern pieces with seams hidden to show just the sew line.

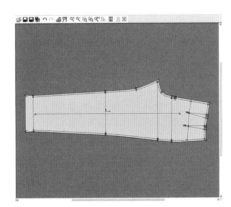

Trouser leg showing a turnback corner (above), and a screengrab of the Seam Menu *in Gerber Accumark (right).*

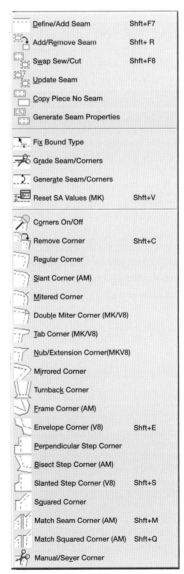

Define/Add Seam		Shft+F7
Add/Remove Seam		Shft+ R
Swap Sew/Cut		Shft+F8
Update Seam		
Copy Piece No Seam		
Generate Seam Properties		
Fix Bound Type		
Grade Seam/Corners		
Generate Seam/Corners		
Reset SA Values (MK)		Shft+V
Corners On/Off		
Remove Corner		Shft+C
Regular Corner		
Slant Corner (AM)		
Mitered Corner		
Double Miter Corner (MK/V8)		
Tab Corner (MK/V8)		
Nub/Extension Corner(MKV8)		
Mirrored Corner		
Turnback Corner		
Frame Corner (AM)		
Envelope Corner (V8)		Shft+E
Perpendicular Step Corner		
Bisect Step Corner (AM)		
Slanted Step Corner (V8)		Shft+S
Squared Corner		
Match Seam Corner (AM)		Shft+M
Match Squared Corner (AM)		Shft+Q
Manual/Sever Corner		

Notches

Notches can be added and removed easily with the click of a button. You are also able to assign different notch types to a piece.

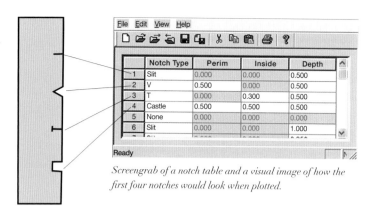

	Notch Type	Perim	Inside	Depth
1	Slit	0.000	0.000	0.500
2	V	0.500	0.000	0.500
3	T	0.000	0.300	0.500
4	Castle	0.500	0.500	0.500
5	None	0.000	0.000	0.000
6	Slit	0.000	0.000	1.000

Screengrab of a notch table and a visual image of how the first four notches would look when plotted.

Dart manipulation

Darts can be manipulated, rotated, combined and distributed easily. Dart legs can be balanced and the computer is able to determine the fold back of the dart accurately (see the equivalent manual technique on page 50).

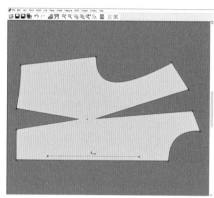 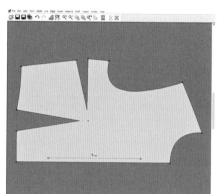

Front bodice before (above) and after rotating the shoulder dart into side seam (above right) with the function Piece>Dart>Rotate.

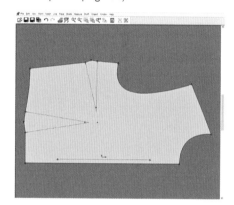

Front bodice with dart filled in using Fold>Close Dart End function.

Adding volume

Adding fullness to pattern pieces is very easy to do. The computer is able to calculate an amount of fullness either in centimetres or percentage and add this fullness evenly through a section whilst making good the line.

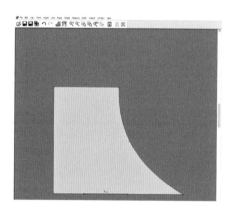 

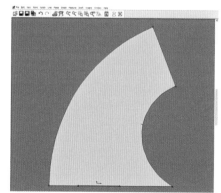 

(Right) Adding fullness to a pattern piece using the Piece>Fullness function. (Far right) Here is the same pattern piece showing slashing and spreading by hand.

Pleats

The computer can easily create pleats, including knife and box pleats, using the Piece>Pleats function.

 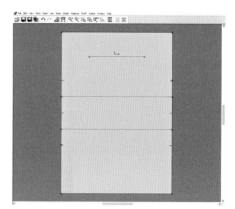

A patch pocket before and after a box pleat was added using the function: Piece>Pleats> Box Pleat.

Working onscreen

With computerized pattern cutting (as with manual pattern cutting), the garment onscreen should be laid so that the garment hem is towards the left-hand side.

Seamed panels

All panels can be drafted on the block and traced off. The pattern cutter can then extract the panel pieces by using the function Piece>Create Piece>Trace or Extract. Copies of the block as a draft can be stored as a reference and returned to when needed.

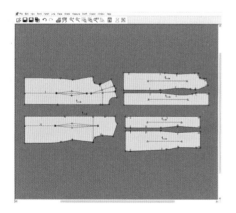

A pattern that has been created by drafting the style lines on to the block. Seams were then added and the pattern pieces saved separately.

Creating common pieces

Pieces where the shape or measurements are taken from an existing piece are made simple on the computer. Pieces such as facings, collars, waistbands and bindings can be made entirely by the program once you have indicated the desired width and parameters that are needed.

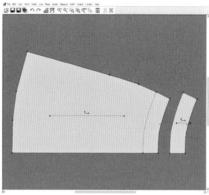

The function will create a new facing piece using the draft line created on to the pattern.

Annotation

The computer can store information for annotations with the pattern piece. This includes grain line, piece name/number/type, cutting information, dates, internal lines or markings and any other instructions. Annotations and information for each pattern piece can be printed on to the piece each time it is plotted.

A fabric code colour fill can also be assigned to each pattern piece to indicate different fabrics, such as self/main fabric, lining and fusing, just as different coloured pens or coloured card is often used when making manual paper patterns.

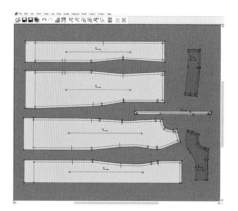

Image shows pieces that are fused indicated with red.

GRADING, LAY PLANNING & OUTPUT

GRADING

Generally, manual grading is very time consuming and labour intensive. A CAD system allows the pattern cutter to grade a style in a fraction of the time it takes to do it by hand. Due to the benefits of time and cost savings, CAD/CAM systems are now used almost universally for grading.

Just like for pattern cutting, the computer is a tool for grading and will not grade for you. When grading the pattern on the computer, the same concepts, theories and principles apply as for manual grading.

Most computer grading follows the Delta method (x/y axis). Grading can be applied to the block and saved. The pattern will then retain the grading during pattern modification. A finished style will then only need checking and tweaking. This also enables a more accurate costing to be made at any time during the garment development stage.

Grading can also be copied easily from one pattern to another. The graded pattern can be viewed as a nest on the system and the sizes can be colour coded to make the size set clearer to view.

LAY PLANNING/MARKER MAKING

A lay plan or marker is created as a template for cutting to help minimize fabric waste as well as for costing the fabric of a garment.

Before a marker can be created, information about the marker needs to be set up. This information needs to include the usable fabric width, number of sizes in the lay, direction (is the fabric a one-way or two-way fabric?) and buffering (allowance around the pattern piece).

The pattern pieces are then brought into the marker and placed in the most efficient and economical way according to the width and parameters that have been ordered. The pieces can be placed by the CAD system automatically, or can be placed by the user to enable more control of the lay plan.

The student or pattern cutter may like to create a lay plan before plotting out the sample pattern in order to save paper and sample fabric. The paper printout can then be placed onto the fabric and the pattern cutter can cut through both the paper and the fabric at the same time.

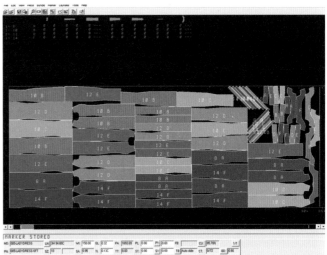

Graded lay plan for a dress in sizes 8-14 using Gerber Accumark Marker Making software.

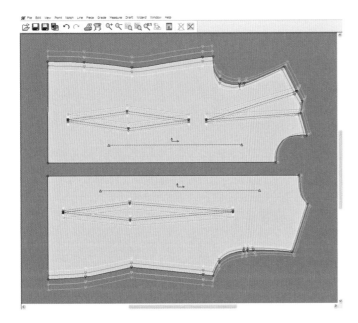

Image shows a graded nest, sizes 8-16. The graded pattern can be plotted (printed) off as a nest (i.e. all the sizes together), or each size can be extracted and plotted off individually.

PATTERN OUTPUT

For transportation of patterns (for example to send to a factory), the most common way is to email the pattern, saving time and courier costs. The addressee needs to be equipped with compatible CAD/CAM software in order to import and open the digital patterns. Some factories have a file converter so that they can accept many types of digital files.

Patterns can also be printed off onto paper or card using a plotter/cutter. The pattern can be reproduced an unlimited amount of times very quickly.

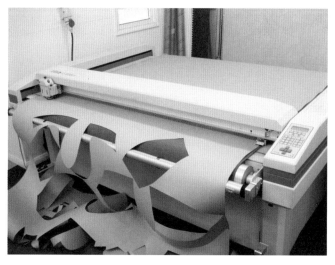

A Gerber Infinity plotter (top) and a card cutter (above).

LOOKING TO THE FUTURE

Pattern cutting must move with the times and embrace technology in order to keep up with the fast-paced world of fashion. The pattern cutter does not necessarily have to operate in an entirely computer focused way, but can combine manual and computer pattern cutting together to suit the needs of the job. Styles that are repeated from season to season and only require small alterations can benefit from being created entirely on a computer system.

Many pattern cutters, however, will still prefer to create the silhouette of a first pattern by hand and continue with the rest of the production process using a CAD/CAM system. The system can then be used to perform repetitive, time consuming tasks such as creating facings and linings, or adding seams and annotations to a pattern.

Many pattern cutters will also say that while computers aid the pattern cutting process, learning to draft paper patterns by hand first can be beneficial in fostering an understanding of how pattern cutting and human anatomy work together, a crucial skill for every pattern cutter. Ultimately, the computer is simply a tool, and is not a substitute for learning pattern cutting skills.

GLOSSARY & ABBREVIATIONS

A

Annotations Marks and instructions added to a pattern to indicate grainline, piece name and season, internal features, different fabrics used, and so on.

B

Bias grain Grainline runs at 45 degrees to centre front and centre back of garment. This gives a stretch quality to the fabric as the weight of the garment combined with gravity makes it relax in length and narrow in width.

Block Basic garment shape from which a pattern is drafted from as a starting point.

BP Bust point.

Button stand Width (vertical or horizontal) within which the button should always sit right along the middle line, on a shirt front for example.

C

CAD Computer aided design.

CAM Computer aided manufacture.

CB Centre back of garment as worn.

CF Centre front of garment as worn.

D

Dart Triangular shape introduced into a garment as a way of removing excess fabric in order to fit the three-dimensional shape of the body; usually applied to woven garment pattern cutting.

Digitizing Digitally entering a physical pattern piece into a computer by entering commands with a digitizing cursor around the outer points of a paper pattern piece.

Draping (*'Moulage'* in French) is also called Draping on the Stand. It means manipulating fabric on a mannequin in order to create a garment design without needing to gauge the shape on paper first. The final paper pattern is created by taking the draped piece of fabric off the mannequin, laying it flat, then tracing the shape onto a piece of paper.

Drill holes Used to mark construction details such as sewing guidelines, position of pockets, buttons and buttonholes, and the ends of darts.

F

Facing Piece of fabric used to finish a section of a garment: in pattern cutting annotation this may be denoted with a different colour.

Flat/working drawing An actual representation, or blueprint, of a garment, drawn to scale and including construction details.

G

Godet A piece of material, usually triangular, inserted into a garment to add fullness.

Grading Increasing and decreasing a sample size pattern to create a range of different sizes. This is most often done by computer in industry.

Grainline Direction of the grain (i.e. warp thread); used to refer to the way fabric is used in a garment's construction, and how the pattern is placed on the fabric before cutting. See *horizontal grain, straight grain* and *bias grain.*

H

Horizontal grain Grainline runs at 90 degrees perpendicular to the centre front or centre back of the garment. Cuffs and yokes of shirts are often cut on the horizontal grain to provide crispness and strength to a folded edge.

L

Lay planning Setting pattern pieces on the fabric in order to minimize wastage. This is most often done by computer in industry.

M

Made-to-measure Custom-made garment created using an individual's exact measurements fitting to a client's specifications.

N

Notches Also known as 'balance marks', these indicate where two sides of a seam are aligned and sewn together. They can also mark construction points such as hip line or knee level on trousers.

P

Pivoting Moving darts on a paper pattern to anywhere on the pattern piece in a 360 degree circular direction, keeping the original point of the dart to absolute origin.

Placket An opening or slit in a garment which aids the wearer in putting it on and taking it off. These can be fastened with buttons, hooks-and-eyes and velcro.

Pleat A fold of fabric introduced to a garment as a design detail or to provide flexibility of fit, also acting as a form of suppression. Pleats are directional folds that are folded with a tangible width that creates the depth of each pleat, from beginning to end. Pleats can be pressed with a steam iron or sewn along their length parallel to the fold. They can also be produced permanently by using industrial solution with synthetic fibres.

Plotter Machine that will output a digital paper pattern.

Princess line Seam that curves from the armhole over the bust and then down the garment to either side of the centre front, eliminating the sharp ends of bust darts.

R

RSU Right side up.

S

Sample size Size to which the first garment is made: this is then graded up and down. This size varies in different markets, but in the UK a size 12 is often used.

Sleeve crown Upper part of the sleeve above the sleeve width.

Sleeve-head ease Depending on the fabric (for example, wool) sometimes an extra allowance of fabric can be added to a sleeve head to allow it to create a fuller sleeve head to imitate and fit the top of the arm at shoulder point.

SNP Shoulder neck point.

Straight grain Grainline is parallel to the centre front or centre back of garment. The warp thread runs down the garment, providing stability, and the weft runs across, allowing for some 'give'.

Suppression Removal of excess fabric to accommodate three-dimensional shape of the body.

T

Toile Test garment, usually made first from calico (plain cotton) and then the actual material intended for the garment in order to test the fit.

Tolerance In woven pattern cutting, an allowance of an extra couple of centimetres must be added on top of the actual circumference measured (e.g. bust, waist and hip) to enable movement and ensure a comfortable fit.

True corners Re-drafting pattern pieces to smooth corners at all the joining points, for example the shoulder neck point, armholes and hems.

Tuck A fold of fabric introduced to a garment as a design detail or to provide flexibility of fit; like pleats they are secured to a seam but do not have a definite directional line – beginning with a tangible width/depth they are left open to move naturally and provide flexibility and volume.

W

Warp Vertical yarn in weaving, running parallel to the selvedge (weft being the horizontal yarn. The warp is the more stable and stronger of the two).

Weft Horizontal yarn in weaving, running at a right angle to the selvedge (warp is the yarn, and the more stable and stronger of the two).

Working drawing/flat An actual representation, or blueprint, of a garment, drawn to scale and including construction details. These usually only need to be drawn in black lines.

Y

Yoke Fitted panel of fabric typically fitted across the shoulders and upper back of a shirt or coat or across the hips of a skirt or trousers, which serves to eliminate darts and acts as a support to which the rest of the garment is attached.

INDEX

SIZE CHART *

HEIGHT: 170CM, (5FT 7IN) (THIS IS ONLY A REFERENCE POINT)

*NB: Size chart should be supplied by the company you are working for, who will have a standard set of measurements according to their market needs. This chart is only an example to explain how to measure the body so as to draft basic blocks.

CIRCUMFERENCE

A	Bust	88cm/34½in	Around the bust line parallel to the bust points.
B	Under bust	74cm/29in	The circumference under the bust, i.e. ribcage. This is especially useful for cutting corsets and for the dress industry.
C	Waist	66.5cm/26in	The smallest circumference joining upper and lower body. Tie a piece of string or a tape measure around the circumference of where waist should sit.
D	Mid hip	85cm/33½in	Circumference of middle of hip length. This is to double check mid-hip area fits well on trousers, skirts and dresses.
E	Hip	92cm/36¼in	The largest circumference below waist, which doesn't always have to be level at the peak of the buttocks. The measurer should also measure up and down to see if measurement increases to the 'true' hip.
F	Front cross shoulder	41cm/16in	Locate shoulder points by visualizing shoulder edge of a sleeveless garment. From shoulder point to shoulder point on the front.
G	Back cross shoulder	42.5cm/16¾in	Same as above, measuring at the back.
H	Shoulder length	12.5cm/5in	Measured from shoulder neck point (SNP) to shoulder point.
I	Cross front (armhole)	35cm/13¾in	SNP measuring downward approximately 13cm (5in), measure horizontally across the front armholes.
J	Cross back (armhole)	38cm/15in	SNP measuring downward approximately 13cm (5in), measure horizontally across the back armholes. Cross back armhole should be generous for arm movement towards front.
K	Neck circumference	40cm/15¾in	As a reference point: there is no exact neck 'line' on a body. This is to double check the pattern while drafting.
L	Head circumference	58cm/22¾in	For pullover garments. If neck measurement is smaller than the head measurement, a fastening MUST be considered.
M	Top of thigh	59cm/23in	Measure this at the very top of thigh, level with crotch.
N	Thigh	52cm/20½in	Middle level between body rise (crotch) and knee.
O	Knee	34cm/13⅓in	Similar to hip measurement, this should increase when bending and moving the knee.
P	Calf	33cm/13in	Middle level between knee and ankle.
Q	Ankle	23cm/9in	Circumference around the ankle bone.
R	Trouser hem opening	32cm/12½in	Depends on the size of feet, this is to consider whether trouser leg opening is practical for the foot to pass through.

VERTICAL MEASUREMENTS

S	Nape to waist	39.5cm/15½in	At centre back, approximately from third vertebrae to waistline.
T1	Hip length	20cm/8in	At side seam length from waistline to hip line.
T2	Mid hip length	10cm/4in	Half way of hip length.
T3	Front body length	43.5cm/17in	From SNP passes bust point to waistline.
T4	Back body length	43cm/17in	From SNP measure down to waistline at back.
T5	Body rise	27cm/10½in	Sitting on a table, measure at side seam from waistline to top of table.
T6	Out seam	110cm/43⅓in	From waistline to the floor measure along the outside seam of legs.
T7	In seam	82cm/32¼in	From crotch to floor. Therefore, outseam should be approx. the sum of body rise and in seam.
T8	From waist to knee	61cm/24in	At side seam, measure from waistline to level of back knee crease.
T9	From waist to calf	92cm/36½in	At side seam, measure from waistline to widest of calf muscle.
T10	From waist to ankle	112cm/44in	At side seam, measure from waistline to side ankle bone.

SLEEVES

U	Armhole	38.5cm/15in	Circumference of armhole passes shoulder point (measure generously).
V	Bicep	26cm/10¼in	Circumference of arm at bicep muscle (measure with arm bent to 90 degree angle).
W	Elbow	27cm/10½in	Circumference of elbow with arm bent slightly.
X	Wrist	17cm/6¾in	Circumference around the wrist bone.
Y	Elbow from shoulder	32cm/12½in	From shoulder point towards back to elbow peak bone.
Z	Sleeve length from shoulder point	58cm/22¾in	From shoulder point towards back to elbow peak bone then to wrist with arm slightly bent.

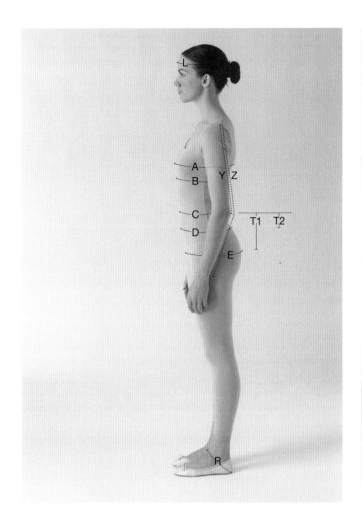

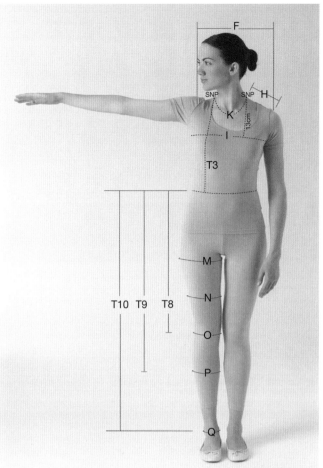

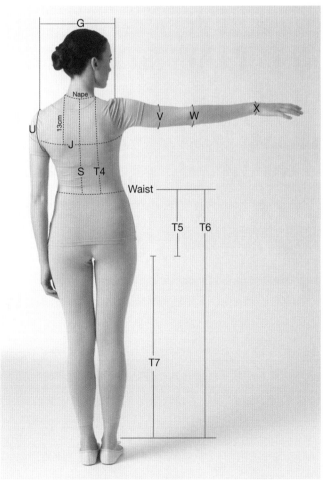

FURTHER READING

Abling, Bina and Kathleen Maggio, *Integrating Draping, Drafting, and Drawing*, Fairchild, 2008

Aldrich, Winifred, *Fabric, Form and Flat Pattern Cutting*, Blackwell Publishing, 2007

Aldrich, Winifred, *Metric Pattern Cutting for Children's Wear and Babywear*, Blackwell Publishing, 4th edition, 2009

Aldrich, Winifred, *Metric Pattern Cutting for Menswear*, Blackwell Publishing, 4th edition, 2008

Aldrich, Winifred, *Metric Pattern Cutting for Womenswear,* Blackwell Publishing, 5th edition, 2008

Aldrich, Winifred, *Pattern Cutting for Women's Tailored Jackets*, Blackwell Publishing, 2001

Armstrong, Helen Joseph, *Patternmaking for Fashion Design*, Pearson Education, 4th edition, 2005

Bray, Natalie, *Dress Pattern Designing*, Blackwell Publishing, 2003

Burke, Sandra, *Fashion Computing – Design Techniques and CAD*, Burke Publishing, 2006

Campbell, Hilary, *Designing Patterns – A Fresh Approach to Pattern Cutting*, Nelson Thornes, 1980

Cooklin, Gerry, *Pattern Cutting for Women's Outerwear*, OM Books, 2008

Fischer, Annette, *Basics Fashion Design: Construction*, AVA Publishing SA, 2009

Holman, Gillian, *Pattern Cutting Made Easy*, Batsford, 1997

Knowles, Lori A, *The Practical Guide To Patternmaking For Fashion Designers: Juniors, Misses, And Women*, Fairchild, 2005

Knowles, Lori A, *The Practical Guide To Patternmaking For Fashion Designers: Menswear*, Fairchild, 2005

Nakamichi, Tomoko, *Pattern Magic*, Laurence King Publishing, 2010

Nakamichi, Tomoko, *Pattern Magic 2*, Laurence King Publishing, 2011

Szkutnicka, Basia, *Technical Drawing for Fashion*, Laurence King Publishing, 2010

Tyrrell, Anne, *Classic Fashion Patterns*, Batsford, 2010

Ward, Janet, and Martin Shoben, *Pattern Cutting and Making Up: The Professional Approach*, 2nd edition, Butterworth-Heinemann, 1987

SOFTWARE SUPPLIERS

Assyst (Germany) www.assyst-bullmer.com
Fashion Cad (Australia) www.fashioncad.com
Gemini (Romania) www.geminicad.com
Grafis (Germany) www.grafis.com
Gerber Technology (USA) www.gerbertechnology.com
Lectra (France) www.lectra.com
Optitex (Israel) www.optitex.com
Pad System (Canada) www.padsystem.com
Telestia (Greece) www.etelestia.com
Vetigraph (France) www.vetigraph.com
Wild Ginger (USA) www.wildginger.com

PICTURE CREDITS

Unless otherwise stated all drawings featured in the book have been created by Alina Moat; all still and toile photography by Packshot.com; all model photography by Simon Pask Photography (model, Angelle Warburton; makeup, Lucie Strong).

The author and publisher would like to thank the following institutions and individuals who provided images for use in this book. In all cases, every effort has been made to credit the copyright holders, but should there be any omissions or errors the publisher would be pleased to insert the appropriate acknowledgment in subsequent editions of this book.

Introduction
p2 ©iStockphoto

Chapter 1
p23 © Stephane Cardinale/People Avenue/Corbis; p26 illustration © Mary Evans/National Magazines; p28 right © Sam Parsons, www.samparsons.com

Chapter 3
p42 left © catwalking.com; p44 © catwalking.com; p49 © esthAlto/Frederic Cirou/Getty; p62 © catwalking.com; p71 top © catwalking.com; p78 all © catwalking.com; p91 left © catwalking.com, right © Warehouse

Chapter 4
p122 top left © George Marks/Getty, bottom © catwalking.com; p125 © catwalking.com

Chapter 5
p137 left © V&A Images, Victoria and Albert Museum, right © Hobbs; p158 top right © iStockphoto

Chapter 6
p210 left © Cornelie Tollens www.cornelietollens.com; p214 © Niall McInerney; p220 top © Darryl Lawrence

Chapter 7
Screengrabs created in Gerber AccuMark and reproduced by kind permission Gerber Technology. All other images courtesy Megan McGuire.

PUBLISHER'S ACKNOWLEDGMENTS

The publisher would like to thank the following:
Mary Gottleib, Parsons School of Design, NYC, US
Sally Selligman, Drexel University, Philadelphia, US
Caryl Court, University of East London, UK
Kevin Almond, University of Huddersfield, UK

AUTHOR'S ACKNOWLEDGMENTS

Dennic would like to thank the following individuals and organizations for their assistance and support in creating this book:

Corinne Andrews
Karin Askham
Eric Bremner
Darren Cabon at LO AND CABON
John, Susan and Beverley Cabon
Sheila Cooke
Dr. Frances Corner
Wendy Dagworthy
Usha Doshi
Helen Evans
Gerber Technology
Henrietta Goodden
Isabel Garabito
Lynne Hammond
Ursula Hudson
Betty Jackson
Carmel Kelly
Mr. Laurence King
Shaun Kirven
Marco Lee
Wendy Malem
Megan McGuire
Beryl Mann
John Miles
Alina Moat
Claire Murphy
Sam Parsons
Evi Peroulaki
Gaynor Sermon
Jan Shefford
Della Shenton
Lucie Strong
Anne Townley
Tera, James and Zachery Thorpe
Angelle Warburton
Julie Wilson
Gloria Wong
Perry Wong
Raymond Yau